FROM WALLFLOWERS TO BULLETPROOF FAMILIES

Children's Literature Association Series

FROM WALLFLOWERS TO BULLETPROOF FAMILIES

The Power of Disability in Young Adult Narratives

Abbye E. Meyer

University Press of Mississippi / Jackson

The University Press of Mississippi is the scholarly publishing agency of the Mississippi Institutions of Higher Learning: Alcorn State University, Delta State University, Jackson State University, Mississippi State University, Mississippi University for Women, Mississippi Valley State University, University of Mississippi, and University of Southern Mississippi.

www.upress.state.ms.us

The University Press of Mississippi is a member of the Association of University Presses.

First printing 2022
∞

Library of Congress Cataloging-in-Publication Data

Names: Meyer, Abbye E., author.
Title: From wallflowers to bulletproof families: the power of disability in young adult narratives / Abbye E. Meyer.
Other titles: Children's Literature Association series.
Description: Jackson: University Press of Mississippi, 2022. | Series: Children's literature association series | Includes bibliographical references and index.
Identifiers: LCCN 2021034582 (print) | LCCN 2021034583 (ebook) | ISBN 978-1-4968-3756-1 (hardback) | ISBN 978-1-4968-3757-8 (trade paperback) | ISBN 978-1-4968-3758-5 (epub) | ISBN 978-1-4968-3759-2 (epub) | ISBN 978-1-4968-3760-8 (pdf) | ISBN 978-1-4968-3761-5 (pdf)
Subjects: LCSH: Youth with disabilities in literature. | Children with disabilities in literature. | People with disabilities in literature. | Characters and characteristics in literature. | Young adult literature—History and criticism.
Classification: LCC PN56.5.H35 M49 2022 (print) | LCC PN56.5.H35 (ebook) | DDC 809/.933527—dc23/eng/20211128
LC record available at https://lccn.loc.gov/2021034582
LC ebook record available at https://lccn.loc.gov/2021034583

British Library Cataloging-in-Publication Data available

for Ed and Charlene

CONTENTS

Acknowledgments ix

Chapter 1. Introduction: Radical Readings of Adolescence and Disability 3

Chapter 2. Wallflowers: Disability as the Young Adult Voice 16

Chapter 3. Fruits: Disability as a Literary Metaphor 37

Chapter 4. Freaks: Disability as a Catalyst for Growth 62

Chapter 5. Accidents: Disability as a Political Identity 85

Chapter 6. Bulletproof Families: Disability as the Unifier 107

Chapter 7. Conclusion: Solidarity in Expression and Action . . . 150

Notes 157

Bibliography 173

Credits 183

Index 185

ACKNOWLEDGMENTS

I want to extend an enormous thank-you to Kate Capshaw, along with Margaret Higonnet and Clare Eby, who've offered invaluable encouragement, feedback, and wisdom from the start.

Marci Korwin, thank you for nearly a decade of keeping me company, engaged in these ideas, (sometimes) hard at work, and (always) awed by figs—and the other things that matter.

I owe and offer a ton of gratitude to June Cummins, Naomi Lesley, and Emily Wender: brilliant teachers and writers, and more importantly, really, really good friends.

Stuart Murdoch, thank you for sharing experiences with ME/CFS, and of course, for singing into existence those strange, beloved adolescents.

Thanks to Pamela Kurth, Stephanie Clark, Darcy Graves, Kris Milledge, Lori Logue, Karey Sego Brandon, Jenny Newton, Greg Cohen, and others at Psychological Health Associates, Homestead of Chariton, and Lucas County Health Center, who model every day how to respectfully and lovingly give care.

For insightful conversations, heated debates, and genuine support, I want to thank Steve Meyer, Mary Meyer, Anshu Wahi, Emma Cohen, Debbie Reck, Arthur Unobskey, Meghan Sweeney, Chris McGee, Jennie Miskec, Ivy Linton Stabell, Victoria Ford Smith, Anna Mae Duane, Chris Geddes, Stevie Jackson, Caraigh McGregor, Elizabeth Duclos-Orsello, Jill Sullivan, Betty Menacher, Denise Fields, Molly Logic, Phil Meyer, Ray Meyer, Linda Baynes, Alex Salvatore, Alex Mendez-Diez, Millie Nemser, Nicole McClure, and Shawn Salvant.

Finally, I thank the mentors and misbehavers in the Children's Literature Association, disabled leaders on Disability Twitter, and Katie Keene at the University Press of Mississippi.

FROM WALLFLOWERS TO BULLETPROOF FAMILIES

Chapter 1

INTRODUCTION

Radical Readings of Adolescence and Disability

To accompany a publishing flurry of disability-themed children's and young adult books in the first few years of the twenty-first century, the American Library Association introduced the Schneider Family Book Awards in 2004. Awarded yearly to novels and picture books that "embod[y] an artistic expression of the disability experience for child and adolescent audiences" ("Schneider"). Literary scholarship about these texts, however, did not emerge so quickly. Following a handful of articles, a special issue of *Children's Literature Association Quarterly*, edited by Scott Pollard in 2013, asked literary scholars to take note of how "the radical work of disability studies scholarship" offers "a fruitful intellectual ground for new ways of reading—and teaching—literature" (Pollard 265). Theoretical readings of disability, he wrote, were "turning normative aesthetics and expectations on their heads" (265). Rather than "radical" scholarship, however, the 2013 special issue was followed mostly by sociological studies of disabled young people and pedagogical introductions to disability studies for K–12 teachers. For instance, Patricia A. Dunn's *Disabling Characters: Representations of Disability in Young Adult Literature* (2014) and Alice Hall's *Literature and Disability* (2016) provide practical backgrounds and frameworks for creating classroom discussions, but they do so by drawing on work already done by Rosemarie Garland-Thomson in 1997 (*Extraordinary Bodies: Figuring Physical Disability in American Culture and Literature*), Ato Quayson in 2007 (*Aesthetic Nervousness: Disability and the Crisis of Representation*), and others working in disability studies.

With this project, I dig into this fruitful intellectual ground and look more deeply into the inseparable literary identities of adolescence and disability. The young adult novels—and narratives in other forms—chosen for this project force rereadings of both adolescence and disability. With play and connection between the two identities, young adult narratives are able to demonstrate their inherent political and literary possibilities. This project illustrates and demonstrates the power that disability-centered readings offer young adult literature, as well as the power that young adult narratives hold to reimagine both disability and adolescence.

Without a doubt, adolescence and disability have long been linked by psychoanalysts and embodied by iconic characters in American literature. Memorable figures, including Beth March in *Little Women* (1868), Helen Keller in her autobiography (1903), Nicole Driver in *Tender is the Night* (1934), Charlie Gordon in *Flowers for Algernon* (1966), and even Hester Prynne in *The Scarlet Letter* (1850) demonstrate the overlap of disability and adolescence, especially as the characters grow into mature sexual identities. William Faulkner's *The Sound and the Fury* (1929) explores the minds of two disabled figures: Quentin Compson, who shows clear characteristics of mental illness, and Benjy Compson, who lives with an intellectual disability. Perhaps most importantly, in the text neither Quentin nor Benjy leaves adolescence; both characters' identities are static: adolescent and disabled. In the novel, Benjy is prevented from entering a sexual adulthood because he is castrated after he—literally and symbolically—"opened the gate . . . and . . . caught" a young girl "in the twilight" (Faulkner, "Appendix" 213; Faulkner, "The Text" 34). Neither welcomed nor tolerated, even when reduced to a desexualized "looney," disabled adolescent Benjy stands as a "judgment" on his family; because that judgment has no place in the Compson narrative, he disappears from the narrative, committed to the State Asylum and named "the Great American Gelding" (Faulkner, "The Text" 8, 139, 164; Faulkner, "Appendix" 213). Benjy's brother Quentin, a student at Harvard, is racked by the sound of his "watch ticking away" and obsessed with distorted sexualized memories attached to his sister and "honeysuckle . . . the saddest odor of all" (Faulkner, "The Text" 163, 107). Mired in guilt and responsibility—not to mention the haunting "round eye of the clock" and a ticking watch—Quentin drowns himself, suggesting a form of depression perhaps amplified by his obsessive thinking (76). Indeed, Quentin "loved death above all . . . and lived in a deliberate and almost perverted anticipation of death," eventually unable to bear "not the refraining but the restraint" of living (Faulkner, "Appendix" 208). Like Benjy, Quentin—finding no acceptable place in the Compson narrative and causing discomfort as a disabled adolescent with unstable sexual preoccupations—is eliminated from the text by his suicide. Neither Compson brother abandons his disabled adolescence, leaving the reader feeling uneasy, as both adolescence and disability are expected to be "overcome." Hardly a work of young adult literature, *The Sound and the Fury* does offer an early suggestion that, in literary representations, adolescence and disability often occupy the same unsustainable, uncomfortable spaces.

LIVES FREED FROM CURES

Outside of—but always relevant to—literary studies, adolescence is widely regarded as a distinct developmental stage based in identity formation. For practical purposes, adolescence in twentieth- and twenty-first-century American literature will be considered the teenage years. Teenagers, "in their search for a new sense of continuity and sameness," consider questions of gender, sexuality, ethnicity, relationships to others, and potential goals, passions, and vocations (Erikson 128). Much like adolescents, disabled people—at least during the twentieth and early twenty-first centuries—are forced to consider and reconsider self-definition, especially in relation to peers and larger institutions. These interpersonal responsibilities require rethinkings of the self, similar to the malleable identities developed and experienced by adolescents. Consequently, because of societal norms that reject dynamic identities, both adolescent and disabled people (are forced to) live in unstable states of identity formation and reevaluation.

Functioning as liminal states, but without distinct beginnings or endings, simple definitions of "adolescence" and "disability" also lose stability. Julia Kristeva's argument that "the adolescent . . . is a mythical figure of the imaginary" with an "open psychic structure," rather than a developing individual, frees the disabled adolescent from starting and ending points, but also makes that identity unreal (Kristeva 135). While I, at least, struggle to hold onto these theoretical contradictions, I find useful the *lack* of definition and *lack* of stability of these identities; I am able to see them as inexorably connected and to reimagine the common characteristics. Still, simply regarding adolescence and disability as the same kind of confusing existence may (unintentionally) reinforce harmful assumptions and representations. If viewed as something less than adult, a disabled character is infantilized, robbed of selfhood; this understanding, of course, relies on the assumption that young people truly *are* lesser-than until they mature. If an adolescent character is viewed as inherently disabled or broken, the reader may hope for a cure, perhaps the entrance into adulthood, which eliminates adolescence altogether; this understanding relies on the assumption that disabled people do need to be cured, fixed, or eliminated. Rather than expecting myself to hold onto the details of these confusing assumptions and representations, I enjoy letting the most effective young adult disability narratives remind me of such problems, while creating something entirely new.

Young adult novels and narratives—however overlooked, dismissed, or derided—find great moments of recuperation in moments that link and play with disability and adolescence. Just as the body of literature can be reclaimed, adolescent and disabled characters can reclaim themselves and find pride, even in their marginalized positions. They can reject notions that their very existence causes discomfort. They can find the power to force radical readings and rereadings. Novels and narratives that I've chosen for this project *remind* readers of problematic representations, and then (the most effective ones, at least) challenge, complicate, and overturn them. Readers are pushed to figure out how and why the narratives surprise and revolutionize disabled adolescents. *The Sound and the Fury*, and the Compson family itself, fail to make room for Quentin and Benjy before the novel's end and before self-acceptance; young-adult literary works, novels that took shape in the mid-1900s, rely on the same dismissive representations and fates of adolescent disabled characters. But many of them, by playing with definitions, labels, and those once-simple tropes, *do* offer places—even homes—for their Quentins and Benjys, and they *do* provide narrative agency to such characters. Young adult narratives, especially those published in the beginning of the twenty-first century, force readers to consider characters' actions, treatments, and representations.

Rather than resolving with celebrated entrances into adulthood, with welcomed cures, with "inspiring" acts to "overcome" hardships, or even with deaths that are able to offer relief to others, radically imagined and understood young adult narratives toy with these traditional endings. With a *lack* of stability or simplicity, these texts do not rely on accepted truths and offensive tropes. Instead, these works of realism, when most playful and empowering, resist distinct endings for disabled, adolescent characters and do not eliminate their Quentins and Benjys; young-adult narrator-protagonists are not asked to adhere to set futures, and many of the narratives end in confusion, *lacking* resolution.

DISABILITIES, DISORDERS, AND ILLNESSES

Generally grounded in feminist, queer, and Marxist theories, disability-studies scholarship cannot and does not ignore political discourse. Disability has its own history and collection of representations, but like gender, sexuality, race, and ethnicity, it is rooted in the body. Disability studies theorists, including Rosemarie Garland-Thomson, Robert McRuer, and Lennard J. Davis, have drawn comparisons between gender, sexuality, and disability, in which otherness is based on the acceptance of an imagined "norm" and a rejection of "imperfect" outliers. However fictional it may be, the corporeal basis of "normality" requires disability to be considered a defining characteristic that is both biological and social. Some of the earliest views of disabled and "visually different" people rendered them "monsters" and "freaks," and then, as understandings of disability became more medically based in the twentieth century, social pressures were placed on normalization through cure and other medical interventions. This medical model of disability, reliant on attempts to normalize, allowed for the emergence of a social model of disability, which sees disability as a social construction, or in other words, as a category produced only by the limitations of social structures in accommodating those with impairments. Postmodernism and Davis's notion of "dismodernism" have disrupted the social model by challenging essentialist understandings of disability as a corporeal "fact," while also challenging "the notion that identity is socially constructed" (232, 235). Such a heterogeneous category of human identity, disability poses countless problems and concerns and lacks group coherence. The general lack of internal coherence and definition may keep disability rights movements stalled in the stages of demanding basic needs of visibility, unity, acceptance, and pride. As of 2020, disabilities are too often understood as identities to be ignored, cured, or forgotten, and internal disagreements prevent the disability community from confidently and easily changing those understandings and assumptions.

Invisible disabilities of chronic illnesses, mental illnesses, mental disorders, and intellectual disabilities are often the most difficult to identify as disabilities; they also appear quite ubiquitously in young-adult narratives. In the Victorian era, mental illness, madness, and melancholia were characterized as rebellions—particularly among possessed women. Then, in the first part of the twentieth century, the rise of psychoanalysis—dominated by figures like Sigmund Freud and G. Stanley Hall—provoked severe treatments for those deemed "mad" or "insane." Extreme treatments continued into the middle of the century, when lobotomies and electroconvulsive therapies were popular treatments. The 1960s, however, brought a distinct change in understanding of mental illness, when French theorist Michel Foucault and American psychiatrist Thomas Szasz both questioned the existence of mental illness; Foucault argued that madness could not be contained in individuals and was instead a product of the categorization of human populations originating in the Enlightenment. Around the same time, the American Psychiatric Association offered a more practical definition of mental illnesses: medical disorders defined in part by social norms. By the 1970s, the newly organized Mad Pride movement gained momentum alongside the disability movement. However, in twenty-first-century disability-pride movements, mental illness—much like intellectual disability—is often relegated to the sides.

Theorizing mental illness has returned to a more medically based model in order to shift, as feminist literary scholar Elizabeth J. Donaldson notes, "from the model of madness-as-rebellion" to a more in-depth understanding of the relationship between biological impairments and social disabilities (Donaldson 104):

> It is possible to begin with the premise that mental illness is a neurobiological disorder and still remain committed to a feminist and a disability studies agenda—an agenda that fights discrimination, advocates for the rights of women and people with disabilities, seeks to dismantle ideologies of oppression, critiques medical discourses of mental illness, and demands equal access to social services and medical treatment—and it is important that feminists and disability scholars begin to think about mental illness in these medical and physical terms. (106)

In order to escape the notion that mental illness is somehow corrupt or otherworldly, and in order to understand mental illness through a disability-studies lens, scholars must return to a bodily, if not medicalized, understanding. Compared to social models of disability, favored in the beginning of the twenty-first century, such a call appears counterintuitive. Risks include reinforcing the need for "cures" and other anti-pride and genocidal-in-theory solutions, but risks of *not* acknowledging the biological bases of mental illness include propagating the notion that madness and melancholia are caused by spirits and used as rebellions.[1]

By returning the mind to the body, I am using this project to allow for more inclusive—while still always messy—definitions of "disability." Perhaps more importantly, with this practical understanding of disability as socially based identity that is ultimately rooted in the body, both disability activists and scholars will be able to move beyond basic demands of civil rights. A return to accepting bodily and biological bases of all disabilities—especially those that are invisible and associated with the mind—allows the disability community to accept its heterogeneous makeup. Rather than separating disabilities, impairments, and illnesses from each other, and rather than ignoring or hoping to eliminate them—tropes that appear frequently in literature and are explored in depth in "Chapter Four: Freaks"—the disability community can use "disabled" as an inclusive, umbrella term for varied identities, each different from the rest, but united together to demand those basic rights and accommodations. Unsurprisingly, perhaps, the young adult disability narratives explored in this project encourage this kind of unity—most explicitly, the narratives in "Chapter Six: Bulletproof Families."

Such a push for inclusivity may provocatively challenge established traditions and beliefs, such as those held by some members of the Deaf community—well known for their pride movements—who reject the idea that Deafness is a disability and instead identify as members of an ethno-linguistic community. The active Deaf community consequently separates itself from other disabled communities and refuses the acknowledgement and acceptance associated with disability and pushed for by activists.

As forcefully illustrated by the young adult narratives examined in "Chapter Five: "Accidents" and "Chapter Six: Bulletproof Families," disabled characters are indeed finding pride in their identities, while keeping their own definitions and labels and *without* distancing themselves from the larger disability community. Great power, these narratives suggest, may be found by accepting—not ignoring—the heterogeneity and variety of identities and cultures within the disabled community. Reducing the use of labels such as "physical disability" and "mental disability"—and instead using "disability" as an umbrella term to include both and more—brings together different groups in a united fight for agency, self-determination, social acceptance, *and* pride. Young adult narratives, especially in the beginning of the twenty-first century, place emphasis on these goals—including choice, self-determination, self-acceptance, and a willingness to embrace all disabled identities—through a number of narrative strategies. Often playful, young adult novels—as well as narratives in other media considered in "Chapter Six: Bulletproof Families"—offer new ways of representing and using disability that result in political and artful texts. The primary texts I've chosen for this project do reinforce claims that literary representations of disability are often patronizing, but they also offer surprisingly effective means for transgressing the traditional bounds, moving closer to achieving these important political goals.

ADOLESCENTS AND THEIR NARRATIVES

In addition to using mental illness to understand larger issues related to disability, I encourage the use of mental illness to map our literary and cultural understandings of adolescence. Certainly, theorist Julia Kristeva provides a suggestion for doing so—for linking adolescence, psychoanalysis, and adolescent literature—by suggesting that "the adolescent novel is a . . . psychological discourse" (quoted in Kidd 140). Critic Kenneth B. Kidd uses Kristeva's notion as a basis for his history of adolescence, from its emergence in relation to the novel in the eighteenth century to the twentieth century, when psychoanalysts like Hall and Freud had begun to study the stage of adolescence, and when the young adult novel began to emerge as a product to be published. By the 1940s, scholars and psychoanalysts understood that "a tumultuous adolescence was the developmental norm" and that nonconformity and rebellion were expected (Kidd 149–69). Literary developments follow suit, and scholars frequently point to the publication of *The Outsiders* in 1967 as an accepted beginning of the young adult literary canon. Popular and scholarly definitions of young adult literature rely heavily on marketing trends, leading to a frequent scholarly dismissal of the body of literature.

Disregarded even more intentionally, perhaps, the young adult subgenre of "problem novels" are often viewed as representative of all young adult literature. Associated with confessional narrators of the mid-twentieth century, problem novels are known for addressing problems and serious issues faced by young people. Consequently, their dismissal is often associated with their structure, which gives more attention to lessons than to stories, characters, or other literary complexities. Very little scholarship exists on this prominent subgenre of young adult literature. Academic discussions of such texts appear tangentially to other analyses, and primary- and secondary-school discussions rarely consider the literary possibilities of the texts.

Explicitly didactic tendencies fall under what critics Jennifer Miskec and Chris McGee have named "the trappings of the problem novel," and like other critics, they argue that attention should be paid to texts that "provide a more nuanced, sophisticated" reading experience (Miskec and McGee 164). In other words, understandings of problem novels suggest that if a young adult text manages to escape the bounds of accuracy and didacticism, it may become literary. However, these more literary young adult narratives simultaneously engage in some of the most familiar and problematic literary representations of disability. Categories of representations have been offered by disability studies scholars such as Thomson and Ato Quayson, but critics rarely consider differently those texts, including problem novels, written for and about adolescents. Critics have neither taken into consideration the ways in which disability and young adult literature interact nor the kinds of power these interactions produce.

Consequently, I am asking scholars to pause at these interactions between disability and adolescence, which occur almost exclusively in the difficult-to-define body of young adult literature. This project considers as young adult narratives those texts that emulate two formative young adult novels, J. D. Salinger's *The Catcher in the Rye* (1951) and Sylvia Plath's *The Bell Jar* (1963), and that do more than *consider* adolescence; they are thematically *focused* on adolescence. *The Catcher in the Rye* and *The Bell Jar*, perhaps the first novels to feature the intelligent, anxious teenaged voice that immediately labels many contemporary young adult novels, are also focused on adolescence. While *The Outsiders* may indeed mark the marketing-based target audience of young adults, I use Salinger's and Plath's novels as starting points for this project in order to use a more textually based definition for the still-nebulous body of young adult literature. The narratives explored here are rooted firmly in adolescence—*and* in disability.

WALLFLOWERS, FRUITS, FREAKS, ACCIDENTS, AND BULLETPROOF FAMILIES

Because young adult literature is defined in this project as a set of texts *about* adolescence, most often *for* adolescents, and most often with a distinctive young adult voice based in disability, these narratives produce literary readings that conflate and complicate. With the play and connection between adolescence and disability, these narratives demonstrate the political *and* literary possibilities for power that are perhaps inherent in young adult literature. Within this literary body, disability appears in—and evolves through—five types of representation: as the voice of adolescence itself, as a literary metaphor, as a catalyst for growth, as a politicized identity; and as a powerful, familial identity. All of these representations contribute to this project's subtitle: *The Power of Disability in Young Adult Narratives*. My intention is to illustrate three (overlapping) ways of interpreting this power: 1) the power that disability brings to young adult narratives to disrupt traditional literary tropes, 2) the strength that transgressive young adult narratives bring to disabled identities and communities, and 3) the social, political, and literary might created by making inseparable disability and young adult narratives.

In "Chapter Two: Wallflowers: Disability as the Young Adult Voice," readings begin with influential novels in the mid-1900s to find the distinctive young adult voice. Marked by traumatic events and language, these adolescent narrators, traced back to *The Catcher in the Rye* and *The Bell Jar*, display unmistakable symptoms of mental illness. The iconic Holden Caulfield and Esther Greenwood narrate with immediacy and urgency; almost always with intelligence, anxiety, and existential questioning; without overt didacticism; and with thematic elements focused around *being* an adolescent. These qualities define almost all young adult narratives, especially those that are marketed as such, and certainly suggest that adolescent voices and disabled voices both inhabit tumultuous, dynamic states of being. Simply, the voice of adolescence and the voice of disability are inseparable; in many ways, both literarily and societally, adolescence is a disability, while disability is a kind of adolescent state.

Chapters three, four, and five examine common representations of disability in literature—and more importantly, the ways that young adult narratives are able to expose these tropes and explicitly challenge their harmful messages. "Chapter Three: Fruits: Disability as a Literary Metaphor" begins with the common literary use of disability to function as a simple difference that provides meaning, restricting disabled characters to simple roles and identities. While these two-dimensional stereotypes allow literary metaphors to work, they simultaneously ignore reality and reinforce the harmful assumption that disability is a problem to be fixed. Some effective young adult novels, however, use disability metaphorically in order to produce greater insight and meaning, while still allowing disability to exist as a medical, social, and political identity. Such complex literary metaphors allow texts to complicate and empower both adolescence and disability—especially by confusing and conflating the identities.

"Chapter Four: Freaks: Disability as a Catalyst for Growth" examines a very specific kind of disabled literary character. The freak—in literature and culture—is marked as disabled, different, or nonnormative; is treated as a supporting character; and is used as a spectacle and catalyst for growth in others. Regarded as one of the most problematic representations of disability, freaks appear so regularly that they often go unnoticed; they are ubiquitous, underdeveloped, not fully human, infantilized sidekicks, and they are used for others' moments of self-realization and self-congratulation. A number of young adult narratives that focus explicitly on disability are, at least by the 2010s, beginning to push boundaries and to experiment with the function and identity of the freak. Chapter four concludes with a discussion of a freak character whose role is questioned and destroyed, in a text that explicitly challenges common assumptions about disabled identities.

"Chapter Five: Accidents: Disability as a Political Identity" reclaims problem novels as important literary and political narratives. While standard problem novels strive for accuracy, deliver didactic messages, and focus on a single problem, others find ways to offer accurate analyses of problems *without* sidelining rich stories and characters. By using disability as a real, politicized identity, the novels presented in this chapter introduce characters, as well as readers, to the goals and actions of disability-rights movements. They simplify neither daily frustrations nor larger, systemic difficulties faced by disabled characters, and they refuse to overly complicate, to a place beyond understanding, disabled lives; the most effective problem novels focused on disability are indeed political and didactic, but they are also artfully told stories.

"Chapter Six: Bulletproof Families" widens the definition of young adult literature from novels (published no earlier than the mid-1900s) to include narratives in other media: nonfiction essays and memoirs, songs, television series, films, and texts in a number of digital media that radically alter narrative formats. These narratives, generally emerging in the beginning of the twenty-first century, reflect and redefine both the narrative voice and the expected uses of disability in young adult novels. By playing with the types of representation examined in chapters two, three, four, and five, these narratives in other media push even further both literary criticism and disability activism. Young adult disability narratives that are delivered through and affected by digital media combine elements of literary criticism, narrative expression, disability theories, and political activism both to create and to represent the solidarity of family-like communities. Popular, accessible, and widely available narratives in digital media emphasize the importance and complication of self-expression, as well as an emerging reliance on authors' authentic voices. These young adult disability narratives encourage a united, multi-voiced community that includes disabled people, allies, and families—through literary texts that are radically different from in-print novels and through political and social strategies that have not yet taken hold.

Chapter 2

WALLFLOWERS

Disability as the Young Adult Voice

The most ubiquitous representation of disability in young adult literature is easy to miss; the immediately recognizable, "authentic" and "normal" voice of adolescence is also a voice of mental illness. Full of confessional urgency, angst, and intelligence, the literary adolescent voice is both definitive of the young adult genre and malleable, debatable, and far from uniform. To illustrate, Stephen Chbosky's *The Perks of Being a Wallflower* (1999), Rachel Cohn and David Levithan's *Nick and Norah's Infinite Playlist* (2006), and Frank Portman's *King Dork* (2006) stand as three very different, yet absolutely typical, young adult novels; the very first page of each welcomes the reader with confessional angst. Such reader-directed openings mimic those of *The Catcher in the Rye* (1951) and *The Bell Jar* (1963), two midcentury novels, with pervasive narrative voices that are thematically focused on adolescence. At the time of its publication in the United Kingdom in 1963, Plath's novel "quickly established itself as a female rite-of-passage novel, a twin to *Catcher in the Rye* [*sic*]—a comparison first noted by one of the original British reviewers" (McCullough xiv). More than moving through a rite of passage, both Holden's and Esther's stories institute complex and nuanced narrative voices, which are now recognizable as "authentically" adolescent.

Indeed, both *The Catcher in the Rye* and *The Bell Jar* are iconic first-person narratives about mentally ill adolescents, and with their remarkably similar voices, they have shaped the standard voice of young adult literature—a voice that's generally not considered ill, or disabled.[1] Mental illness and adolescence, however, are locked together. In tracing the developments of both psychoanalysis and young adult literature, scholar Kenneth B. Kidd turns to J. D. Salinger's *The*

Catcher in the Rye, which he calls "both a psychological and a literary work," as well as "a case history of us all" (156, 169). If adolescence sounds like Holden Caulfield, then adolescence sounds like mental illness; consequently, if adolescents are expected to display symptoms of mental illness, then mental illness is "normal" during adolescence, and a mentally ill teenager like Holden may represent "us all." Indeed, as this chapter illustrates, young adult literature directly borrows from two *mentally ill* adolescent narrators: Holden Caulfield and Esther Greenwood. Adolescence, understood biologically and psychologically, is *not* the same as severe mental illness, but because of the influence of Salinger's and Plath's texts, young adult literary portrayals represent them as one and the same. Specifically, the iconic Holden Caulfield and Esther Greenwood narrate their tales with immediacy and urgency; with thematic elements *focused on* what it means to be a young adult; and in narrative voices marked by intelligence, anxiety, and existential questioning.[2] Young adult literature must be positioned as a set of texts—largely emulating *The Catcher in the Rye* and *The Bell Jar*, that are written *about* adolescence, most often *for* adolescents, and most often with a distinctive, mentally ill narrative voice.[3]

Because Holden's and Esther's voices, which echo each other, reign as archetypically adolescent voices, effectively and authentically voiced young adult narrators may also be considered mentally ill—or at the very least, they demonstrate qualities of the mentally ill archetypes. Like Holden and Esther, literary young adult narrators are:

1. intelligent, urgent, and solitary;
2. judgmental and overly sensitive;
3. obsessed with sex, death, and truth;
4. existentially distressed by adolescence; and
5. symptomatic of mental illness.

With such qualities, Holden and Esther reflect clinical criteria of depressive and other episodes, *as well as* qualities typical of adolescents. Both groups of people are expected, in Western cultures, to grow up, change, and cure their current conditions, but looking a bit more closely at the adolescent narrators of these novels, however, reveals secrets for finding security, or "normalization," without change and without "cures." Even if mental illness is found only implicitly, these wallflower-like narrators do display symptoms of (generally depressive) disorders. Consequently, literary authenticity is achieved when adolescence itself is represented as mental illness. The novels ultimately suggest acceptance; these narrators find solace when they accept themselves, *refusing* the notion that they must grow, change, or be treated. These literary adolescents offer suggestions that not only align with twentieth- and twenty-first-century psychological treatments but also remove the stigmas faced by both adolescents and the mentally ill. Radically disabled, they control their narratives and refuse change.

INTELLIGENT, URGENT, AND SOLITARY

In his famous opening words, Salinger's Holden explains, "If you really want to hear about it, the first thing you'll probably want to know is where I was born" (1); he continues to regard his "lousy childhood" as a part of his story but of course, he claims that he doesn't "feel like going into it" (1). Go into it he does, urgently explaining to his reader—the "you" he addresses immediately—his tales of being shuffled from prep school to prep school, always cynical and always somewhat of a loner. He gets expelled for poor grades but not for a lack of intellect, made clear when he tells his reader how he "read[s] a lot of classical books" and when he writes a beautiful homework assignment for his roommate because he's a "hot-shot in English" (18, 28). In much the same vein, Plath's Esther writes not for herself but for an implied audience, one she desperately needs and one that needs explanation. Esther's loneliness—moving along without close friends and feeling "very still and very empty, the way the eye of a tornado must feel" (3)—is offered to her reader alongside clues of her intelligence. For starters, she *is* the supposed envy of girls across America, having "won a fashion magazine contest, by writing essays and stories and poems and fashion blurbs," but more importantly, Esther's entire life and history has been defined by "good marks and prizes and grants of one sort or another"; at age nineteen, she is already "champion[ed] for graduate school at the biggest universities in the east . . . [with] promises of full scholarships all the way" (3, 25, 31–32). Like Holden before her, Esther defines the young adult voice with her intellect, which separates her from others, leaving her a loner who writes to someone who might understand. Consequently, both Esther and Holden, like their twenty-first-century descendants, have alienated and separated themselves as independent intellectuals, but both demonstrate at least some desire to connect,[4] a characterization that fuels their stories and creates the kind of existential angst that has come to define the adolescent voice.

Also angst-ridden and searching for an understanding confidant, Charlie, the narrator-protagonist of *Perks*, begins his epistolary story by directly addressing a reader—much as Holden does—someone he simply calls "friend":

> I am writing to you because she said you listen and understand and didn't try to sleep with that person at that party even though you could have. . . . I just need to know that someone out there listens and understands and doesn't try to sleep with people even if they could have. I need to know that these people exist. (Chbosky 2)

Charlie's "friend" is never revealed but remains the recipient of his thoughts throughout the novel, the story of Charlie's first year of high school. Charlie begins the academic year—like so many wallflowers—as a loner, but Charlie's loneliness is amplified by the loss of his two best friends: his schoolmate Michael to a recent suicide and his aunt Helen to an earlier, more mysterious death. Quickly targeted as "one of the most gifted people" that his English teacher Bill has ever met, Charlie is assigned extra reading and writing, while receiving lectures asking him to consider why he might be content as a loner (181):

> "Do you always think this much, Charlie?"
> "Is that bad?" I just wanted someone to tell me the truth.
> "Not necessarily. It's just that sometimes people use thought to not participate in life."
> "Is that bad?"
> "Yes." (24)

Such conversations with Bill quickly alert Charlie to a problem in being a wallflower and create an urgency in trying to change himself and connect with his peers. The safest choice for a friend, since "Michael is gone, and Susan hangs around different boys now, and Bridget is still crazy, and Carl's mom sent him to a Catholic school, and Dave with the awkward glasses moved away," is Patrick from shop class, who "seemed like the kind of guy you could just walk up to at a football game even though you were three years younger and not popular" (18, 19). Even so, Charlie's personality has already grown so introverted that, when new friend Patrick tells him he is insightful, Charlie notes, "I didn't know that other people thought things about me. I didn't know that they looked" (38). Like Holden and Esther, he wanders through school and life assuming he is alone and desperately trying to make uncomfortable connections, separating himself from social functions, and participating internally rather than externally.

Also intelligent loners, the eponymous narrator-protagonists in *Nick and Norah's Infinite Playlist* write alternating chapters, and like Esther, they provide enough exposition to suggest that they are telling their tales to outside readers, rather than recording intimate thoughts for themselves. Nick immediately separates himself from his friends and bandmates by introducing himself as "the nonqueer bassist in a queercore band who is filling the room with undertone" (Cohn and Levithan 1). Norah similarly separates herself, but does so with harsh judgments of her closest friends, primarily Caroline, the "groupie bitch," whom she "loves" but "always [has] to think about" (10). Both somewhat out of place at the queercore show, Nick and Norah alert their readers to their singularities, bound to wind up next to each other at the bar. Neither is particularly happy, but each—like the other narrators—relies on wit and intellect, particularly Norah, who agonizes over her decision to take "a gap year on a *kibbutz* in South Africa over Brown" (11, emphasis in original). Nick's intelligence is described as a more creative, yet equally admirable one, as he writes song lyrics that make Norah think, "I would give body parts to have a guy write something like that for me" (18). And of course, Nick eventually does. The lead-up to Nick's writing song lyrics for Norah provides the central plot of the short novel, which captures a desperate desire for intimate connection, along with an intense fear of trusting others. Nick confesses that he is not ready for "being open. Being hurt. Liking. Not being liked. Seeing the flicker on. Seeing the flicker off. Leaping. Falling. Crashing," while Norah almost simultaneously tells him, "I think you're nice to me and that scares the fuck out of me" (61, 63). True disciples of Holden and Esther, Nick and Norah tackle a loneliness that does, however, become a kind of "twoliness" in Nick's chapters, as well as all-encompassing, urgent desires for change from their current states of heartache and "malaise" (173, 51).

Naturally, *King Dork*—called "a window into what it would be like if Holden Caulfield read *The Catcher in the Rye*" by the *New York Post* on its back cover—begins with an intelligent loner in distress. Narrator Tom clarifies to an outside reader that "it started with a book," *The Catcher in the Rye* (Portman 1). Tom quickly explains to his reader that he is a dork, "small for [his] age, young for [his] gender, uncomfortable in most situations, nearsighted, skinny, awkward, and nervous. And no good at sports" (5). He even explains at the outset of his story that he is not only an outcast, but a smart one: "I suppose I fit the traditional mold of the brainy, freaky, oddball kid who reads too much, so bright that his genius is sometimes mistaken for just being retarded" (5). Less mature and creatively intellectual than the other narrators, Tom does begin his story in the same way and places himself in the same position of being an intellect looking for connection—a student searching for fulfillment outside of school. As his story continues, Tom reveals that his outside reader is also a teenager by using phrases and sentences such as "your school" and posing questions such as "What would you have done?" (11, 290). Tom is fraught with desires to connect—to his reader, to his past, to his family, to sexual partners, and even to his closest "friend," an untrustworthy boy named Sam (295). Tom prides himself on being able "to give . . . [adults] the old freaky-youth-genius treatment," but his consistent reminders to the reader about his intelligence, coupled with rather simple sentence structures and an explicit hatred of "*Catcher in the Fucking Rye*" set Tom apart from the other narrators (182, 92).[5] Still, even with, and perhaps *because of*, his pervasive self-consciousness, Tom's character echoes the others from the start; he is a lonely intellectual (so he claims, at least) who strives to connect in part through an urgent telling of his own story.

JUDGMENTAL AND OVERLY SENSITIVE

As they attempt and nevertheless refuse connections throughout New York City and New England, Holden and Esther complicate their already angsty dispositions; throughout *Catcher* and *The Bell Jar*, the sensitive narrators demonstrate emotionally unstable propensities to feel extreme empathy and sympathy, as well as to feel strong judgments toward themselves and others. These self-aware narrators feel too much too strongly, and their later young adult peers mimic the emotional and critical manners in their respective narratives. Holden, of course, well-known for his use of the word "phony," is disillusioned by nearly every person and institution he encounters. It's as though he cannot *not* feel so much so completely—simultaneously insulting and loving everything inside of him and everything he observes, including his headmaster's daughter, whom he describes with insult and sympathy:

> I liked her. She had a big nose and her nails were all bitten down and bloody-looking and she had on those damn falsies that point all over the place, but you felt sort of sorry for her. What I liked about her, she didn't give you a lot of horse manure about what a great guy her father was. She probably knew what a phony slob he was. (3)

So many of Holden's criticisms, particularly of what he perceives to be phoniness, are inextricably connected to great admiration and sympathy for humanity. In the above passage, for example, Holden notices this young girl's "bloody-looking" nails, but if anything, her faults and areas of vulnerability *appeal* to him, and he likes her, though with much more strength and consideration than one may expect from a sixteen-year-old describing a girl he'd sat next to just once. When confronted with more meaningful encounters and memories of family members, friends, and former teachers, Holden suggests very strong emotions but shows lesser actions—such as kissing heads and making dates—in a way that almost keeps true connection at arm's length.[6] Like Holden, Esther, established as a loner who resists true connection, similarly approaches the world with a painful mix of judgment and feeling, worrying about her own behaviors while both criticizing and sympathizing with others. Perhaps as an attempt to protect her sensitive inner-self, Esther uses biting humor and praises intelligence throughout her narrative. Like Holden's, Esther's insults are peppered with sensitivity and confusion, as when she "spent an hour kissing a hairy, ape-shaped law student from Yale because [she] felt sorry for him, he was so ugly" (146). Critical and consistently self-aware, Esther also wrestles with extreme surges of emotion at seemingly inconsequential moments:

> I didn't want my picture taken because I was going to cry. I didn't know why I was going to cry, but I knew that if anybody spoke to me or looked at me too closely the tears would fly out of my eyes and the sobs would fly out of my throat and I'd cry for a week. I would feel the tears brimming and sloshing in me like water in a glass that is unsteady and too full. (100–101)

While Esther may control her tears more effectively than Holden, she still feels overwhelmed, while unable or unwilling to connect with others. She is drawn to "people in crucial situations," and although they make her sick, she knows that "if there was a road accident or a street fight or a baby pickled in a laboratory jar for me to look at, I'd stop and look so hard I never forgot it" (13). She cannot look away from those she disdains and with whom she so often sympathizes, and she looks at herself with the same judgmental eye.

In *Perks*, Charlie explains that he's "pretty emotional," even adding, "Some kids look at me strange in the hallways because I don't decorate my locker, and I'm the one who beat up Sean and couldn't stop crying after he did it" (Chbosky 8). As sensitive and self-reflective as any narrator, Charlie knows he beat up classmate Sean in self-defense and acknowledges he didn't "understand why Sean wanted to hurt" him, considering how small and quiet he is (7). Like Holden especially, Charlie feels empathy while watching others, even when it makes his thinking more difficult; when he learns that his sister has been abused by her boyfriend, he writes, "I could see this boy at home doing his homework and thinking about my sister naked. And I could see them holding hands at football games that they do not watch.

And I could see this boy throwing up in the bushes at a party house. And I could see my sister putting up with it. And I felt very bad for both of them" (12). He feels sorry for this boy, even though he finally tells his teacher Bill about the abuse. Nothing is simple for Charlie. He feels "ashamed" for going to the high school football game and doesn't "know exactly why," but he does know that he is not "popular enough to go" (18). Further shame arises after he meets and spends time with new friends Patrick and Sam, stepsiblings, because "that night, I had a weird dream. I was with Sam. And we were both naked. And her legs were spread over the sides of the couch. And I woke up. And I had never felt that good in my life. But I also felt bad because I saw her naked without her permission" (21). His emotion makes it difficult for him "to 'participate' like Bill said" (28), but he continues to try throughout the novel, and he eventually spends most of his free time with Patrick, Sam, and their friends. His self-awareness and self-consciousness never subside, however, and when Sam begins dating a boy named Craig, he knows his reader will assume he is "jealous of him. I'm not. Honest. It's just that Craig doesn't really listen to her when she talks. I don't mean that he's a bad guy because he's not. It's just that he always looks distracted" (48). Charlie wants Sam to find someone who will love and appreciate her simply for being her, and when he imagines he could be the one, his feelings overwhelm him. Rarely as harsh as the other narrators, Charlie does express dislike for Mary Elizabeth, his girlfriend for a brief time, because—much like Charlie's characterization of Craig—she shows a distinct lack of concern for others and gives him gifts in order to "expose [him] to all these great things" that he doesn't care about at all (129).

Presenting themselves almost as twenty-first-century versions of Holden and Esther, the narrators in *Nick and Norah's Infinite Playlist* are both emotional, sensitive, self-aware, and—in Norah's case—judgmental. In the middle of their magical night together, Norah's ex-friend and Nick's ex-girlfriend Tris barks advice to Norah: "You and he are not the one-night-stand types. You're all sensitive and shit. Don't go too fast" (Cohn and Levithan 131). Sensitive they are, as Nick feels anxiety when Norah "looks at [him] with this total incomprehension, like she's watching footage of the world being blown up, and [he's] the little blurb on the corner of the screen saying what the weather is like outside, and Norah hides behind self-judgments by defining herself as a "straight-edge, responsible valedictorian bitch" who is also "an insufferable music snob," while actually valuing sentiment and loyalty, "the best parts of Nick" (42, 11, 90). Reminiscent of both Holden and Esther, Nick realizes that he is "self-conscious" while dancing and does his best to free himself "from everything but the chords" (77). Norah, on the other hand, looks outward and apologizes for being rude to a cabbie, acknowledging, "I bet he's a really nice dad. I bet his daughters make his favorite foods from Kazakhstan for him and nag him about getting his prostate checked regularly" (105). These two narrators feel swells of emotion about strangers, about each other, and about their own movements. They interact with each other in a way that is both flirtatious and painful in its overanalysis and incessant evaluation, always filled with judgment and sensitivity:

> "What's up?" I shout. And she looks at me like she's forgotten I exist. This means she's also forgotten to guard herself from me, so I have a moment when I see the sentences behind her eyes. *I can't do this. This is too fucking hard.*
>
> I change my question. I say, "What's wrong?" And just like that, her sentences are shut behind a screen. But I'm curious. Yes, I'm damn curious. (23)

Their curiosity propels them, and their intense emotion makes them echo Holden and Esther as narrators.

Also intensely emotional and judgmental, as well as occasionally sensitive, *King Dork*'s Tom navigates through his world of "High School Hell," where he assumes his writing is "too complex for the robots [teachers] to grasp" and where the kids who aren't losers are "psychopathic normal people" (Portman 10, 14, 13). Filled with insults—many of which are simply, and startlingly, offensive regarding others' genders, sexualities, and disabilities—Tom's narrative is written in anger and self-consciousness. Through most of the novel, he even regards his family coolly, noting unemotionally that his "mom spends a great deal of time crying" (25). Tom admits that "it's not fair that I'm so unaccommodating" to his parents, and when complimenting his stepfather, Tom's sentences are laced with insults directed both at his stepfather's attempt to connect and at societal norms in general (27):

> Little Big Tom had done everything wrong and had broken a great many well-established, TV-dramatized, "Dear Abby"–certified rules about parental conduct with regard to respecting people's privacy whenever drugs are not involved, but I've got to say that in the all-important stage known as Making Amends by Trying to Purchase Affection and Trust with Extravagant Gifts, he had really come through. (135)

Tom eventually cuts his family some slack, even putting his "arm around [his sister] kind of awkwardly" and "kiss[ing his mother] on the cheek" when discussing his father's death (263, 270).

OBSESSED WITH SEX, DEATH, AND TRUTH

Holden and Esther have doubtlessly defined a young adult manner of speech and behavior, and through their tales of accepting adolescence, they have also set guidelines for the *content* of adolescent thoughts. Both narrators are preoccupied by ideas of sex, death, and truth, and both recall and experience traumatic events. Holden bluntly explains his own sexuality—"I don't mean I'm oversexed or anything like that—although I am quite sexy" (54)—and his desire to set boundaries because, he explains, "Sex is something I really don't understand too hot. You never know *where* the hell you are" (63). His brother Allie's death, as well as death in general, similarly occupy Holden's thoughts, such as when he worries he'll catch pneumonia and imagines himself being buried, "surrounded by dead guys," after a funeral (155). Such preoccupations lead Holden to ponder truth and authenticity, as he suspects people and institutions of being "phony" and frequently goes into more detail, as when he observes a crowd in New York: "You never saw so many phonies in your life, everybody smoking their ears off and talking about the play so that everybody could hear and know how sharp they were" (3, 9, 126). His seemingly superficial and endless judgments betray a profound desire to understand himself, his relationships with others, and his relationships with both life and death. Esther—Plath's alter ego known for suicide attempts—ponders death and dying throughout her story; like Holden, she also obsesses over sex and truth, and these preoccupations connect with each other. Esther encounters men who disappoint and abuse her sexually, and who lead to her obsession with truth and purity: when she finally loses her virginity to a professor named Irwin, she worries that "Irwin had injured me in some awful obscure way, and the while I lay there . . . I was really dying" (232). She also seeks truth, or weight, in death, as she devours articles about suicides and suicide attempts and "paperbacks on abnormal psychology" in order to understand her own depressive symptoms (158). Before attempting, or beginning to attempt, suicide four times in the novel, Esther explains, "The thought that I might kill myself formed in my mind coolly as a tree or a flower" (97). Her thoughts about suicide and death are relentless—and always connected to her suspicions of hypocrisy and a desire for truth.

While Charlie searches less explicitly for truth in *Perks*, his entire journey is one of self-discovery, as he learns about his aunt Helen's death and his resulting emotions, caused by sexual abuse. Consequently, the entire novel revolves around a quest for truth, specifically about sex and death, which are understood through traumatic experiences. When he realizes that Helen had abused him, Charlie is kissing his longtime crush Sam, who encourages him to be honest: "I don't want to be somebody's crush," she tells him. "If somebody likes me, I want them to like the real me, not what they think I am. And I don't want them to carry it around inside. I want them to show me, so I can feel it, too" (Chbosky 201). Charlie allows himself to feel—and feels much more than expected. Earlier in the novel, he echoes Holden's insecurities by asking his reader, "Do you know what 'masturbation' is? I think you probably do because you are older than me," and then explaining how he *tries* "not to feel ashamed" when he does masturbate (21, 27). Self-consciousness, shame, and insecurity carry over into Charlie's understanding of sexual relationships between people. When he witnesses sexual assault at a party, he tells Sam and concludes, "I couldn't tell if she was sad or just knew more things than me" (32). His assumptions are that he knows very little about sex, but he also possesses a mature acceptance of Patrick's secret relationship, which he poetically describes as "a stolen type of kissing" (36). Similarly, the death that remains present throughout the book is perhaps a stolen type of death, as it exists mainly in poetry and in memories that are "hard to remember" (3). Charlie has experienced his friend Michael committing suicide, as well as his aunt Helen's death "in a terrible car accident" on his seventh birthday, and both memories haunt him (90). In addition to reciting "some kid's suicide note," Charlie falls in love with the song "Asleep" by the Smiths, with lyrics—"sing me to sleep" and "deep in the cell of my heart / I really want to go"—that allude to suicide (Chbosky 73, 62; Morrissey and Marr). Indeed, Charlie, though he does not express any desire to take his own life, surrounds himself and is surrounded by death, as he learns about sex through an unintended search for truth.

Less morbid perhaps than the other stories, *Nick and Norah's Infinite Playlist* still echoes the thought patterns of archetypal narrator-protagonists, as both narrators are heartbroken by the loss of past lovers and are embarking on a new romance. Nick and Norah are obsessed with sex and romance, and they seek truth and honesty. Norah seems to channel Esther's preoccupation with purity by noting again and again that she is "frigid," as well as Holden's uncertainty by explaining, "I have no idea how to do this 'date' thing" (Cohn and Levithan 54). Nick, on the other hand, worries less about his sexual knowledge and finds more excitement in all things romantic, believing that every time he sees his ex-girlfriend, "from now until I die, she will leave me for good," and viewing Norah as the "one hopeful chord in this cacophony" (26). Both explicitly identify as straight, but still show more comfort with sexuality than the other narrators; Nick appreciates physical affection from his male friend Dev, and Norah supposes that "there's just *sexuality*, and it's bendable and unpredictable" (148, original emphasis). Such realizations illustrate the duo's consistent desire for honest communication, because, as Norah points out to her reader, "I'm all for sarcasm, but sometimes it's tiring" (68–69).

King Dork, on the other hand, is driven by mystery: Tom searches for truth about a girl ostensibly named Fiona who kisses him at a party, about his maligned associate principal Mr. Teone, and—most importantly—about his father's life and death. All force him to consider sex, death, and truth. Even without mysteries to solve, Tom is a fourteen-year-old boy and announces bluntly, "It seems as if I am always horny" (Portman 51). As inexperienced as Charlie, Tom approaches sex with the same self-deprecation and nervousness as the other narrators. He notes that, when Fiona puts his hand on her stomach, "it was so surprising. I knew I was supposed to kiss her, but I wasn't sure how to go about it exactly" (73). By the end of the novel, Tom has "struck up an illicit, blow-job-oriented relationship" with two different girls, and he even considers that he might be "in love" with one of them (297, 302). Not as integrally connected to sex as it is for some of the other narrators, death does surround Tom's character. Much as Charlie "want[s] it all to stop spinning" when he thinks of his aunt Helen, Tom becomes "disoriented and light-headed" with pressure in his chest when he thinks of his dad (Chbosky 94, Portman 22). When he discovers that his father's car accident "wasn't straightforward," he focuses almost completely on learning the truth; though he never learns for sure if his father died by suicide, homicide, or accident, he eventually concludes that "life is weird" (42, 315).

EXISTENTIALLY DISTRESSED BY ADOLESCENCE

In his central metaphor of watching "little kids" and running "to catch everybody if they start to go over the cliff," Holden Caulfield becomes "the catcher in the rye," a preserver of childhood (Salinger 173). Fraught with emotion and preoccupied with matters of life and death, teenaged Holden demonstrates nostalgia for times past and anxiety over his future. When he tries to return to his childhood spot at Museum of Natural History, "all of a sudden [he] wouldn't have gone inside for a million bucks," because—his reader must assume—he knows he cannot return to an age he's already left (122). Holden is alone as an adolescent, remembering being told that he "had no direction in life" and feeling forced to confront an uncertain future (59). Pressure to find a future, coupled with nostalgia, Holden gets "depressed as hell again" when his friend Sally refuses to run away (133); Holden, of course, knows that adulthood will "be entirely different," even though Sally cannot understand what he means "at all" (133). In his anxiety, Holden is alone. Esther, too, remains alone as she sits in the crotch of a metaphorical fig tree, watching all of her potential futures "wrinkle and go black" as she delays her transition into adulthood (Plath 77). Like Holden, she remembers a past that felt more promising, when "studying and reading and writing and working like mad was what [she] wanted to do," but she is already in the middle of the "terrible, terrible fall" Holden is approaching (Plath 31, Salinger 186): "After nineteen years of running after good marks and prizes and grants of one sort and another, I was letting up, slowing down, dropping clean out of the race" (Plath 29). Before reaching adulthood, Esther is ready to resign, exhausted by imagined futures: one with a husband, "getting up at seven and cooking him eggs and bacon and toast and coffee," and another as an editor, "in an office full of potted rubber plants and African violets my secretary had to water each morning" (84, 39). These futures are mutually exclusive for Esther, and the realization that neither one is likely leaves her to believe that she "was only purely happy until [she] was nine years old," just before her father died (75). Esther, like Holden, mourns the loss of childhood and fears the uncertainty of a future that seems to hold only disappointment.

On the brink of the twenty-first century, Charlie faces a similar position of being both young and old, feeling "both happy and sad and . . . still trying to figure out how that could be" (Chbosky 2). His story begins the night before high school, to which he is "really afraid of going," and in the way Holden sees children falling off a cliff, Charlie falls into a world where his old friends are gone, and where his new teacher begins giving him extra coming-of-age books (6). Charlie's own tale not only begins at the onset of high school, it also coincides with wondering why he is "this way": a wallflower who cries too easily (2). Eager to find self-understanding, Charlie combs his childhood for answers and acknowledges that he and his family are changing; his parents worry about his brother in college and about his sister's applications to college, but Charlie—still growing—is taken to buy new clothes:

> It's like when we were little, and we would go to the grocery store. My sister and brother would fight about things that my

> sister and brother would fight about, and I would sit at the bottom of the shopping cart. And my mom would be so upset by the end of shopping that she would push the cart fast, and I would feel like I was in a submarine.
>
> Yesterday was like that except now I got to sit in the front seat. (54)

Through his first year of high school, Charlie begins smoking cigarettes, experiments with sex and drugs, learns how to go to parties, and discovers something new with each letter he writes. He is caught in a world that is changing, and discoveries about his past and predictions for his future change as wildly as his adolescent present.

Having already finished high school, Nick and Norah are teetering on the far end of adolescence—more like Holden and Esther. Especially through Norah's narration, anxiety about adulthood emerges, and the two narrators are standing "at the crossroads of the world," on the brink of a new relationship and unsure of how to spend the next year (Cohn and Levithan 153, 11). Like Esther, Norah imagines various futures but assumes she faces "a lifetime of loneliness" and will "dedicate [her]self to good deeds," while Nick spends more of his narrative trying "to get past the past" (92, 60). He has been devastated by the end of his last romantic relationship, and in Norah finds someone who believes she has "lost [her] virginity and [her] whole youth" to her own ex-boyfriend (48). They both agonize over wasted time and worry about future plans, occasionally finding comfort in music with nostalgia and hope: "suddenly Hunter and Dev launch into a fucking *Green Day* cover, and we're all seven years old again and dancing like we spit out the Ritalin while Mom wasn't looking. We become this one flailing paramecium mass, fever-connected as the guitarist riffs electrons" (22). The music-centered adolescence experienced by Nick and Norah is an anxiety that unites them, even though each feels alone.

In *King Dork*, Tom is even more existentially alone, but his criticisms of other adolescents—both fictional and around him—display notable angst about adolescence. Tom criticizes Holden Caulfield and even suggests that the "mythical fantasy about saving children from falling off a cliff" is "pretty goddam phony and all," but his reading of

Holden's chief metaphor actually shows the same desire to preserve a kind of childhood innocence (Portman 245, 246). Tom imagines that he is *in* Holden's field of rye, which he describes as his teenaged existence—where someone inevitably starts "hiring a psychiatrist to squeeze the individuality out of you, and making you box till first blood, and pouring Coke on your book, and beating you senseless in the boys' bathroom, and ridiculing your balls"—and forgets that "little kids" inhabit Holden's rye (Portman 246, Salinger 173). Viewing Holden as a villain, rather than savior, Tom explains that "just when you think you've found the edge of the field and are about to emerge from Rye Hell, this AP teacher or baby-boomer parent dressed as a beloved literary character scoops you up and throws you back into the pit of vipers. I mean, the field of rye" (Portman 247). Tom is no longer one of those "little kids," and lingers in the emotional and social difficulties of adolescence. At times nostalgic, Tom tries to see his mother through his now-deceased father's eyes, as a "quirky and goofy and charming" woman, in order to make his present situation more bearable (24). He dreams of future possibilities, when he might find a girlfriend to join "A Sex Alliance Against Society" or when everyone will "wake up and realize that we were right about everything all along" (133, 248). Perhaps not as well-articulated as those of the other narrators, Tom's situation is one that straddles childhood and adulthood, and it is one in which he is not at peace.

SYMPTOMATIC OF MENTAL ILLNESS

Most important in naming Holden and Esther the archetypal adolescents are their symptoms and treatments for mental illness. Neither is explicitly diagnosed, but both narrators exhibit behaviors and thoughts that fit diagnostic criteria for depressive disorders. Holden, of course, uses words such as "depressing," "sad and lonesome" almost as frequently as he calls people phonies, and in a few moments, he even contemplates suicide: "I wasn't sleepy or anything, but I was feeling sort of lousy. Depressed and all. I almost wished I was dead" (Salinger 50, 51, 90). In addition to suicidal ideation, Holden meets criteria of several mental illnesses, and he does finally reveal that, in addition to speaking to his reader, he has had to answer questions made by "this one psychoanalyst guy they have here," situating himself in some sort of treatment center for those with mental illnesses (213). Residence in a psychiatric hospital accounts for a large part of Esther's story, in which mental illness is not simply implied but is thematically important.[7] After her first dose of electroconvulsive therapy, she nearly attempts suicide twice with razor blades, a method she "thought . . . would be easy, lying in the tub and seeing the redness flower from my wrists, flush after flush through the clear water, till I sank to sleep under a surface gaudy as poppies" (Plath 147). Then she tries to hang herself but realizes "that my body had all sorts of little tricks, such as making my hands go limp at the crucial second, which would save it, time and again"; next, she tries drowning, but finds herself "floating, without effort" (159, 161). Finally, swallowing a bottle of pills and hiding in "a dark gap" under her house's breezeway nearly kills her, and she ends up in a hospital (168). Beyond suicide attempts, Esther—as already discussed—shows signs of depression when she cannot take a photograph without risking "tears brimming and sloshing" and when she takes to her bed and can no longer "see the point of getting up" (101, 117). Like Holden, Esther lives, through her entire narrative, with strong symptoms of depressive disorders.[8]

Twenty-first-century narrator Charlie begins his story by explaining how he "never did stop crying" to his guidance counselor after Michael committed suicide (Chbosky 4). Eventually, Charlie reveals that he has been going to psychiatrists since Aunt Helen died, and while he does not offer any diagnoses, he describes "going to a bad place" that gets worse when he "think[s] about it too much" (74). Charlie's bad place reminds him of "when you look at yourself in the mirror and you say your name. And it gets to a point where none of it seems real" (74). His brief losses of reality recall the nearly psychotic symptoms of both Holden and Esther, and Charlie also feels simply "too sad" and guilty when remembering his aunt (92). Seeing a psychiatrist, "who is a very nice man," is part of Charlie's routine, but he also works hard to prevent falling too deeply into his bad place; he also feels worse when his doctor asks him "questions about when [he] was younger" because "they're starting to get weird" (103, 173). Ultimately, Charlie decides that his "psychiatrist's questions weren't weird after all," because he remembers that Helen had abused him, and he ends up "sitting in a doctor's office" after blacking out (205, 208). He stays in the hospital for two months, and though his problems are neither solved nor cured, he realizes that "it's okay to feel things" (212).

Feeling strongly throughout their narratives, Nick and Norah are not treated for mental illness and probably fail to show symptoms severe enough to require any treatment; however, the narratives in *Nick and Norah's Infinite Playlist* are filled with words and phrases of despair. Nick states dramatically, "The streets are empty. I am empty. Or, no—I am full of pain. It's my life that's empty," and even Norah notices early in the novel that he "looks so depressed and defeated" (Cohn and Levithan 26, 31). Norah herself is described as looking like "a statue of someone totally defeated," and she thinks Nick's broken car "is like a fucking metaphor for [her] sorry-ass life: STALLED" (23, 28). The narrators may not have depressive disorders, but they make quite clear to each other and to the reader that their adolescent lives are full of heartache and defeat. In one of the novel's more philosophical moments, Norah explains to Nick a piece of Jewish theology that she appreciates, *tikkun olam*: "Basically, it says that the world has been broken into pieces. All this chaos, all this discord. And our job—everyone's job—is to try to put the pieces back together. To make things whole again" (143; original emphasis). She tells Nick that, while she's unsure about god, she "absolutely believe[s]" that "the world is broken" and that "we're becoming more and more fragmented" (143). Broken and fragmented, both Nick and Norah express existential sadness, despair, or madness, which Norah says becomes "more confusing" and "more complicated" the older she gets (143).

Also confused by his world, Tom is so lonely that he describes his best friend Sam as "the closest thing I have to a friend, and he's an all-right guy. I don't know if he realizes that I don't bring much to the table, friendship-wise. I let him do most of the talking. I usually don't have a comment" (Portman 8). Distancing himself, coupled with an extreme lack of self-confidence, result in an angry narrative voice that seems to combat vulnerability. However, regarding his father's death, Tom admits, "When I get nervous or worried about something, I do this weird thing with my ears. They start to itch way on the inside and I have this urge to move them back and forth on the outside, trying to relieve the itch" (29). A relatively minor physical quirk, his "ear thing" emerges, along with a lack of sleep, when his "day-to-day life [is] kind of weird" due to his sudden sexual encounters with girls and his discovery of a secret code inside his father's old books (30, 165): "I was constantly in this frantic, anxious state, all wound up" (165). Tom does see a psychiatrist at his mother and stepfather's demand, and though he considers the doctor "by far the most intelligent adult [he's] ever talked to," he calls her profession little "more than a shameless racket" (182). It's through psychotherapy that Tom learns his father is assumed to have committed suicide, but rather than allow Tom to work with a doctor he trusts, his mother "fire[s] her on the spot" for not simply prescribing "pills [to set him] on the road to being more normal" (262). Become "more normal" Tom does not, and he continues to speak to his reader with anger, sadness, and self-deprecation.

All four (turn-of-the-)twenty-first-century narrators—Charlie, Nick, Norah, and Tom—doubtless speak to their readers with urgent sadness and despair as they search for truth with overwhelming emotion. The only places in their narratives that offer peace or self-acceptance are moments in which they knowingly experience life in the present—without nostalgia for the past or worry about the future. These moments are few, and the novels superficially suggest that, as long as the narrators are adolescents, they will suffer. Underneath this surface-level sadness, however, the narrators, when mindfully present, find themselves. Archetypal Holden experiences a fleeting moment of peace when he tells his sister Phoebe, "I like it now. . . . I mean right now. Sitting here with you and just chewing the fat and horsing—" before she interrupts him (Salinger 172). Esther, though she worries that "the bell jar, with its stifling distortions," could descend upon her at any time, ends her story with a departure from the psychiatric hospital in a gesture of hope (Plath 241). Most explicitly, Charlie "feel[s] infinite" when driving with his friends and listening to music "because the song was that great and because we all really paid attention to it. Five minutes of a lifetime were truly spent, and we felt young in a good way" (Chbosky 33). Charlie identifies this feeling as a kind of reveling in the present moment. When Nick and Norah channel Charlie's sense of infinity by imagining "an infinite playlist" of songs for each other, Nick notes that his "heartbeat accelerates. I am in the here, in the now" (Cohn and Levithan 174). Even Tom, the most miserable critic of all, refuses to include the expected "character arc stuff" in his narrative, but he does include a brief "Outro," in which he simply enjoys band practice (Portman 303, 325).

While Tom, Nick, Norah, and (maybe) Charlie do not exhibit the kind of mental illness that hospitalizes Holden and Esther, the turn-of-the-twenty-first-century narratives are "authentically" adolescent because they mimic *The Catcher in the Rye* and *The Bell Jar*. All three of the turn-of-the-twenty-first-century novels employ narrator-protagonists who use words and anecdotes suggesting mental illness; they are intelligent loners, speaking with urgency; they approach the world with intense emotion, judgment, and sensitivity; they obsess over sex, death, and truth; and they express anxiety over the very nature of adolescence, with nostalgia for the past and worry over the future. While these narrative characteristics may be *due to* mental illness for Holden and Esther—and for Charlie—all of the narrators speak in the "authentic" young adult voice.

Whether demonstrating diagnoseable mental illnesses or simply living in the madness and despair of tumultuous adolescence, they adopt similar voices. These narrator-protagonists find peace only in brief moments spent in the present, which delivers a rather subtle message that adolescence is only a time for peace or acceptance when the past and future are forgotten. These narrator-protagonists do not await cures or change into adults to save themselves; they simply let themselves be. Tom refers to his misery as the "familiar monotony of standard, generic High School Hell" and explains that most adolescents feel "overwhelmed and desperate," but when Charlie feels infinite, "just let[ting] the wind rush over [his] face," he feels the power of mindfulness, awareness, and acceptance (Portman 10, 244; Chbosky 213). Generally powerless and underdeveloped, the inherently disabled adolescents in these young adult narratives have the power to control their own lives—and to both recognize and find moments of peace. More often than not, disability is not simply represented by literary adolescents; disability *is* adolescence, and adolescence disability.

Chapter 3

FRUITS

Disability as a Literary Metaphor

Literary texts—both about adolescence and not—that use disabilities as symbols of unwanted societal or personal characteristics are identified quite easily as harmful. To work, such texts require two-dimensional characters, with unrealistic, stable, and static conditions, rather than dynamic and living disabilities. Commonly, disability works metaphorically as a shallow representation of societal otherness or as a signifier of tragedy, which perhaps provokes wisdom or insight. However, to increase the viability of young adult literature as a *literary* body of work, scholars sometimes praise texts that veer away from accuracy and reality, texts that use identifiers such as disability to symbolize or represent something more abstract. Young adult narratives, such as M. T. Anderson's *Feed* (2002), that *do* use disability metaphorically may be noted, as by critics Jennifer Miskec and Chris McGee, for having "more nuanced, sophisticated representation[s]" (Miskec and McGee 164). Anderson's dystopian novel employs self-injury, often a symptom of mental illness, "as a metaphor for something much broader" (163). Both physical lesions and the characters' desire to create those lesions demonstrate the power of commercialism, which can make self-injurious behavior fashionable:

> On Monday, I went into School™ and I was sitting in homeroom when I saw that Calista had her hair up in this new way, and on the back of her neck was this total insane macro-lesion that I never even saw before. I guess I was looking at it kind of *Holy shit!*, because Quendy sat down next to me and chatted, *Impressed? Ain't even real.* (Anderson 183)

Miskec and McGee insightfully argue that the lesions, like the behavior that creates them, function both as literal "body modification" and as "comment[s] on the overlapping nature of the body, of power, and of corporate culture" (Miskec and McGee 175). In order to understand the text's comment on the *problem* of corporate culture, the reader must view self-harm as a *problem* that could and should be eliminated. For disability to represent a larger, more abstract problem or brokenness, the reader and the text's characters must indeed prefer nondisabled identities.

However, complex, three-dimensional, disabled characters that function metaphorically, at least in part, appear in young adult novels that work to understand and represent adolescence. *Because* these characters are not portrayed realistically, and instead with elements of fantasy, symbolic comparisons are generally more complex and less focused on actual disabilities. Notably, disabled adolescent characters in *The Virgin Suicides* (1993) by Jeffrey Eugenides and *The Secret Fruit of Peter Paddington* (2005) by Brian Francis are used metaphorically to achieve greater insight into both personal and societal questions.[1] Further, the novels simultaneously use comparisons and connections with adolescence to allow, quite radically, for disability to be considered a medical, social, *and* political part of human identity.

In *The Secret Fruit* Peter's body and "popped out" nipples rebel against and criticize his queer fantasies (Francis 1), and in *The Virgin Suicides* the Lisbon sisters' suicides illustrate "the imprisonment of being a girl" in an American suburb (Eugenides 43). While these uses of disability *could* be read as common, symbolic "problems," they are too experimentally portrayed, and they are linked with both adolescence and its developing sexuality. Disability in *The Secret Fruit* and *The Virgin Suicides* represent the "disabling" effects of adolescence, making both disability and adolescence unwanted; at times, disability catalyzes plot and character development, by relying on pity and inspiration, but nearly always disability complicates and confuses traditional literary metaphors. Adolescent sexuality becomes a disability, and disability is defined by tumultuous self-discovery and the discomfort it provokes in others. In achieving such simplistic definitions and characterizations, however, the two novels resist traditional uses of tropes. The symbolic nipples and suicides verge on the fantastical—Peter's nipples speak to him and the Lisbon girls are turned into mysterious, ephemeral creatures without diagnosed mental illnesses—which allows the literary metaphors to rely on fantastic disabilities to symbolize problems. The concrete manifestations of larger, more abstract concerns—Peter's nipples and the Lisbons' suicides—are not realistic, and they represent both abstract concerns and real disabilities: Peter's nonnormative fat body and the Lisbons' probable mental illnesses. With complexity and confusion, both of which keep disabled characters fully developed, the novels resist simple readings. Similarly, while neither disability nor adolescence is expected to remain by the novels' ends—much like traditional uses and understandings that force both identities to disappear with cures or growth—the characters in *The Secret Fruit* and *The Virgin Suicides* choose their own fates. They and their disabilities—both real and fantastical—may disappear, but they do so on the characters' terms.

THE LISBON GIRLS' SEXUALIZED SUICIDES

Frequent and overwhelming suicides in Eugenides's Lisbon family function most simply as a metaphor for unstable, adolescent female sexuality. As is echoed in *The Secret Fruit*, the strong emphasis on emergent sexuality reinforces the idea that adolescence, marked by developing sexual identities, is itself a disability. Eugenides uses first-person plural narration by a group of adolescent boys—technically men who are remembering adolescence—who try to understand why the Lisbon sisters, their ethereal and adolescent neighbors, all killed themselves during one year in the 1970s. The novel revolves around the men, who have never left adolescence and have instead "[become] custodians of the girls' lives" to retrace "a path that [leads] nowhere," because the mythologized story yields no satisfying answers (Eugenides 224, 238). Indeed, the text points to the girls and their suicides as a metaphor, as "a symbol of what was wrong with the country" and as a clear representation of "today's teenagers' overwhelming anxiety" (231, 94). But the narrators' refusal to accept these interpretations suggests that the metaphor works in a far more complex way. As the narrators retrace the Lisbon family's tragedy, from Cecilia's death to her sisters' deaths, they demonstrate the use of suicide to blur boundaries between disability and "health" and between metaphor and reality. Meanings behind suicide and depression in *The Virgin Suicides* evolve over the course of the novel, refusing to become a trite or restrictive metaphor that flattens characters and posits disability as a "problem." The girls' suicides move from representing the torment of becoming a female adolescent in suburban America to representing the agency and sexual freedom they demand. They are ethereal versions of girls-becoming-women who reject the space between purity and assumed immorality; throughout, the Lisbon girls and their suicides never become stand-ins for real mental illness, by conflating adolescence, disability, sexuality, reality, and the metaphysical.

As the tale begins, with a recollection of the final suicide (Mary's) quickly followed by a more in-depth account of the first (Cecilia's), suicide demands to be understood as a metaphorical trope. In mainstream understanding, as well as according to the American Psychiatric Association, suicide is often a symptom of mental illness, a characteristic of disability. In Eugenides's novel, however, the girls are seen by a psychiatrist, but because of the exaggerated natures of their deaths, suicide is more than a symptom; they are not simply mentally ill. The girls attempt to end and do end their lives with the most dramatic and expected methods: Cecilia "slitting . . . wrists like a Stoic while taking a bath" (3), Cecilia "falling onto the fence that ran alongside the house" (30), Bonnie "kick[ing a] . . . trunk out from under herself," Mary "put[ting] her head in the oven," Therese "stuff[ing herself] with sleeping pills washed down with gin," Lux poisoning herself in the garage "in the front seat, gray-faced and serene" (216), and Mary ultimately going to sleep "in a sleeping bag . . . full of sleeping pills" (237). Dr. Hornicker, their psychiatrist, similarly behaves more literarily than medically, thinking "it best to humor" Cecilia after she has slit her wrists and dismissing "psychological counseling" (16, 143).

Dr. Hornicker and the novel allow the girls' fantastical disabilities to function explicitly as metaphors, as responses to adolescence. In what the narrators consider Cecilia's "only form of suicide note," the youngest Lisbon answers her doctor's question about the suicides' causes: "'Obviously, Doctor,' she said, 'you've never been a thirteen-year-old girl'" (7). With the proclamation, Cecilia quickly makes clear that suicide in the text is the only rational response to female adolescence, and the novel's sensory descriptions reaffirm the suffocation of the girls, who live in "gauzy chambers of canopied beds . . . [which house an] effluvia of so many young girls becoming women in the same cramped space" (9). The girls' suffering is viewed by the 1970s suburban community as a "contamination of tragedy," but the girls themselves do not show typical signs of illness; instead, they show signs of emergent female sexuality, evident in "the odor of all those cooped-up girls" (38, 23). While the narrators imagine "the imprisonment of being a girl, the way it made your mind active and dreamy," other neighbors note that the girls, on the verge of womanhood, simply lack a place to be themselves: "'That girl didn't want to die,' [Mrs. Buell] told us. 'She just wanted out of that house.' Mrs. Scheer added, 'She wanted out of that decorating scheme'" (43, 17).

Finding a way out of their house, symbolic for "the imprisonment of being a girl," evolves into the primary concern of the Lisbon girls and the novel; following Cecilia's suicide, emphasis on the girls' situations and reasons to die moves from a simple *emergence* of female adolescence to the repression and oppression of it. Not medical and only viewed as tragic by onlookers, the suicides become an understandable—even powerful—escape from societal norms, subverting the traditional use of disability as a metaphor to showcase a "problem." Instead, the "problem" in the novel is represented by those people and societal norms that keep the girls hidden. Mr. and Mrs. Lisbon become more aggressive in keeping their daughters at home, locked in a house described by its "signs of creeping desolation" and "growing disrepair," and enforcing strict rules intended to preserve "for all time the unstimulating stage of the Lisbon girls' infancy"; in fact, "It was well known that Mr. and Mrs. Lisbon didn't allow their daughters to date, and that Mrs. Lisbon in particular disapproved of dances, proms, and the general expectation that teenagers should be allowed to paw one another in back seats" (89, 94, 25, 68). Perhaps *because* their parents refuse to allow the Lisbon sisters to become sexualized adolescents, the girls' sexualities become their primary characteristics. Lux, in particular, possesses a "singleness of purpose, . . . [a] total lack of inhibitions, . . . [and a] mythic mutability that allowed her to possess three or four arms at once" (87)—at least when her "promiscuity" is not restrained. Lux's escapes from her parents' control force the narrators to remember the sisters as "feverish creatures, exhaling soupy breath, succumbing day by day in their isolated ward" (87, 158).

So sexualized and occasionally caught "copulating on the roof with faceless boys and men," the Lisbons risk becoming two-dimensional characters that do function as simple metaphors: their suicides represent repression and oppression, the impossibility of female sexuality in mainstream American society, and a shocking and empowering escape from that society (145). The novel, however, prevents such a narrow reading. When the Lisbons are allowed to attend their school's homecoming dance, they—without warning—are fully realized characters, who still "didn't look depressed" and who suddenly possess individual personalities (123): "skittish Bonnie, shrinking from the flash; Therese, with her braincase squeezing shut the suspicious slits of her eyes; Mary, proper and posed; and Lux, looking not at the camera but up in the air" (118–19). The narrating boys, their dates, at once become silent, "too overwhelmed by the Lisbon girls' volubility. Who had known they talked so much, held so many opinions, jabbed at the world's sights with so many fingers?" (124). Refusing to remain a group of undifferentiated symbols for emergent female sexuality, the girls are real individuals, real characters. The tragedy of their position as "trapped beaver," as one of the boys appropriately if crudely explains, grows more acute and painful (165): "For even as the house began to fall apart, casting out whiffs of rotten wood and soggy carpet, this other smell began wafting from the Lisbons', invading our dreams and making us wash our hands over and over again. The smell was so thick it seemed liquid, and stepping into its current felt like being sprayed" (165). The smell of sexuality and maturity suffocating under the guise of innocence and purity further emphasizes suicide as an escape from a stifling home and society; the girls are "carnal angel[s]" surrounded by the "precision" of "an elaborate escape plan" (148, 212).

As they find agency and become powerful in their plan to escape from suburbia, with "everything laid out on a grid whose bland uniformity the trees had hidden," the Lisbon girls serve as manifestations of adolescence itself (243). Adolescence, like the Lisbon adolescents, is highly sexualized and closely monitored. The girls' impossible position of being caught between childhood and adulthood leaves only suicide as an escape, and this position is illustrated by a number of secondary metaphors. The Lisbon sisters are likened to ephemeral fish flies, to dying elm trees, and even to smoke rings made by the narrating boys. When the reader first meets Cecilia, the youngest Lisbon and first to die, she is nothing if not a metaphor for her own short life.

> She was standing by the curb, in the antique wedding dress with the shorn hem she always wore, looking at a Thunderbird encased in fish flies. "You better get a broom, honey," Mrs. Scheer advised. But Cecilia fixed her with her spiritualist's gaze. "They're dead," she said. "They only live twenty-four hours. They hatch, they reproduce, and then they croak. They don't even get to eat." And with that she stuck her hand into the foamy layer of bugs and cleared her initials: *C.L.* (4)

Undaunted by the layer of dead bugs, Cecilia makes herself one of them, knowing that she too will "croak" in about twenty-four hours and finding comfort in the flies' "senseless pattern of ecstasy and madness" (187). Fish flies reappear throughout the text, always connected to the Lisbons; when the narrators suggest that "Lux Lisbon [is] bleeding between the legs," her maturing sexuality is paired in the same sentence with "the fish flies [that make] the sky filthy" (10). As the girls become trapped in their deteriorating house, surrounded by crude neighbor boys, the fish flies die in numbers, making the air in their neighborhood "no longer brown but blue," but the Lisbons with a "crust of dead bugs over [their] lives," "coat[ing their] windows, making it difficult to see out" (56, 201). The fates of the flies inspire the Lisbons to escape.

Like the flies who die before experiencing life's joys and pains, the Lisbon girls are surrounded by dying elm trees, as though they—like elements of the natural world struggling to survive amid suburban developments—are fated to early deaths. Adolescence, as commonly understood, is a temporary stage of life, but generally not with an ending so abrupt or final; the Lisbon girls, however, live only as adolescents in the novel, and those identities cannot survive. When the narrators suggest, from reading Cecilia's diary, that the girls "understood love and even death," they also account for Cecilia's "despair[ing] over the demise of our elm trees," trees that disappear over the course of the novel, only to be replaced by saplings "selected for their 'hardiness'" (44, 90). When the sisters link arms around their family's own elm, they only succeed temporarily in their fight against the Parks Department, because even though the girls "feel the trees would survive better on their own, and . . . place the blame for the disease on human arrogance," that arrogance prevails (182). The metaphor, however, cannot be ignored, and it is as though the Lisbon sisters wage an unsuccessful fight against human arrogance that prevents them from surviving "better on their own." Such hints in the text, which reinforce the impossible position of the girls—as sexual women or permanent adolescents or those kept hidden—continue even in the novel's most light-hearted moments, such as when the sisters and their dates drive to the homecoming dance:

> Parkie Denton lowered the front window while Lux smoked. She took her time, exhaling through her nose. At one point she jutted out her chin at Trip Fontaine, rounded her lips, and, with a chimpanzee profile, sent forth three perfect smoke rings.
>
> "Don't let it die a virgin," Joe Hill Conley said. He leaned into the front seat and poked one. (125)

While the boys do their best to prevent the girls from dying before maturity, the Lisbon girls succeed in their own plan by committing suicide shortly after their one night of "look[ing] so cheerful" and "talk[ing] so freely" (132). Rather than staying trapped and silenced, the Lisbons find the agency to leave as drastically as they are treated. The text does not *force* them to disappear, with unwanted deaths or forced "correction," but the characters themselves choose something else.

Eugenides allows journalists in the text to voice the importance of adolescence in the girls' suicides, making much of the metaphor explicit with "conclusions such as these: 'Psychologists agree that adolescence is much more fraught with pressures and complexities than in years past. Often, in today's world, the extended childhood American life has bestowed on its young turns out to be a wasteland. . . .

Self-expression can often be frustrated. More and more, doctors say, this frustration can lead to acts of violence'" (96). However, complicating the metaphor, and even mocking this simplistic and pathetic reading of suicide, the narrative questions "the truth" and works to create a mythology, with the girls "pass[ing] beneath the great school clock, the black finger of the minute hand pointing down at their soft heads" (97, 100). Something far more mysterious is at work with the Lisbons, and even when Dr. Hornicker tries to diagnose Cecilia's sisters with post-traumatic stress disorder, the narrators reassure that "Cecilia's suicide had assumed in retrospect the stature of a long-prophesied event" (157). In some passages, Cecilia's suicide is so mythologized that she and her still-living sisters are described together as "becoming shadows" and "slowing sinking" (187, 186). Such a positioning of the girls, as existing in a space between life and death, is impossible, much like the need for adolescent, sexualized women, trapped in twentieth-century societal norms, to live as ephemerally as fish flies. Ultimately, the narrators reject all medical explanations of the suicides, and agree that the Lisbons' deaths "came as predictably as seasons or old age," and that nothing short of prophesies could "explain why Cecilia had killed herself in the first place" (220). The "mystery of their despair"—made more mysterious by their seeming lack of sadness—combined with both otherworldly and overtly naturalized descriptions of the Lisbons, separates them from medical understanding; by the end of the novel, they are as "unreal as the news" (221). Mythologized and forever misunderstood, the sisters use very real suicides to make clear the impossibility of sexually evolving adolescent women in twentieth-century American society.

PETER PADDINGTON'S JUDGMENTAL NIPPLES

Peter Paddington is a fat, queer adolescent with popped-out talking nipples, who is committed to "fixing" his identity in order to make himself "normal" (1). A quick reading of *The Secret Fruit of Peter Paddington* suggests that Francis uses fantastical nipples as a physical deformity reminiscent of those in fairy tales and freak shows, which "defy the ordinary and mock the predictable, exciting both anxiety and speculation," in order to make concrete an abstract "problem," such as emerging queerness (Garland-Thomson, "Introduction" 1). Asserting that his deformed nipples must be read as an extraordinary, freak-like trait, Peter fears that someone will call "photographers to take pictures [of him] to include in one of those 'Freaks of the 20th Century' books" (91). However, Francis's text does far more than use deformed nipples as a metaphor for what Peter understands to be a socially "deformed" sexuality; Francis also creates a protagonist with at least two disabilities (fatness and extraordinarily large, talking nipples) and two abstract sources of turmoil (sexuality and adolescence). While the novel's thrust may rely on swollen nipples as a metaphor for sexuality, Peter's multi-faceted character refuses a simple reading of either sexuality or disability as a problem to be solved, ignored, or embraced. Both Peter's nonnormative body and sexuality are further complicated by his fatness and adolescent anxieties. By blurring the lines between actual, politicized disability and fantastical disability, *The Secret Fruit* forces readers to consider literary complications, political implications, and potential offenses of using disability as metaphor.

That disability and sexuality are so connected to adolescence, especially in this text, raises even more questions: is Peter punished with disability (deformed and metaphorical nipples) because he is queer, because he is fat, or because he is an anxious adolescent struggling with identity? Because Peter lacks one dominating identity trait and instead occupies many, the use of metaphor in the text is confused and blurred. Even Peter lacks a clear understanding of himself: "It's like all the other boys are normal, except for me. . . . And I'll think to myself, 'They don't have Bedtime Movies. They're not fat. They don't have taped-up nipples.' It's like being a boy is the easiest thing in the world for them" (74–75). The Bedtime Movies, or fantasies, always follow Peter in sexual and romantic pursuits of men; his growing awareness that he may not conform to a normative sexual identity is expressed—in his mind, at least—through physical abnormality in the form of popped-out nipples that resemble cherries. Additionally, even the one stable identity trait that Peter seems to accept, his male gender, is questioned—perhaps because he is an adolescent being thrust into adulthood. Peter's identity, without a doubt, demonstrates how literary representations of disabilities may work successfully as metaphors without robbing characters of complexity and humanity. *The Secret Fruit* links reality and metaphor, or the material and abstract, in a way that leaves the metaphors richer and more effective than those used in more well-known novels. It also refuses simplistic readings of disability-as-literary-metaphor used to propel young adult novels, like *Feed*, into a higher literary status. Certainly, Peter's narration makes it difficult for the reader to determine which "problems" are real and which are imaginary, and Peter himself connects and confuses his perceived problems by simultaneously trying to "get normal nipples," "lose weight," "get a boy friend" (not a sexual or romantic boyfriend), and "act confident" (100, 101). Peter's nipples serve as a metaphor for the bodily betrayal felt by queer adolescents, for unstable literary and political portrayals of fatness, and for abstract effects of adolescence.

To some extent, metaphor is very straightforward in *The Secret Fruit*, as Peter's emerging and panic-inducing nipples parallel and make physical his emerging sexual desire for men. The nipples themselves are referred to by Peter as cherries, and this clear connection to "fruit," a common and often derogatory term for a gay man, resonates most forcefully in the novel's title and in Peter's final Bedtime Movie fantasy, when he finds himself fearing that his "cherry nipples will come popping out and then they'll know. . . . Everyone will see the fruit . . . [he is] trying to hide" (276). This physical growth of "fruits" on Peter's chest allows an unarticulated fear and passion to become material and visual, a trope within the novel that interviewer and sex-advice columnist Dan Savage clearly references when asking Francis about Peter's sexuality:

> All adolescents feel a sense of estrangement from their own bodies during puberty. For gay adolescents, that sense of estrangement is made more intense by feelings of betrayal—'How could my body be doing this to me!' I think that's the animating idea of your novel. As a gay man, what was your reaction when your body informed you that, like it or not, you were going to be gay when you grew up? (Savage 7)

While Francis's answer fails to explicitly engage with these "feelings of betrayal," he does suggest that realizing one is not straight may become an "emotional—and sometimes physical—tug-of-war with [one] self," which implicitly reaffirms a link between the emotional/abstract and the physical/concrete (7–8). And in the novel, those nipples that are described with such physicality, emerging "round and puffy and not the two pink raisins they used to be" and that feel "soft as a rose petal," emphasize the betrayal Peter feels when he notices classmate Andrew Sinclair's "long eyelashes, blue eyes, and really thick brown hair" and when he masturbates to thoughts of "Billy [another boy he knows] and his parachute pants" (Francis 4, 75, 167).

Beyond functioning as physical manifestations of sexuality, Peter's nipples do far more than make him feel like the kind of "visual novelty" of myths and folktales that so often represent larger dilemmas (Garland-Thomson, *Staring* 161). The nipples speak; they remind Peter of his taboo desires and goad him into acting upon them. Silent until the novel's fourth chapter, the nipples' first words to their owner come in response to Peter's realization that "all they want to do is grow" (61):

> "Maybe if you were normal, we'd be normal, too," they say. "Did you ever stop to think about that?"
> "You're cruel!" I tell them. "I'm perfectly normal."
> "Who are you kidding? You can't even go out and find a boy friend."
> "You're terrible! Don't say another word or I'm going to get the ice cubes. I mean it!"
> The truth is, my nipples are right. I do need to get myself a boy friend. (61–62)

Peter's and his nipples' use of the phrase "boy friend," of course, offers a meaningful glimpse at his deliberate refusal to acknowledge that what he truly wants is a boyfriend (one word). The nipples continue to threaten exposure, telling Peter that he's "really starting to bug" them and that they will "tell everyone [his] secret" (82). Obvious to the reader, but maybe not as obvious to Peter, that secret is his sexuality, rather than the nipples themselves, but because Francis allows his metaphor to risk clarity for complexity, the nipples' threats are less obvious. When they push Peter to "pick that phone up [to call Andrew] and make [him]self a boy friend," it is unclear whether they are urging him to find a *boy friend* in order to become "normal" or pushing him to find a *boyfriend* in order to satisfy his true desires, thus rejecting "normality" (82). Similarly, when Peter considers calling another crush of his, the nipples ask, "Do you really think this is a good idea?" and they insist that they are "the only ones telling the truth" when they explain, "Mr. Hanlan doesn't like you. Not in the way you want him to, anyway" (234). While the nipples may protect Peter from embarrassment in this case, they still voice truths that Peter will not allow himself to voice, because he very much wants Mr. Hanlan to like him sexually.

Peter acts according to his emerging queerness only twice in the novel, and in both instances, his nipples are involved in "mak[ing] . . . [him] do these terrible things" (163). Rather than blame his own desires, Peter separates himself and blames the physical manifestations of them. When Peter finds himself touching a sleeping Billy Archer on New Year's Eve, his nipples start "vibrating" and can hear "only the sound of [his] heart" (158).

> "Put your hand on his leg," my nipples whispered from beneath the tape.
>
> "No," I said. "That's wrong."
>
> "He touched you first," they said.
>
> "No," I said again. My nipples were evil. "It's wrong."
>
> But my nipples took control of my hand and the next thing I knew, it was on Billy's ankle.
>
> "Stop it!" I whisper/screamed to my nipples. "He's going to wake up at any second!"
>
> It didn't do any good. My nipples had a mind of their own. I watched as my hand moved further and further up Billy's red pant leg and past the black triangles. And then, my hand stopped over Billy's dink. I couldn't catch my breath and I was afraid I'd start coughing and then Billy would wake up and give me a knuckle sandwich.
>
> "Take my hand away," I told my nipples.

> "But then he might wake up," they said.
>
> My nipples had a point. It was better just to leave it there. (159)

Again, the nipples walk a line between *protecting* Peter from embarrassment, by warning him that Billy "might wake up" if Peter moves his hand, and *encouraging* Peter to act, by initially urging him to touch the boy. After touching Billy's "dink," Peter explains that he thinks about Billy while putting "the showerhead on [his] dink to make sperm," and he explains that the showerhead "is evil" for making him think things he doesn't "want to think" (167). For Peter, his nipples and the showerhead allow him to separate himself from thoughts he perceives to be wrong, and his reader understands that Peter's nipples and showerhead express what he has been taught about normality and acceptability.

The second time Peter acts upon his secret desires, the nipples adopt a more protective role, questioning him after he "put[s] on one of [his] mom's bras and stuff[s] a pair of socks into each of the cups," wears a black dress with pearl earrings and heels, and dances around his house to Olivia Newton-John, only to be seen by Uncle Ed peeking in the window (186). When Peter berates himself for doing "something very bad" and "let[ting] a Bedtime Movie . . . come to life," his nipples both comfort and argue with him (190):

> "Aren't you getting a little carried away?" my nipples asked.
>
> "No," I said. "And I don't remember asking you for your opinion."
>
> "Don't get angry at us. *We're* not the ones who put on a pair of pantyhose."
>
> "You think you're so much better than me, don't you?" (191)

Quick to argue with him and criticize his pantyhose, the nipples offer an interesting lesson to Peter about his experiment with gender identity; their suggestion that he has gotten "a little carried away" may help him understand that his secrets are not quite as "bad" as he thinks they are, but they may also suggest that a trans- or nonbinary-gender identity is not what Peter desires. While Peter imagines himself as Brooke Shields in "a shiny pink dress" and as a beauty-pageant contestant named Vanessa with blonde hair and a "voice [that] touches people" in his Bedtime Movies, being or acting as a woman does not transfer into his waking life (17, 58). While his intimate moment with Billy Archer becomes an active sexual fantasy for him, Peter regrets his foray into gender exploration, and his nipples make clear that *they* did not approve of his wearing women's clothes. Francis reinforces the nipples' reading of Peter's identity in his interview with Savage, explaining, "Whenever I allowed myself a gay fantasy, whether it be sexual or romantic in nature, there was always some kind of catch. Like, I had to be bullied into it. Or it was what *all* the guys did after football practice. Or I happened to look like Heather Locklear. That was the only way I could rationalize my desires" (Savage 11). Perhaps like Francis, Peter imagines himself as a woman not because he questions his gender, but because he must try to rationalize to himself his attraction to men. While *The Secret Fruit* is not autobiographical, Francis offers an explanation for the lessons Peter's nipples try to teach him; not only do they function as a speaking physical manifestation of his desires, they know what he has yet to consciously realize about himself.

The nipples' words of wisdom, indeed, guide Peter in understanding and potentially accepting his identity as a gay adolescent. Not quite ready to listen to his nipples, but eager to solve the mystery of their emergence, Peter believes that his "deformed nipples [formed] because of . . . [his] subconscious. . . . The subconscious is a very tricky thing, . . . [and] when bad things happen to people, it's because their subconscious secretly wants the bad things to happen" (15): "Maybe we *do* make bad things happen to ourselves because we think we deserve them. Maybe we *need* to be punished for thinking things we shouldn't" (16). Though he does not consciously explain the content of his "incorrect" thoughts, Peter realizes that he is "being punished for the Bedtime Movies" that "play over and over in . . . [his] head until . . . [he falls] asleep at night . . . [and] make . . . [him] feel bad" (16–17).

Just as the fruit-like nipples represent his sexuality and the warnings he feels compelled to follow, Peter's physical treatments of the nipples allow the text a metaphor for sexual repression. When they first emerge as Peter is getting ready for school, he says, "This is the last thing I need," and he tries to "cure [him]self" by rubbing ice cubes on his nipples to make them shrink (4, 6). When ice fails and Peter realizes that the nipples will not normalize so easily, he begins an evolving regimen to hide his nipples, which of course suggests a regimen to hide his sexual desires:

> I went straight to my room with my Scotch tape. I took off my sweatshirt and made a Scotch tape "x" across each of my nipples. I put my shirt back on and stood in front of the fan. I thought it was very smart of me to fake wind.
>
> The Scotch tape isn't too bad, although it makes my skin crinkle under it. It looks like I have many-pointed nipples now. They're stars, which are better than cherries any day. (12)

Because the Scotch-taped stars itch, peel, and leave him still feeling self-conscious, Peter moves onto wrapping masking "tape around [his] chest three times every day before [he goes] to school. It holds much better than the Scotch tape, but it's hard to breathe, and when [he] pull[s] the masking tape off at night, it hurts" (62). He hurts himself in order to hide his nipples—and presumably his sexuality, as well. Though Peter nurses his nipples and tries to care for them by "rub[bing] some of [his] mother's skin lotion on" them, he refuses to let them be seen, just as he refuses to acknowledge his gayness (96). At his most extreme, Peter begins using an elastic bandage purchased for wrapping ankles; every morning, he wraps it twice around his chest, held "in place with a safety pin," compromising his ability to breathe and angering his nipples, who argue, "Serves you right for squishing us down with that stupid bandage" (234, 240). Eventually annoyed with Peter for asking them to become "normal," the nipples tell him to get used to who he is and who may become, because he cannot ignore his physical desires. Peter's elaborate treatments to hide his nipples, the nipples' words, and the nipples physical manifestation work to mirror adolescent queerness with layers and complexity—a far cry from flat representations of disability to represent more abstract social or personal "problems."

While the use of popped-out talking nipples as a metaphor for emerging queerness forms Peter's central narrative in the novel, his nipples and sexuality are both inexorably linked to a second disability: fatness.[2] Already self-conscious, Peter is also subjected to torment from his peers due to his fat frame: "'Hey look! It's Peter Fattington.' . . . Brian sat there looking at me for a couple of seconds. He was chewing on his bottom lip. 'All right,' he said, getting up from the table. 'Let's go. This pig's making me sick, anyway'" (143). Notably, Peter finds a voice and a bit of confidence *before* deciding to improve his health and to lose weight; while the end of the novel follows Peter attempting to exercise and eat more healthily, he does *not* require a more socially acceptable, normative body in order to care for others and for himself—both measures of growth that come with self-confidence and a bit of self-acceptance.

Much more complex than a two-dimensional fat adolescent that stands in for larger problems, Peter feels betrayals that are firmly rooted in his body. The talking nipples clearly originate in Peter's own imagination—for he knows that "it's weird how your mind can make you believe things that aren't really true. Especially when it comes to yourself"—but the actual state of his nipples, puffy and red, are a part of his actual body. Because those nipples appear above his "big white stomach" as a part of his "'I need to lose weight' kind" of boobs, they are a part of his fatness, and his fatness becomes a part of his burgeoning sexuality (1). This is also a connection made by fat activists—both in individuals' perceptions of themselves and in critics' understandings of societal intolerance of fat bodies and non-straight sexualities. Though he tries not to admit it, Peter lusts after Billy Archer, Mr. Hanlan, and Andrew Sinclair, "the most fashionable boy in 8th grade," and he acknowledges that "before [he can] even think about asking him to be friends, [he'll] have to lose a lot of weight, shave [his] legs, change [his] personality, and cure [his] nipples" (12). Peter's shame for feeling sexual in a fat body, combined with his shame for having gay fantasies, provide an explicit link between coming out as fat and coming out as queer, both of which are also linked to his cherry-like nipples. Using these implied connections to his advantage, Peter is able to choose which identity to reveal first. After passing out while running in his elastic bandage, Peter fears his secrets have been exposed, only to discover that he can hide the more shameful ones by admitting to his fatness: "The good thing is that my mom doesn't know about my nipples. When she asked me why I'd wrapped the bandage around myself, I told her that I did it to look thinner" (242).

Such an admission draws a sharp comparison between coming out as fat and coming out as gay, and it makes clear that, for Peter, being gay is a much more difficult task.

The tasks of repressing his sexual desires and hiding his deformed nipples become more urgent once Peter's fatness has been acknowledged; while exposing one shameful part of himself, coupled with attempts to lose weight and become "normal," he is reminded by his nipples that his sexual identity is less likely to change or to normalize. Peter is learning that he is decidedly not "normal" or straight, an identity he feels pressured to fill. No matter how hard he tries, he cannot normalize his desires the way he attempts to normalize his body. Whereas Peter can force himself to attend aerobics classes and can even enjoy exercising to Jane Fonda, he continues to wrap up his nipples, who eventually learn some manners, even as he continues to fantasize about Mr. Hanlan.

Queer, fat, and socially taboo, Peter's Uncle Ed functions as a more traditional, two-dimensional "freak" in the text, and just as freakshow audiences in the early twentieth century "simultaneously identified with and were repulsed by the performers," Peter sees a repellent version of himself in Ed (Thomson, *Extraordinary* 66). In Uncle Ed, fatness represents queerness and social abnormality; for Peter, Uncle Ed is the visual representation of a future he fears most. Peter knows that he is "not the fattest person in [his] family, Uncle Ed is," and Peter's mother explains that Ed has never married because he was "smothered": "The sun just rose and set on Eddy, there was no doubt about that. Now look how he's turned out. Can't cook for himself. Can't clean. Can't even wash a towel. And not a wife in sight for miles. And then, of course, there's the other thing" (Francis 25, 95). When Peter asks about that "other thing," his mother refuses to elaborate and begs him to promise he will never "become like him" (95). Unpleasant at family dinners, embarrassing in public, generally in a red Hawaiian shirt, and often calling, "What's in the news?" Uncle Ed surfaces throughout the novel as Peter's dreaded, secret future: "I started to see someone in the mirror. It was a face worse than the Devil. And before the Hawaiian shirt got any clearer, I blinked really hard to break the spell and blew out the candle" (94, 102–3). Though Peter's mother never explains that Ed is gay, and instead focuses on his inability to care for himself, the nipples tell Peter that he and Ed are "both the same" when Peter fantasizes about sex and gender identity, suggesting that Peter knows that Ed is more than fat (191). When Peter finally sees Ed flirting with another man, "leaning into the counter toward Mr. Bernard," he watches with curiosity and then heads home as fast as he can, unable to articulate his discomfort (270). The novel's final scene, a Bedtime Movie, in which Peter is a "normal" teenage boy playing football, results in his "not running *to* something, but running *from* something," and when he finally looks up, he "spot[s] someone in the distance, standing between the goal posts. 'What's in the news?' he asks" (276). The threatening nature of Ed's character—a trait often found in characters with disabilities, illustrating "that anyone can become disabled at any time" (Garland-Thomson, *Extraordinary* 14)—does not dissipate when Peter begins losing weight, and as the novel draws to a close, Ed's fatness becomes another metaphor for sexuality—this one far more ominous and realistic than popped-out talking nipples.

Frightening visions of the future—like that of Ed between the goal posts—allow *The Secret Fruit* to conflate disability and adolescence. For Peter, freakish nipples, fatness, queerness, and adolescent anxieties cannot be separated; his talking nipples work as a metaphor, a concrete manifestation of adolescence, and at the same time, Peter's adolescent mind mirrors life with a disability. Such a connection between all of Peter's identities allows the metaphorical nature of the novel to succeed without shallow symbolism. Whereas Garland-Thomson notices that "stereotypes in life become tropes in textual representation," Peter resists becoming either one (Garland-Thomson, *Extraordinary* 11). His extraordinary characteristics are conflated with his very real and even ordinary preoccupations, and the text itself refuses to let its reader find comfort by simply assuming that the physical parts of Peter stand in for his emotional turmoil. Peter's narrative moves so quickly from one concern to another that those concerns are inseparable, and when he thinks of one (such as his attraction to Andrew Sinclair), the others (particularly his weight and his nipples) quickly enter his thoughts: "Andrew is the most fashionable boy in 8th grade and I think we could be friends some day. But before I even think about asking him to be friends, I'll have to lose a lot of weight, shave my legs, change my personality, and cure my nipples" (12). With these overwhelming concerns, seemingly so unique to Peter, the character quickly becomes a typical adolescent, and the metaphorical nature of his nipple-disability may represent all of adolescence, weighted by self-discovery and concerns about peer groups. Typically adolescent, Peter acknowledges that "things started to change in 7th grade," when he "started taking sex ed" and realized that "everyone was divided off into groups" (67). For Peter, his nonnormative body and nonnormative desires are linked so firmly to social anxieties that he knows he cannot succeed as one of the normal adolescents "because they [are] thin and [have] normal nipples" (267).

In many ways, the novel allows the disabled and decidedly nonnormative Peter to function as the ordinary adolescent. It also allows Peter to grow by responding to underdeveloped disabled characters who are forced into the margins. The social hierarchy in Peter's school extends to the larger community and to his family, both of which continue to posit him in the position of nonnormative outcast. For Peter to gain self-awareness, notable secondary characters function as traditional freak-like characters who teach Peter important lessons. Unlike Ed, with his socially marginalized and threatening presence in the novel, Peter's sisters—Christine and Nancy—offer a rather transgressive view of fatness as a signaling moral goodness and kindness. Both ordinary sisters, who are "always bugging [Peter and] calling [him] a Momma's Boy," Nancy is fat, while Christine is thin (6). Familiar tropes of disabled characters representing personalities, the sisters achieve enormous power by inverting the usual connections. Nancy, who "is never on a diet for very long," is introduced as a sympathetic character, "upset because . . . she has to buy her clothes at Suzanne's, the fat women's clothing store" (26). Nancy's fatness highlights the social stigma caused by a world in which thinness and appearance are valued—perhaps especially among adolescents. Nancy's responses to stress, including skipping her prom for an all-you-can-eat dinner with her boyfriend, seem reasonable; her character resists pity because of the cruelty with which she treats Peter, but she remains sympathetic. Christine, on the other hand, used to be "the fattest of all three" siblings, but by the novel's beginning has lost weight and has separated herself from her family; Peter knows that "Christine thinks she's better than Nancy and me just because she's thin and has opinions and works at Peoples Jewelers" (30, 31).

With the contrast between sympathetic Nancy and cruel Christine, Peter's sisters create a binary in which fatness is equated with moral goodness, which makes Peter's pressure to lose weight more difficult to stomach. Christine's cruelty climaxes when Peter runs to Christine to escape bullies: "When she noticed me, her whole expression changed. It was like she was scared of me—almost as if I was going to come into the store and do something bad to her. . . . Christine mouthed two words to me. 'Go away'" (144–45). Back to her brother, Christine represents normative views of fatness—and perhaps gayness, as they are so connected in the family and text—and she occupies the same role as normative bullies. Nancy, on the other hand, resists such cruelty—until she herself loses weight. After being humiliated by a photographer, Nancy dumps her fat boyfriend, finds "a best friend named Bubbles, dyes her hair blonde, and spends all evening in front of the mirror. She has lost 40 pounds" (224–25). Along with such superficial changes, Nancy refuses to eat junk food and becomes self-righteous, insulting her family members and taking all social cues from Bubbles, who "isn't very smart, uses Lee Press-On nails, and wears jeans so tight she has to lie on her bed every morning and pull up the zipper with a coat hanger" (226). When Peter sees "her collarbone sticking out from underneath her skin," he realizes that her unpleasant demeanor is linked without question to her thinness and to what Peter calls "a whole new Nancy Paddington" (231). With the transformation of Nancy's character, Peter realizes the sacrifices he would need to make in order "to become a new and improved Peter Paddington" (100). Yet when Peter eventually decides to improve his health and also strive for a more normative body, Christine and Nancy grow kinder toward him. Only after Peter borrows a headband to wear jogging does Christine say to her brother, "You don't embarrass me. . . . So don't think that" (260). Peter ultimately fails at jogging, but he is accepted by a person whose moral quality he has criticized throughout; the text, therefore, refuses to let Peter find comfort in changing himself. If he succeeds, he may be welcomed by his formerly fat sisters, but to do so, he risks becoming a "new" person like they've become, embarrassed by family and impressed by the superficial.

Consequently, while inverting stereotypes associated with body size, the novel still uses a body type—in this case, thinness—as a metaphor for abstract social ills. For the Paddingtons, goodness is associated with fatness.

Also semi-disabled secondary characters, Peter's friend Daniela and acquaintance Jackie Myner work to shape Peter's growth by provoking self-awareness. In the beginning of the novel, Peter criticizes others for being outcasts, showing a profound lack of awareness of himself in relation to his adolescent peer group; Jackie, for example, is derided by Peter, their classmates, and their teacher not only because she is "the ugliest girl in the whole school," but also "because Jackie stutters and it takes her a very long time for her to say anything" (12, 14). Her disability-based ostracism is further explained in relation to Peter when he defines the social groups in his grade:

> Then there are people that don't fit into any group. Like Jackie Myrner, who as well as being the ugliest girl at Clarkdale is poor and stutters and doesn't dress very well. Sometimes, I'll see Jackie trying to talk to Arlene Marple. Arlene doesn't belong to any group. That's because she has dandruff and B.O. and wears sweatshirts with kittens on them. But even Arlene doesn't like to be seen with Jackie. That's how bad it is for Jackie.
>
> I guess I don't belong to any group either, but I'm not like Jackie or Arlene. Even though I'm overweight and have deformed nipples, I never stutter. And there's no way I'd be caught dead wearing a kitten sweatshirt.
>
> Back in September, I started hanging out with the Goody-Goody girls, but that was only because most of them were in my home ec class and Margaret goes to my church. Then, Brian Cinder noticed me trading stickers with a couple of the girls at recess.
>
> "Look at Peter Paddington," he said in a high voice, "he's just one of the girls." (70–71)

No matter "how bad it is for Jackie," a character who possesses a noticeable stutter, Peter refuses to place himself in a similar category. He may be mocked for hanging out with girls rather than boys, he may go to great lengths to hide his nipples and queerness, and he may fear that fatness keeps him from popularity, but he tells himself that he is "not like Jackie," largely because he doesn't stutter. Also illustrating Peter's lack of self-awareness, his relationship with his only true friend, Daniela, similarly allows him to elevate himself. While not identified as disabled, Daniela is socially different, at least to Peter; she looks unusual, is "a little stupid" because she failed sixth grade, and "still wets the bed" (42).

Both Jackie and Daniela turn Peter into an ordinary adolescent protagonist who grows with help from marginalized, disabled characters (a familiar trope explored in "Chapter Four: Freaks: Disability as a Catalyst for Growth"). What Peter learns from Jackie and Daniela, of course, is that he is one of them. When he finally sees "Daniela in a way [he] hadn't before . . . [and] realize[s] that even though she had a plugged-up nose and split ends and still wet the bed, she was [his] friend," he feels compassion for the first time (212). Learning to accept his friend also allows him to begin accepting himself. He sees himself in Daniela: "It was weird, but for once, I knew exactly how Daniela felt. Even though I never served tables or had a nun for a teacher, I felt like 'they' had won in my life, too. 'They' were the people that thought Daniela and I were losers. 'They' thought they were better than us, just because they were thin and had normal nipples and didn't wet the bed" (267). Such epiphanies occur a number of times, as Peter gains awareness and compassion, but his struggle for self-acceptance is not over, because in the same moment that he realizes he "*was* Jackie Myner," he also "want[s] Jackie gone" (254). Peter is not yet comfortable with himself, just as Jackie and Daniela are not comfortable as outcasts, and while they provoke moments of growth, they do more than simply offer dire situations. Daniela, at least, becomes more important to Peter and integral in his plan to change, but rather than changing in response to humiliation, as Nancy did, Peter's need to change becomes more urgent and all-encompassing. "Daniela, we've got to take control of our lives," he says, with greater awareness that their stigmatized identities are affecting their futures and happiness (268). Through his observations of and interactions with fellow outcasts Daniela and Jackie, as well as with his sisters, Peter grows a modicum of self-awareness and begins to create a more realistic plan for "self-improvement," or normalization. Self-improvement, however, is never assured. Peter cannot be fat without also being an adolescent, also having talking nipples, and also being queer.

In order to feel happiness and a sense of belonging, Peter must change a number of things about himself and his life—including eliminating his disabled traits. Understanding Peter requires a messy connection between disability, adolescence, and sexuality—both real and fantastical. When Peter and Daniela refer to their neighbor and former-paperboy John Geddes, his age and assumed intellectual disability are inseparable because he is "too old to be a paperboy" (Francis 38). When Peter asks, "What kind of thirty-five-year-old plays birthday games with his mom?" Daniela quickly explains, "A retarded thirty-five-year-old" (38). The characters suggest to the reader that societal norms put more pressure on adults than they might children and adolescents to conform—were John still an adolescent, his behaviors would not be worth questioning, but because he is "too old" to pass as an adolescent in that liminal state of development, his nonnormative intellect becomes the target of laughter and criticism. Both Peter and Daniela grow to accept themselves and each other as disabled—at least socially—but they do not accept the disabled paperboy. Adolescence remains a time for development and emerges as a time for acceptance; however, just as the threat of Ed standing between the goal posts awaits Peter at the novel's close, so the threat of adulthood suggests a far less accepting and accommodating world for those with disabilities.

Both *The Secret Fruit of Peter Paddington* and *The Virgin Suicides* use metaphor to do what Miskec and McGee admire in Anderson's *Feed*, but these novels do so in a way that resists theoretical and political criticism. Peter's nipples and the Lisbons' suicides are complicated and confused, allowing for more complex readings and more interesting characterizations. Unlike most novels written for and about adults and young adults, *The Secret Fruit of Peter Paddington* and *The Virgin Suicides* use disability as metaphor without demeaning disability or adolescence. In neither novel can a reader push aside adolescent sexuality or fantastical disability, even when characters work to eliminate—through death and through weight-loss—those characteristics. Novels that use disability metaphorically to represent adolescence, or that use adolescence as an explicitly disabled identity, are able to achieve literary complexity by creating characters that resist easy interpretation and definition and by placing those characters into worlds that are both overwhelmingly realistic and impossibly fantastical. If, as Davis suggests, disability is "the identity that links other identities" (Davis, "The End of Identity" 233), adolescence too may offer a time when nonstable identity categories are allowed to flourish—not without difficulty for the disabled and adolescent characters, as societal and outside pressures push them to eliminate their nonnormative characteristics, but with a celebration in the narratives themselves.

Chapter 4

FREAKS

Disability as a Catalyst for Growth

While any disabled character may be reduced to a "freak," or may proudly embrace a label like "freak," only some disabled characters are used as literary "freaks." In literary narratives, freak characters—especially children and adolescents—sacrifice dignity and humanity in order to advance plotlines, catalyze growth, and inspire others. They serve to help other characters, along with readers, appreciate what they have, put their problems in perspective, and never give up—because if a freak keeps trying, so can anyone. A traditional freak is a usually secondary character, marked as nonnormative, who operates as a spectacle and as a catalyst for the development of others; they are essential to stories that test the morality and ethics of more prominent characters. Reviewing representations of intellectual disability, Alison C. Carey draws attention to the "special child"—moral, innocent, selfless, and sometimes visionary—who illustrate goodness and simplicity; they provoke pity, sympathy, kindness, and wonder (Carey 7). Villainous freaks, too, are simply marked by ugliness or deformity in order to provoke hatred and perhaps pity; they further story arcs and offer conflicts.

People and characters of all ages who are "visually different" have been known since antiquity as monsters, freaks, and sometimes simpletons (Garland-Thomson, "Introduction" 1). Evolving from these marvelous monsters, who once inspired awe, deviant characters began to serve as examples of medical horror stories (3). At the expense of their own humanity, freaks of all kinds allow readers and watchers to confront bodily differences, contemplate what it means to be human, and reaffirm their own "normality" by seeing what they, presumably, are not. Especially in sensational freak shows of the mid-1800s to the mid-1900s, western culture, and literature, spectators stare to indulge in curiosity and horror. Theorists who study "freakery" have focused their attention on visual disabilities, monster-like deformities, and deviant bodies, rather than on invisible disabilities. Additionally, few have looked specifically at how freak figures function *specifically* in young adult narratives. Carey's special children, of course, are invisibly, intellectually disabled adolescents, but they have been used since the earliest forms of storytelling. Young adult novels—only emerging in the mid-twentieth century—use both visible *and* invisible freaks in order to experiment with representations in stories about adolescence.

Unsurprisingly, most young adult narratives with disabled characters do employ the traditional kinds of shallow, inspiring freak characters: positioned carefully as siblings, sidekicks, and best friends. Even progressive, critically acclaimed, beloved novels, such as *Sweet Whispers, Brother Rush* (1983) by Virginia Hamilton and *Becoming Naomi León* (2005) by Pam Muñoz Ryan, use these traditional roles. A number of morality-driven, didactic novels—such as Rodman Philbrick's *Freak the Mighty* (1993) and R. J. Palacio's *Wonder* (2012)—work to complicate and question the treatment of disabled characters, but often reinforce patronizing representations and even introduce others. These novels, which use freaks to elicit kindness and moral growth, almost *always* reaffirm the disabled character's humanity by emphasizing their intelligence; strange looking freaks may need wheelchairs, walk with unusual gaits, or attract stares, but because they are smart, the texts explain, they are human. While able to bring social acceptance to visibly disabled freaks, such texts further separate and stigmatize intellectually disabled people. However, characters *with* intellectual disabilities, chronic illnesses, and mental illnesses are the ones that allow young adult narratives space to experiment both narratively and politically. Ron Koertge's *Stoner & Spaz* (2002), for instance, harnesses the power of invisibly disabled characters to expose the freak's role, question it, and even turn it on its head; ultimately, the role of the freak in *Stoner & Spaz* is filled simultaneously by many and no characters.

SIMPLE, CONVENTIONAL FREAKS

Both well-received young adult novels, Hamilton's *Sweet Whispers, Brother Rush* and Ryan's *Becoming Naomi León* feature disabled siblings that act as simple catalysts for growth in their nondisabled protagonists. These traditional literary freaks elicit sympathy and pity, and they also serve to further emphasize the struggles of their abled siblings.

In *Sweet Whispers, Brother Rush*, fourteen-year-old protagonist Tree confronts the past through communication with the ghost of her uncle, Brother Rush. By doing so, she discovers the continuing repercussions of American slavery and racial oppression, illustrated by her uncle's and brother's disabilities. Tree's older brother Dab has an intellectual disability, as well as what is eventually revealed to be porphyria—affecting nerves and skin—both disabilities that force Tree to adopt an "adult," or caregiver, position. Dab functions in the story as a responsibility for Tree. With a mostly absent mother, Tree must care for Dab, and because of Dab's intellectual disability and mysterious bouts of illness, she must also worry about making dinners, taking care of her household, and dealing with Dab-related emergencies; "Tree! You got to always have him on your *mind*," she reminds herself, "else something bad could happen" (Hamilton 41). She loves her brother, but the text makes clear that she has had to take care of him to such an extent that she has forgotten about herself, as she feels "filled with worry over Dab for so long" when his porphyria worsens, and she realizes she is simply a "kid taking care of Dab" (140). When Tree's character shows growth near the end of the novel—when she begins to have hope that "things [will] be different by way then. [They've] . . . got to be different"—her hope is inspired by reflecting on Dab's sickness and death (143). Because he has died, she stops berating herself for thinking of anyone other than her brother. Tree sees a world outside of her home, her brother, and her ghost-uncle. She expresses anger toward her mother and even takes moments to reflect on her own situation: "She thought about herself and how empty she felt. She thought about Dab and M'Vy's [her mother's] love, and about porphyria. Last, she thought about being out on her own. She didn't know, yet, about that" (214). For the first time in the novel, Tree sees a future with options; suddenly gone is her responsibility to care for a disabled brother, the freak who was known in the neighborhood as a kind of spectacle, for "shucking and jiving with girls" and for needing to be sent "where they puts people lak him, . . . some retarded" (42, 51). Dab is a familiar literary freak, and he unintentionally serves as a textually important burden to his sister.

In death, Dab forces Tree toward self-understanding and even simple self-awareness; contributing didactic and moral lessons to the text, Dab's character pushes readers, like the characters, to feel sympathy for the simplistic yet sexualized boy. As Tree reluctantly acknowledges, "He was seventeen and he wasn't smart" (13). The reader is encouraged to see Dab in this way, to feel pity for the intellectually disabled boy with a "sweet, empty look," and to feel sympathy for both simple Dab and burdened Tree, adolescents who have been left "alone together" (16, 17). Dab is also marked physically by porphyria, a disease that Tree's mother explains could be symbolic: "traced to South Africa and a Dutch settler. Then, it became a *colored* porphyria and made its way to America probably through the slave trade" (183). Emphasizing the freakish nature of the disease that has marked her family, Vy asks her daughter, "Ain't it strange, black men get a disease where no light can touch their skin?" (183).[1] Though the other characters in the novel are complex, Dab remains simple and elicits only pity and sympathy: he is not smart, he has porphyria that makes him ill, he is always kind, he is the victim of child abuse and neglect, and he ultimately dies. The final lines of the novel even celebrate Dab's sympathetic simplicity, how he used to wear "his shuffling light shoes" while moaning and wearing his bathrobe (37); Tree's old family friend and new parental figure, Miss Pricherd gives "Tree one of her toothless grins. And she did a little dance in her slippers," an homage to Dab's shuffling dances (215).

In *Becoming Naomi León*, Owen—another intellectually disabled brother—forces his sister Naomi to self-reflect and grow, while allowing characters and readers to pity him and test their moral compasses. A visibly "deformed" freak, Owen was "born with his head tilted to one side and scrunched down next to his shoulder," talks with "a permanent frog voice," and has one leg that's shorter than the other (Ryan 4). His prominent otherness makes him noticeably different from his peers, and his personality—perhaps in a guided attempt to encourage readers to feel pity and sympathy—is characterized by his speaking "in a dreamy sort of way" and having a "never-ending good nature" (21, 34). In the novel, Owen's presence tests Naomi's morality by permitting her to love and accept him the way he is and the way he accepts himself, as "a Funny Looking Kid," without medical treatments designed to normalize his appearance (115). Owen's disabilities also serve to further their mother's villainous role in the text, as she *would* prefer he received treatments and were made to look more "normal." While artfully dealing with stronger themes of ethnicity and familial culture, *Becoming Naomi León* quietly uses a freak to teach lessons about acceptance, tolerance, and love. Much like *Sweet Whispers, Brother Rush*, the novel demonstrates what Ato Quayson explains as using a disabled character to serve as a measurement of ethical standing and what Rosemarie Garland-Thomson categorizes as using human spectacles to elicit responses from other characters.

DEVELOPED, COMPLICATED FREAKS

Freak the Mighty and *Wonder*, both popular and frequently taught, employ the freak character more deliberately and attempt to complicate representations of disability. Startlingly, *Freak the Mighty*'s Kevin, also called Freak, and *Wonder*'s August, usually called Auggie, are more developed than traditional disabled sidekicks. Both novels work to blur lines between primary and secondary characters; to play with narrative techniques, to offer disabled characters a modicum of self-awareness; to question what it means to be disabled; and to allow the disabled characters themselves to change, grow—and *almost* find pride in their disabled identities. But in their development, the texts ultimately compound problematic messages. Kevin and Auggie demean themselves with self-deprecating humor, accept their roles as simplified helpers, and find acceptance in the texts only from other nonnormative characters. Most troublingly, both narratives prevent self-acceptance and eliminate their characters' disabilities.

Freak the Mighty and *Wonder* are both tales of early-adolescent, visibly disabled boys who make friends and change lives. Most simply and most traditionally in *Freak the Mighty*, Freak—described as having "a normal-sized head, . . . [while] the rest of him is shorter than a yardstick and kind of twisted in a way that means he can't stand up straight and makes his chest puff out" (Philbrick 8)—lives to give his friend Max confidence in himself and his intellectual abilities, and he dies to force Max to "write it all down," to grow and remember, while readers are left with nothing but sympathy and admiration for Freak, who "knew from a very young age that he wasn't going to have a very long life" (151, 157). The novel straightforwardly teaches that friendship can change lives and that people—especially those like Max, who is huge and looks like his criminal father, and Freak, who is a tiny, deformed boy with "crooked legs" (2)—are often much more than they first appear to be.

Wonder, published almost twenty years after *Freak the Mighty*, tells essentially the same story. Auggie is a fifth-grader with a craniofacial disorder, "'single nucleotide deletion mutations' that made a war on his face," and other genetic differences that are "just incredibly bad luck" and cause very noticeable physical deformities (Palacio 104, 105). After being homeschooled, Auggie attends his first year in an actual school, where he—of course—teaches others about acceptance, tolerance, and kindness. After forming shallow friendships, being hurt and bullied, forming genuine friendships, and being physically attacked by older students from another school, Auggie finally receives "the Henry Ward Beecher medal . . . to honor students who have been notable or exemplary . . . [along with] the strength of one's own courage" (303). Auggie notes that his receiving the award has made "everyone kind of teary-eyed and wet-cheeked" and that "everyone started taking pictures of" him, illustrating growth and self-satisfaction achieved by his nondisabled peers (307). Though Auggie "was just smiling a big fat happy smile for all the different cameras clicking away" (307), his happiness is barely relevant; without a doubt, the charming, honest freak has been placed on a stage and in front of cameras, a very familiar and problematic image. Garland-Thomson's descriptions of P. T. Barnum's famous American "freak shows" of the nineteenth and twentieth centuries, which "challenged audiences not only to classify and explain what they saw, but to relate the performance to themselves, to American individual and collective identity" (Garland-Thomson,

Extraordinary 58), capture quite accurately Auggie's school assembly and award presentation:

> The freak show is a spectacle, a cultural performance that gives primacy to visual apprehension in creating symbolic codes and institutionalizes the relationship between the spectacle and the spectators. In freak shows, the exhibited body became a text written in boldface to be deciphered according to the needs and desires of onlookers. (60)

Smiling Auggie is presented, by his school administrators and by the text itself, as an object for the audience, who feel sympathy and find self-affirmation of their morality, as well as relief of their own physical normality. Auggie teaches and relieves, while the crowd stares and takes photographs of the freak enclosed in a "big tight huddle as parents clicked away like we were on a red carpet somewhere" (Palacio 307). These characters, presumably like the novel's readers, are rewarded for (finally) accepting a freak, who is awarded and displayed simply for being himself. As much as readers may feel moved and pleased that Auggie "wasn't even thinking about [his] face," they cannot forget the context of his smile and the spectacle that has allowed readers to grow (307). Rather, they are simply able to ignore the smile's craniofacial context, which enables them to ignore a prominent part of Auggie's identity; the text does not make room for Auggie to be proud of his entire being, including both his smile and deformities.

Auggie and Freak, however, are not so simplistic that they are voiceless; both characters are able, if not always willing, to speak up for themselves and to work for acceptance. In doing so, they both rely on demeaning and self-deprecating humor. The young adolescents do their best to make friends by telling jokes, and they make their peers laugh—at their own expenses. Freak begins by "tell[ing] robot stories that are so strange and funny" and poking fun at his new friend Max by calling him a "big moron" (Philbrick 27). As situations and storylines become darker and more complicated, so too do Freak's quips; he mocks nearly everything and everyone, and he uses his physical appearance to enhance the humor: "'Please, sir, more gruel,' he says, holding up his plate and making a funny face where his tongue sticks out sideways, and Gran laughs so hard" (94). His humor is largely lost on Max, who suspects Freak believes what he says, but Freak exaggerates the notion of his being a medical wonder, a human spectacle, with a kind of dark humor, in order to make Max smile. Freak's stories are revealed to be untrue, of course, and Max is left with an elaborate "lie," a "remarkable fantasy," a complex exaggeration and joke that Freak created for himself and for his friend (156, 157).

Humor in *Wonder* is a bit less dark, but Auggie—like Freak—uses demeaning and self-deprecating jokes as social lubricant throughout the novel. Even though he knows the names people call him—"Rat boy. Freak. Monster. Freddy Krueger. E.T. Gross-out. Lizard face. Mutant"—Auggie faces enormous hurt when he hears one of his two real friends, Jack, say about him, "If I looked like him, seriously, I think that I'd kill myself" (79, 77).[2] Later, once Jack apologizes and stands up for Auggie against the fifth grade's *real* bully Julian, their grade divides itself into two "official sides," and "for a while, the 'war' was all we walked about" (177, 208). As tensions begin to lessen, Auggie takes control by earning friends through humor:

> Like the other day I saw Maya writing a note to Ellie on a piece of Uglydoll stationery, and I don't know why, but I just kind of randomly said: "Did you know the guy who created Uglydolls based them on me?"
>
> Maya looked at me with her eyes wide open like she totally believed me. Then, when she realized I was only kidding, she thought it was the funniest thing in the world. (209–10)

Though he makes himself the butt of a joke, Auggie—presumably like the text's reader—sees his social life improving, because "six months ago stuff like that would never have happened, but now it happens more and more" (210). Even earlier in the text, Auggie shows that his go-to method for easing the discomfort of nondisabled peers is to make a joke about himself, allowing others to laugh both with and *at* him. While Auggie's jokes may indeed dispel tension in social settings, they also position Auggie as someone at whom it is acceptable to laugh. When he and Jack laugh about another student's reaction to Auggie, prompting Jack to ask if Auggie is "always going to look this way," and whether he "can't get plastic surgery or something," Auggie "smile[s] and point[s] to [his] face. 'Hello? This *is* after plastic surgery!'" (64). Both laugh so hard that they are reprimanded by a teacher; on the surface, Auggie is having fun, but again, he is positioning himself as a not-fully-human freak who tests other characters' moralities with friendship.

Auggie even dismisses his mother with self-deprecating jokes, telling her, "We're kind of like Beauty and the Beast," when she comments that his friend Summer is "very pretty" (56). But the jokes, of course, disguise very real feelings and insecurities that Auggie only occasionally reveals:

> "Why do I have to be so ugly, Mommy?" I whispered.
>
> "No, baby, you're not . . ."
>
> "I know I am."
>
> She kissed me all over my face. She kissed my eyes that came down too far. She kissed my cheeks that looked punched in. She kissed my tortoise mouth.
>
> She said soft words that I know were meant to help me, but words can't change my face. (60)

Even if comforted by kindness and sympathy, Auggie never stops wishing for a "change." Words may not offer such a cure, but Auggie, his mother, and the novel itself could offer words that suggest pride and acceptance rather than sympathy and denial. Words, certainly, could change his perception of his face, but in *Wonder*, Auggie is always marked as a freak, earning fear or pity.

Not only are Auggie and Freak forever marked as human spectacles and used to inspire others, they—because they are more developed than the shallowest literary freaks—even *accept* their roles as sidekicks. By doing so, the freak characters do expose their demeaning literary positions to the reader, but the narratives themselves do little to challenge those positions. Just before Freak dies in *Freak the Mighty*, his heart literally and metaphorically "too big for his body," his final conversation with Max is entirely composed of reassurances, explanations, and inspirations (Philbrick 157): "'I'm not coming home,' he says. 'Not in my present manifestation'" (149). Freak accepts that his role is to comfort Max, tell him not to be afraid and then tell him to open a book on the table. "That's for you," Freak explains calmly, unable to point with his finger, but wise beyond his years; "I want you to fill it up with our adventures" (150). He tells Max that, though he wanted to record their adventures himself, he "won't have the time," so he leaves Max with resounding confidence (151): "It's all in your head, Max, everything you can remember. Just tell the story of Freak the Mighty, no big deal" (151). And in the very end, Max has indeed told their story by "writ[ing] a book. . . . No big deal" (160). Yet the reader knows with great sentimentality that Max's intellectual achievement is a very big deal.

Toward the end of his own story, Auggie makes clear that he understands, at least in part, his role at school and in his family (and consequently in his text). He listens to his principal describe the Henry Ward Beecher Medal and even starts "paying attention, for real now," because "Mr. Tushman's voice cracked a bit, like he got all choked up" (Palacio 303). Of course, the medal goes to Auggie, the "student whose quiet strength has carried up the most hearts," and who is able to encompass "something like greatness" (304). Without recognizing patronizing or condescending overtones—especially considering that this award traditionally has "acknowledg[ed] volunteerism or service to the school," which Auggie has not done—"people started applauding before Mr. Tushman's words actually registered" to Auggie (303, 305). Like a freak in a freak show, Auggie takes the stage to the delight of others, as the recipient of an award that names his existence a "service" for others. When the words do register, Auggie *almost* articulates the problem with using a freak to illustrate and improve others' morals, before cutting himself off and simply accepting his role:

> I wasn't even sure why I was getting this medal, really.
>
> No, that's not true. I know why.
>
> It's like people you see sometimes, and you can't imagine what it would be like to be that person, whether it's somebody in a wheelchair or somebody who can't talk. Only, I know that I'm that person to other people, maybe to every single person in that whole auditorium.
>
> To me, though, I'm just me. An ordinary kid.

> But hey, if they want to give me a medal for being me, that's okay. I'll take it. I didn't destroy the Death Star or anything like that, but I did just get through the fifth grade. And that's not easy, even if you're not me. (306)

Auggie and *Wonder almost* unexpectedly begin to address that his presence at school and in the auditorium is a way for others to cultivate sympathy. Auggie allows himself to "imagine what it would be like to be . . . somebody in a wheelchair or somebody who can't talk" and to imagine himself as a starer who questions humanity and makes "sense of ourselves and our world" (Palacio 306; Garland-Thomson, "Introduction" 1). So close to challenging the use of his disability as a "difference that signals meanings," Auggie stops himself—as the text stops philosophically with him (Garland-Thomson, *Extraordinary* 11). Rather than push himself, his peers, and his reader to understand how unfair it is to rob the freak of his humanity in order to reconfirm the humanity of others, he thinks, "But hey, if they want to give me a medal for being me, that's okay" (Palacio 306).

Sufficiently pitied and admired for their inner strength, Auggie and Freak *remain* freaks, accept their roles as freaks, and as they find friends and allies, align themselves only with other outsiders. Clearly, the novels suggest that nonnormative characters should remain outside of the mainstream. As Auggie's mother tells him following the school's cliquey science fair, "I guess it's true that like seeks like" (207). Indeed, Freak's only real friend in *Freak the Mighty* is Max, who stands out as a poor student, who is bigger than everyone else and closely resembles his father, imprisoned for killing Max's mother (Philbrick 19–25). Max's own self-consciousness allows him to feel empathy for Freak, and the pair becomes one strong being, Freak the Mighty, "walking on high" (141). Still, other than Freak's mother, Max's grandparents, and Freak's doctor, the pair make no other strong connections and find few allies; in the novel, the most that "normal" kids do is chant, "Freak the Mighty! Freak the Mighty! Freak the Mighty!" when the duo marches around a classroom as a foolish spectacle (78). Though most characters differ from sociological norms in some way, the text suggests that, yes, like seek like, and the freaks will always be a part of a separate group.

The same dynamic of separation appears in *Wonder*. Part of the novel's complexity is that the characters' stories and situations are revealed little by little, but by doing so, Palacio perhaps unintentionally reveals—little by little—that everyone who befriends Auggie is also an outsider. His first friend at school, Jack, quickly realizes that "a kid like August doesn't stand a chance in middle school," and the text later reveals that Jack has been marginalized for years because his "parents are not rich" and live in "the section of North River Heights where people don't want to park their cars" (Palacio 14, 149). Auggie's second friend at school, Summer, has been "asked . . . why . . . [she] hang[s] out with 'the freak' so much," and is clearly identified as biracial (119, 127). Not only is Summer nonwhite, she is considered a "a bit out there" by other students (144). Further, Auggie's loyal sister is differentiated from other students simply *because* she is the freak's sister and loaded with responsibility and guilt; her boyfriend Justin and her former best friend Miranda both support and love Auggie, but of course they are outsiders, too. Justin is a "cool enough dude" who has "underprotective . . . neglectful . . . self-involved" parents and "tics [that] are always there . . . a few hard blinks now, the occasional head pull"; Miranda is a compulsively lying product of a difficult divorce, which at the very least, makes her feel "othered" and alone (184, 192, 190, 236–37). In many respects, *Wonder* appropriately illustrates that not many people in Auggie's world, like people in the real world, fit molds of normality, but the text also subtly suggests that everyone who is willing to empathize and be friends with Auggie is *already* an outcast of some kind. The novel very explicitly advocates kindness, but It does so with potentially harmful sympathy—as characters pity Auggie, as opposed to listening and working to understand his experiences—rather than empathy. Anyone may feel empathy and exhibit nonpatronizing kindness; in *Wonder*, however, othered characters feel empathy, presumably because of similar experiences, while the majority of Auggie's community feels sympathy, pity, and sorrow for the other(s). *Wonder* may echo and further demonstrate messages delivered in *Freak the Mighty*, a text in which secondary characters receive far less attention, but for the most part, do not show empathy toward or accept the othered protagonists.

Though certainly not direct challenges to the literary freak, *Freak the Mighty* and *Wonder* both attempt to make their characters more *human* in their stories.[3] Both novels do blur lines between primary and secondary characters; allow disabled characters some agency; and begin to question what it means to be disabled. In Philbrick's *Freak the Mighty*, Max is undeniably the narrator and protagonist—and even the implied *author* of the text—but two slight identifications begin to blur the distinction between primary and secondary, or more importantly, between Max and Freak. Most notably, the novel's title *Freak the Mighty* refers to the identity that Max and Freak inhabit when they become one; they share an identity by physically joining together, using a combined name, and sacrificing individuality. In Freak's words, "We're Freak the Mighty, that's who we are. We're nine feet tall, in case you haven't noticed" (Philbrick 39–40). Less explicitly, but equally as important, Max's and Freak's identities merge with Freak's death, when Max must record their "adventures," "the story of Freak the Mighty" (150, 151). It is, of course, one story, and by writing this text, Max has attempted to give a voice to *both* of them, illustrating the success and confidence found in their union.

Narratively, *Wonder* is a very different text entirely; it gives voice to all of the principal adolescent characters by changing narrators with each "part," or section. Even though Auggie-the-freak does not narrate the entire novel, he does speak for himself for a full three-eighths of it. As the only narrator to receive three parts, including the first and last, one could argue that Auggie the freak is *the* principal character, and all others secondary. In any case, all six adolescents are able to speak for themselves, both about themselves and about Auggie's situation and identity. With so many narrators, a reader may consider whether *Wonder*'s "appeal relies not on the individual strivings of the main character but on a vision of a community transforming itself" (Wheeler 338). While Elizabeth A. Wheeler argues that this is representative of "social change" and told "from the rarely explored viewpoint of the kids involved, rather than the adults" (338), she fails to note that young adult novels are *usually* told from an adolescent's perspective and that the individual experience of the disabled character *should* be privileged over the community's experiences—after years of relegating the freak to the sidelines.

Still, Freak and Auggie both exhibit some complexity, show a bit of personal growth, and *almost* find pride in their identities. In addition to almost—but never—allowing their disabled characters pride, *Freak the Mighty* and *Wonder* both almost—but do not—redefine what it means to be disabled. In *Freak the Mighty*, disability is portrayed both as something permanent, for Freak, and as something much more fluid and even "curable," for Max, whose poor performance in school is *sometimes* labeled a "learning disability" (Philbrick 19). Without a doubt, Freak occupies the role of freak in the text, but Max introduces himself as "a butthead" (4); he has been placed in separate classes at school for students with learning disabilities and understands that he is "different." Max may indeed be disabled, but the novel only deals with it to illustrate how Max grows and becomes more successful in school. His tutor explains his sudden academic improvements by saying, "As you know, heh heh, my personal opinion has always been that you're lazy and stubborn and you didn't *want* to learn" (81). Ultimately, Max's maybe-disability is simply eliminated; while the reader perhaps finds the tutor's accusations of Max being "lazy and stubborn" insulting and hurtful, the reader must also believe that Max's performance at school *has* changed, doubtlessly due to inspiration from Freak (81). Consequently, the novel stops short of changing literary uses of disability; instead the use of terms like "learning disabled" and "lazy" only further confuse and demean disabled identities.

In *Wonder*, Auggie is explicitly *not* disabled, and the text furthers harmful understandings of "disability," "special needs," and "inclusion." The only redefining of disability that *Wonder* accomplishes is to further stigmatize it. Just as Auggie's mother tells him he's not ugly, his principal Mr. Tushman reassures parents in an email that the school "is not an inclusion school" (Palacio 60, 162):

> As for your other concerns regarding our new student August, please note that he does not have special needs. He is neither disabled, handicapped, nor developmentally delayed in any way, so there was no reason to assume anyone would take issue with his admittance to Beecher Prep—whether it is an inclusion school or not. (163)

While Auggie's mother and principal may be attempting to explain to both Auggie and his community that he is not *wrong* or *bad*, they do so by denying his disability, rather than by accepting it as a current and important part of his identity. The characters in *Wonder* either convince themselves that kindness is all it takes to cure disability—at least the social elements—or ignore the heterogeneity of the disabled community. They uniformly refuse to understand disability and a character trait worthy of pride and confidence. While Mr. Tushman states that Auggie "is neither disabled, handicapped, nor developmentally delayed," Auggie himself cries, "I'm not retarded!" (Palacio 163, 218). Wheeler suggests that the novel allows readers to "focus on how he feels instead of how he looks," which sounds progressive but actually just removes disability from the text (Wheeler 340). Auggie may have a "remarkable face," but he is not disabled, he may have severe hearing loss, misshapen features, and a mouth that makes eating difficult, but he is not disabled (340). Auggie and *Wonder* ultimately do nothing to further movements for disability visibility, acceptance, and rights.

Both *Freak the Mighty* and *Wonder* make disability something to deny, cure, or ignore, and neither text offers the possibility of confidence or *self*-acceptance or pride in a disabled identity. Freak dies, Max is cured, and Auggie simply is not disabled. While both texts do complicate representations of disability—questioning treatments of disabled people, placing disabled characters in central roles, and attempting to play with familiar tropes—they fail.

REVOLUTIONARY FREAKS

In a quite radical retelling of the adolescent freak's story, Koertge's *Stoner & Spaz* exposes the traditional literary freak, uses humor to question and challenge it, and ultimately destroys it. *Stoner & Spaz* is written in the typical "wallflower" voice by narrator-protagonist Ben Bancroft, a sixteen-year-old movie buff with mild cerebral palsy, who immediately presents himself as a freak with an "anomalous human body, at once familiar and alien" (Garland-Thomson, "Introduction" 1). The reader does not receive a freakish physical description of Ben through another's eyes—already a great departure from the trope of the traditional literary freak as a secondary, observed character. Still, he criticizes himself as he "limp[s]" and "drag[s his] foot" in the first few pages, and he even asks for a discount "since it's Monster Week" at the local movie theatre (Koetrge 1, 3, 2). Separating himself from what he perceives to be a mainstream culture, Ben paints himself as a true monster, "the resident spaz" and identifies with Christy Brown, celebrated Irish author with severe cerebral palsy who wrote *My Left Foot* (1954), an autobiography that was adapted into a film in 1989 (23); Ben knows Brown's story enjoyed success because "everybody likes to see people triumph over adversity. And he had some serious C.P." (11). Aware of such expectations, Ben knows that his role is to experience "life as an eavesdropper," present only to provide a life-affirming story of triumph over adversity as "a bit player in the movie of life. Listed at the tag end of the credits: Crippled Kid" (8, 30). *Stoner & Spaz*, however, is *Ben's* story; the reader experiences a version of "the movie of life" as told by a usually sidelined freak. By granting Ben total control of narration, Koertge's novel not only gives voice to a character usually relegated to the sidelines, it also gives that character a chance to grow and change as much as, if not more than, the characters he influences; Ben has a strong, developed, and distinctly young adult voice, with self-awareness and self-consciousness.[4] Without a doubt, Ben is not given the portrayal reserved for a typical freak, but at the same time, *because* Ben sets himself up as the disabled figure seen "gimping down the aisle," his character becomes more of an anti-freak or a freak-in-protest (5).

Like other freak characters, Ben immediately connects with other outsiders, many of them patrons of his favorite cinema: "Misfits and Luddites. Castaways and exiles. And all of us alone" (3, 4). Even the individuals with whom he grows close are outsiders: Colleen, who is known by "everybody who wants weed" and who follows a "regimen of self-destructive behavior," and Marcie, a divorced single woman who "had bypass surgery before [she] was forty" (32, 50). Initially at least, Ben has accepted his role as a freak meant to help others grow, has aligned himself with other outsiders, and uses sometimes-self-deprecating humor to ease social situations. Like Freak and Auggie, sixteen-year-old Ben has taught himself to relieve tension with humor, often to describe his self-perceptions; he corrects himself after writing, "Then I stalk away," with a quick revision: "Oh, all right—then I *limp* away" (Koertge 17; emphasis added). Ben's narrative is riddled with self-directed insults, but as it does for Freak and Auggie, humor helps Ben with social interactions. When Ben assures Colleen that, when she's "totally sober," she will "find [him] pretty easy to resist," he welcomes casual, affectionate teasing from and with his friends (83). Upon meeting Marcie, he explains that he lives with his grandmother and is an "orphan," so when Marcie arrives at their house for brunch, she greets Ben by saying, "If it isn't the orphan" (36, 48). Ben finds comfort in this known joke between them and notes Marcie's "nice smile, so I smile back" (48). As a freak, Ben accepts laughter, but it also takes him time to get used to ironic, inside jokes that reaffirm, rather than weaken, friendships.

Through the text, Ben's character finds pride in his identity without denying his disability, and the entire cast of misfit characters push questions of what it means to be disabled and what it means to function as a literary freak. Ben is a disabled adolescent with self-awareness and the ability to tell his own story—a story of adolescent identity-finding with new friends and experiences. Ben learns about *himself*; he realizes that many of his self-perceptions, such as assuming he is simply ignored as "the resident spaz," are not quite accurate (23). For instance, when Ben gets into Colleen's car, he "point[s] at the door. 'I'm the one who's supposed to be helping you'" (56). Rather than rely on narrative melodrama by showing Colleen feeling sympathy or feeling inspired by Ben's perseverance, the text allows the characters to speak honestly and candidly:

> "And you would [help me], too, if I was the spaz."
>
> It's funny how different that sounds when Colleen says it; it's not so much a name as a fact. Or maybe coming from her, it isn't like the brickbat people usually hurl at me.
>
> I turn sideways, fall back into the seat, and haul my gimpy leg in as Colleen walks around to her side. (57)

Ben's cerebral palsy is becoming "a fact" that he learns to accept as others accept it. By the novel's conclusion, the text makes clear that *Ben* is the one who has grown and changed. Ben becomes more aware of himself, too, as when acquaintance tells him that his problem is not his C.P., but "those clothes your grandma makes you wear. And how you think you're better than everybody else" (118). Rather than continuing to rely on arrogant judgments, Ben is the one who learns acceptance and kindness. He finally realizes that his grandmother's comments about "people like that" and about how "we're judged by the company we keep" have been conditioning him into being, or at least presenting himself as, a snob (15, 38):

> "You started it [Colleen tells him]. You want to blame your mom and dad because you're a snob, go ahead. But it's bullshit."
>
> "A minute ago I was just a loser. Now I'm a snob, too?"
>
> Colleen holds out her hand and lifts a finger for every name: "Don Secoli is in a wheelchair, and he's Mr. High School. Karen Radley's practically deaf, and she still plays drums in some garage band. Doris Schumacher's blind, but all you have to do is say one word to her and she knows who you are. Get over yourself, okay? (73)

Similarly, Marcie teaches Ben that his disability is not an alienating part of his identity; she demonstrates knowledge and comfort when she first meets him:

> I show her my bad arm, the fingers curled into a pathetic little fist.
>
> "Not a stroke, I hope."
>
> "C.P."
>
> "But not dyskinetic."
>
> "No, spastic."
>
> "Ah, well, you were lucky."
>
> "That's the title of my autobiography: *Ben the Lucky Spaz*." (35)

With trust and comfort, Marcie furthers Ben's development by urging him not to "[waste] this incarnation," by teaching him how to create and produce his own film, and by assuring him with gentle teasing that he is a typical adolescent (87). Ben doesn't search for acceptance by trying to overcome, deny, or ignore his disability. Instead, he *finds* it with help from Colleen and Marcie, who never ignore his disability but also illustrate that—in Colleen's words—*all* "bodies are really interesting. All the shit that happens to them, and they just don't quit" (149–50). With kindness and confidence, Ben rebels against his grandmother's guidelines, changes his hair, has sex with someone he cares for, and is accepted to a film festival (153). He finds success, growth, and pride in himself, including his disability.

Stoner & Spaz, though, does more; the novel destroys the traditional role of the literary freak. By creating his own role, Ben demonstrates that disabled people want neither unwanted attention nor diverted eyes, and that they are able to be sexual without being dangerous, and he captures the difficulty of challenging assumptions. Ben finally reconsiders staying as "invisible as the sign that says NO RUNNING, the one nobody pays any attention to," because while avoiding freakshow-like spectacles and stares, he has also avoided nearly all human touch, something he had blamed on others' discomfort with his body (Koertge 23):

> "Grandma, in the last three years, except for you, [Colleen is] the only person who actually touched me, actually put her hands on me." I shake my stunted arm at her. "She touched this, she touched my stupid leg. It was like it didn't matter. When I was with her sometimes I felt like John Travolta in *Saturday Night Fever* bopping down the street carrying that can of paint." (127)

With confidence, Ben's entire world expands. Rather than simply exposing the problems reinforced by freak characters, *Stoner & Spaz* is a narrative of a visibly disabled, wallflower-like narrator-protagonist with adolescent self-consciousness. Ben allows himself to appreciate affectionate touch, through hugs from Marcie: "I let her. I want her to. My C.P. doesn't matter to her. It never has. She puts her arms around all of me" (161). Ben remains very aware of this kind of touch, noting each time Colleen "leans into" him, "leans against" him, and when he "put[s his] arm around her" (108, 137, 135). And when Colleen finally says, "Kiss me like they did in those old movies," she and Ben talk about the self-consciousness he feels about his disabled body (148). Ben warns her, "I don't look too good with my clothes off," and he even asks to wait until dark falls, but Colleen refuses to wait or to close her eyes (148). "Shut up," she tells him. "You want somebody's eyes closed, close your own" (145). After sixteen years of feeling like an untouchable freak, Ben gets told that his "ugly" body is a—sarcastically stated—"big fucking deal" (149). Ben's acceptance of sexual touch from Colleen comes as no surprise, because the text has allowed him to think about sex and feel sexual from the beginning—when Colleen makes his body feel "like being plug into a wall socket" and by learning about sex "as an eavesdropper" (7, 8). Marcie hands him condoms with great nonchalance before leaving town: "Take some. You're going to be all alone with your girlfriend" (142).

Though unsurprising in this narrative, Ben's expressions of sexuality are radical moments for a freak; some disabled characters, like Freak and Auggie, are absolutely sex-less, while other disabled adolescents—like Dab in *Sweet Whispers, Brother Rush* and Benjy in *The Sound and the Fury*—are dangerously sexualized. Anna Mollow and Robert McRuer further explain that "rarely are disabled people regarded as either desiring subjects or objects of desire" (1). Ben is allowed to be both, and instead of showing "tragic deficiency or freakish excess," he flirts with a girl who promises to "show [him her] tits" and he prepares for a kiss by licking his lips, "because that's what people do in movies" (Mollow and McRuer 1; Koertge 19, 77).

Further breaking the restrictions placed on freak characters, *Stoner & Spaz* allows Ben to connect with other—not exclusively disabled—adolescents by filming a documentary, *High School Confidential*. Ben talks with kids known for academic work (Koertge 115–18), for athletic associations (118–22), for being black teenaged mothers (122–25), for being the gay man who's "been out since sixth grade" (129), and for being "a one-woman Afterschool Special . . . [with] booze everywhere" (145). Using Marcie's advice to "start with . . . [his peers] defined by race and sexual preference and [then] move deeper," beneath initial presentations for complex truths, Ben asks about self-identifications, assumptions, observations, hopes, and future plans (141). The final film shows his peers explaining what they feel "really shitty" about, even among their friends; *High School Confidential* becomes an exploration of intersecting identities, and it even draws a crowd at the gallery that is "actually not that little" (140, 160, 159). In the photograph taken of the filmmakers, Ben begins to see himself more accurately: "There's my picture. And nineteen others: black guys, Hispanic girls, Chinese guys, Vietnamese girls—it's a regular UNICEF card" (157). Always conscious of his visible disability, Ben finally regards it with the same acceptance that he does others' identity traits. He demonstrates how disability deserves space in the "multicultural quilt" of society, allowing the novel to suggest that activism could be in his future (Davis, "The End of Identity" 233).

Quite simply, Ben fails to function as a freak. He lacks the ability to elicit sentimental, emotional responses, and Marcie's character doesn't even need those responses. While she does need and value friendship, and while she is unsure of a lifetime of unfinished beginnings, working "here, there, hospice work one year, classes at Caltech the next," she is never tricked into relying on inspiration from others (87). Marcie doesn't need Ben as a catalyst for moral growth, and she isn't desperate for someone to pity in order to reinforce her own identity. Even Colleen, who *is* a character laced with desperation and who often uses Ben as a sidekick, refuses to let him save her. He very nearly inspires Colleen to seek treatment for drug abuse and addiction, simply by existing—by being "the nicest guy" and "the cleanest, soberest guy in the world" (26, 135). Ben supports her when she "suck[s] on the joint," tells him about being sexually abused when she was "fucking ten years old," and he bluntly tells her, "Colleen, you're a drug addict," when she is "all, like, woozy and shit," but his help is not enough (69, 70, 71, 133). He does not possess ethereal wisdom or demonstrate brave perseverance; all Ben can do is care about his friend, who is not able or ready to accept his help, who is not "cured" in the text.

Though presented as a self-described "Monster," who assumes he is "the one who's supposed to be helping," he doesn't help (105, 56). Marcie, however, succeeds at inspiring, while Colleen provokes pity and growth; *they* are the ones who disrupt definitions of disability, along with the roles and effects of disabled characters. Colleen, very obviously, could occupy the role of disabled freak; she is a mentally ill sidekick who is "passionate about drugs" and "like[s] getting high" (114, 153). Colleen is viewed as a social freak by her peers, and she would almost certainly earn diagnoses of mental illnesses if treated. "I know I smoke too much [marijuana]," she tells Ben, but still, she "continue[s] despite knowledge of having a persistent . . . psychological problem"

(Koertge 76, American Psychiatric Association 509). Colleen is a physically noticeable secondary character—"Her hair is tufty and ragged. She's as pale as a girl in a poem about maidens and moonlight" (4)—who accompanies narrator-protagonist Ben on a journey of growth and understanding. She never shies away from touching Ben, and she speaks to him with frankness and honesty he's never before heard; because Colleen sees him as "normal," Ben begins to see himself that way. Colleen inspires and evokes passion, even as she slumps, exhausted; she teaches Ben to take chances, to not always follow rules, and to really try to live—because when he does, he "feel[s] really good" (63). Perhaps that relegates Colleen to the simple role of catalyzing plot and character growth, which allows Marcie to elicit inspiration and moral development.

Like both Ben and Colleen, Marcie is nonnormative; she lacks the visible markings of a freak, but is recovering from bypass surgery, which requires she "watch what [she] eat[s]" because, under her smock, she looks "like the bride of Frankenstein" (50). Marcie also offers lessons, as freaks ought to do, that affect other characters in meaningful ways. Less didactically than traditional freaks, Marcie does expose Ben to other ways of approaching life by explaining her routines of a "little meditation, a little prayer, a little tai chi, and . . . a little bit in the way of the wind and water" (85–86). This kind of inspiration, however, is due to Marcie's quiet acceptance, confidence, and openness, as opposed to difficulties she's overcome or opportunities she will never have. Marcie follows a Buddhist teacher who "warned me about wasting this incarnation, and all the time he's got this huge grin on his face" (87). She imparts that intentionally nonspecific wisdom to Ben, and sometimes her wisdom also reaches the more erratic Colleen. "What do you guys see at school?" she asks them; "Are kids passionate about things? Ben's in love with movies. What are you in love with, Colleen?" (Koertge 88). Colleen's only answer is later revealed to be "drugs," but Marcie refuses to give up on either of them. Ultimately, Marcie settles into the role of mentor, rather than freak. Still, with her less obvious identity traits, combined with her quiet ability to elicit more development in Ben than he does for her, Marcie demonstrates that the role of the freak does not have to be so easily defined or identifiable. Implicitly, her character raises questions about needs and relationships, about assumptions and stereotypes, and about literary tropes. Explicitly and obviously, though, Marcie keeps her emotions private, lives her own life, and offers her adolescent friends support and advice.

With roles far less stable than expected in a disability narrative, Colleen and Marcie challenge familiar literary tropes of disabled characters, and in some ways, work to redefine disability. In the very end, Colleen—maybe the dominant freak—does disappear from the narrative, "buzzed" and "speed[ing] away" in a car, while Ben "feel[s] for the slip of paper" that carries a new acquaintance's email address (168). Then he catches up with his grandmother, Marcie, and the other filmmakers. Just as Dab and Freak ultimately die once their narrative duties have been filled, "outlining the complex moral choices open to the protagonist[s]," and leaving others with hope, Colleen is gone (Quayson 38). Her disability no longer fits in the text.

In other young adult disability narratives that use freak characters, including of course, *Freak the Mighty* and *Wonder*, critics and readers claim to have found helpful, empowering messages. Wheeler even asserts that *Wonder* "is staging "a revolution," because the primary characters feel inspired to change their school community (335). Another overwhelming message in the text, as well as in *Freak the Mighty*, is that "like seeks like" as an explanation for behaviors; specifically, nonnormative characters—generally those who represent marginalized groups—may quietly join together, but the looming power of normality will keep those characters in the margins (207). Readers hardly find revolutions in these messages. They may learn to tolerate, with pity, those who are different from them, but just as audiences at freak shows stared in order to confirm their own normality, normative characters in *Wonder* and *Freak the Mighty* learn that, as long as they are kind, they may leave the freaks on the margins. Only in *Stoner & Spaz* are notions of normality and the role of the freak inverted, challenged, and nearly destroyed. Only in *Stoner & Spaz* are all characters potential-freaks, while the expected-freak becomes a confident anti-freak. This reversal of a common trope forces complex readings, especially of how literary representations of adolescence and disability reflect and impact social attitudes. *Stoner & Spaz* is narrative that presents a revolution.

Chapter 5

ACCIDENTS

Disability as a Political Identity

Accidents of Nature (2006), Harriet McBryde Johnson's semi-autobiographical novel set in 1970, begins with a prologue about an old "forty-five acre tract [of land] that had been planted in pine" and left to "absentee owners" before becoming the ground below Camp Courage (1). Because the pine trees were not managed according to a human desire for a "regiment of uniform straight trunks, ideally suited for the market," they grew dense and disorganized: "thin and thick, twisted and shapely, bent and straight" (2–3). Johnson concludes her prologue with a short paragraph written about these trees, which serve as metaphors, as well as a very literal stage, for a cast of disabled (human) characters:

> They were products of what is called the natural law of survival of the fittest. But their fitness was not defined by human needs, or market forces, or any grand design. In truth, they did not survive because they were fit. Rather they were proven fit because they survived. They survived by accident. (3)

Johnson shows little interest in arguing that the trees are "normal" or that they are actually—underneath all of those "trunks twisted" and "limbs . . . so entangled"—the same as all of the other trees on the coastal plain of North Carolina (2). Rather, Johnson acknowledges and even celebrates that these trees are accidents, that "they *survived* by accident" (3; emphasis added). The accidents in Johnson's novel, of course, are not trees; they are disabled young adults, but like Johnson's trees, the characters' disabilities, caused by disorders, mistakes, and accidents, become important parts of their political and social identities.

Accidents of Nature, Terry Truman's *Inside Out* (2003), and Ginny Rorby's *Hurt Go Happy* (2006) all offer didactic lessons using disabled characters; they are problem novels. More importantly, these three young adult texts, which disrupt shallow problem-novel expectations, are disability narratives, which stand as complex works of literature that simultaneously explore and respond to political and social movements. A truly exceptional problem novel, *Accidents of Nature* places ample attention on political lessons, but does so by delving into complex and compelling social issues. Johnson uses her text as a political treatise, as a way to consider and ponder the complexities of identities (specifically disabled identities), and she refuses to patronize by including theoretical ideas and provocative experiences. While the adolescent characters in *Accidents of Nature* may follow expectations for young adult literature by "tell[ing] the reader what they have learned" (Trites, *Disturbing* 71), these characters are not finished learning, they are not taught by authoritative adult characters, and their problems are *not solved*. Johnson's text serves as a model for what problem novels may be: convincing, educational, didactic, as well as complicated, ambiguous, difficult, and provocatively unfinished. *Inside Out* and *Hurt Go Happy* offer heavy-handed lessons and are also unquestionably literary—with thoughtful language, developed characters, engaging stories—as well as politically powerful—with complex messages about disability. They include conflicting and questionable messages, which draw attention to the *importance* of accuracy, particularly in reality-based narratives.

COMPLEX MESSAGES

Even with intertwined themes and developed characters, *Inside Out* and *Hurt Go Happy* explicitly deliver dominating messages about disability as a politicized identity, along with complicating lessons about human connection and animal-human connection. In doing so, the novels resist simplicity and even offer provocative discrepancies. *Inside Out*'s ending, for instance, illustrates both the limitations and possibilities of uniting literary and political writing, and *Hurt Go*

Happy, even with forceful messages, never aligns itself with traditional political views. Literary openness in these texts both complicates didactic messages and allows the reader to think critically about civil rights and human understanding.

Trueman's *Inside Out* is the story of narrator-protagonist Zach Wahhsted, an adolescent living with schizophrenia, presented as a medicalized mental illness, a disability, and a social issue (or problem) that begs for understanding and action. In the novel, Trueman uses direct descriptions to draw attention to Zach's medically explained disability, and he offers parallels to other socially marginalized identities, illustrating that Zach must be respected as an adolescent *with* schizophrenia, rather than *in spite of* his schizophrenia. As a character, Zach quickly distances himself from "everyone else," and the text shows that he does not always trust—or feel—instinctual reactions, that he struggles reading social cues, and that he routinely sees and hears "weird stuff" (4). Zach elaborates and continues to show his nonnormative behaviors, until he finally announces to the teenagers who are threatening him with guns, as well as his reader, "I'm sick, that's my problem; I take medicine two times every day" (5). By the time the novel includes explicit information on "psychotic mental disorders, such as schizophrenia," the reader has witnessed Zach hearing voices that tell him he is a "*stupid wong-gong, a long-gone, wong-gong*," and working "to decide if this situation is real or not" by using all of his senses (12, 6). The text also has demonstrated that Zach gets "massively confused" because he's "not normal"; consequently, the reader experiences symptoms and effects of living with schizophrenia (7). Zach knows to expect such behaviors from himself and in no way tries to hide his illness or disability. With blunt honesty, he explains that he is not "normal," but prone to confusion: bothered by "two psycho-killer enemies [voices he hears] named Dirtbag and Rat," and stuck in a body that, "most of the time, feels like a foreign country" (7). Beyond Zach's personal acceptance and willingness to identify as someone "sick," who "started to hear voices and got all confused and had to go to the hospital," Trueman's narrative includes other voices—such as excerpts of notes from Zach's psychiatrist—which teach the reader about Zach's disability from another perspective (73). Because Zach remains a likeable narrator-protagonist, the reader is encouraged to empathize with and accept him as he is, even when others' accounts don't exactly match.

In the text, Zach is, without question, a schizophrenic adolescent, and he is consistently portrayed without sentimentality or judgment. On his own, he displays a need for acceptance and pride and moves beyond simple acknowledgement of his disability; with his supportive mother and doctor, Zach creates an identity for himself that includes—and even emphasizes, never with shame—his disability. He knows, for example, that according to societal norms, he is "sick and messed up," but he has the awareness and confidence to recognize that other people—especially "these two kids" robbing the café he is in—"aren't so different" from him; indeed, they are "messed up," as are other people he encounters, and Zach recognizes that, in being *different*, they "are kind of the same" (81). The pride, or maybe the company, that he finds in being different allows Zach to remember that he is "okay" (20). When comfortable with reality, Zach shows confidence and barely notices when the other hostages and one of the robbers—younger-brother Joey who's nicknamed Stormy—throw names at him like "retard," "fruitcake," "nut job," "loony," "moron," "idiot," and more (13, 41, 42, 52, 53). Rather, Zach ignores derogatory names and responds to their outbursts and questions calmly and honestly; his eclectic behaviors are simply a part of what makes Zach a perceptive human, more than the sum of his symptoms. Observant and intuitive, Zach interprets that the way Alan/Frosty—the older brother/robber—half-smiles means that "he's scared too," and Zach understands that Joey/Stormy is upset because of the way that "he keeps staring at the floor and won't look up" (17, 45). Part of Zach's ability to perceive things he may not instinctively understand comes from keen observation and the connections he is able to make to his own memories of "being scared" before he "got sick" (15). In the novel, at least, Zach earns respect and acceptance, and he demands to be treated with dignity. He demonstrates strong ethical convictions by volunteering to help the brothers, though he suspects that turning them in "would be the 'appropriate' thing to do"; he also notes that Alan and Joey, who are also "messed up," have learned to trust *him* (81). Both Zach and the narrative itself allow him the role of hero.

In the end, however, the reader receives a rather surprising and complicating final chapter that begins, "Three months later . . . " (116). The text that follows—designed as an article from the *Spokane Intelligencer*—recaps the novel's events: most importantly that "Zachary Wahhsted, a teen hostage and apparent hero of the coffee-shop saga, committed suicide at his mother's home just a week ago" (116). In this news article, Trueman is direct and summarizes that Zach "had struggled for several years with schizophrenia. This disease is a chemical brain disorder that frequently leaves victims haunted by phantom voices and unable to define or deal with reality as we know it" (116–17). The article concludes with words from Zach's psychiatrist Dr. Curtis:

> "For Zach to have survived all the dangers of the hold up only to die by his own hand, a victim of the dangers inside himself, is tragic. Unfortunately, deaths like Zach's are all too common in patients suffering from schizophrenia," Curtis concluded. "Zachary Wahhsted was a good kid who had a terrible illness. He was much beloved; he'll be missed." (117)

In its final chapter, *Inside Out*—while ignoring Zach's self-acceptance and pride—demonstrates quite strongly that disability is worthy of sympathy rather than pride. Trueman's conclusion summarizes Zach as an adolescent who "struggled," who was a victim "haunted by phantom voices" and who was vulnerable to "dangers inside himself" (116, 117). Consequently, *Inside Out* ends as a "tragic" story of "a terrible illness," told in words that evoke pity and sympathy (117). Contradicting its earlier messages on par with disability-rights activists, *Inside Out*—perhaps in an attempt to achieve literary complexity—refutes what could have been a forceful political message. In some ways, by allowing the novel to present two conflicting understandings of Zach's schizophrenia, Trueman creates a thoughtful, open-ended narrative. At the same time, the political cry for taking pride in disabled identities is muted; to end on a note of pity reinforces harmful messages that advocate for pity and protection, rather than empathy and dignity. While Trueman's narrative may conclude with Zach as a tragic, subhuman character, Zach himself makes clear throughout his tale that schizophrenia is a permanent part of his identity, and with support and strategies, he does more than manage himself; he takes action and feels pride in that action.

Also featuring a disabled adolescent who develops strength and agency, Rorby's *Hurt Go Happy* takes on cultural conflicts and conversations within the Deaf community as it follows thirteen-through-sixteen-year-old Joey. In limited third-person narration—not quite, but reminiscent of, the wallflower voice—Joey accepts, understands, and creates a highly politicized and proud identity—that includes her disability. Joey's deafness, from the beginning of the novel, is a medicalized condition, and Joey is not a part of the politicized Deaf community (which uses *Deaf* with a capital 'D' to refer to cultural identity, and *deaf* with a small 'd' to refer to hearing impairment). *Hurt Go Happy* does touch upon issues of cultural identity and even "DEAF PRIDE," but it does not explicitly represent the Deaf community as the "disenfranchised" and separatist group with considerable "community empowerment" (Rorby 169; Hamill and Stein 391, 390). Even so, the novel assures readers from the beginning that Joey accepts deafness as being a part of her identity; her domineering mother Ruth, on the other hand, ignores both adolescence and disability and acts as though Joey "were still a *child* and that her life was *normal*" (Rorby 46; emphases added). Because Ruth hides her daughter's disability, along with her family's "secrets" of abuse, Joey's medical history is not frequently detailed in the narrative or in her life; her hearing loss, however, is distinctively marked as a visible disability by "scars behind her ears" that she hides by keeping "her hair medium length and bushy" (93, 32, 99). Joey never denies or forgets her deafness, and the medically based "FM system," accompanied by "big bulbous headphones," that Joey has to wear in order to hear her teachers prevents others from forgetting it, too (39): "She had to carry a microphone from class to class for . . . [teachers] to wear on a cord around their necks and two boxy little amplifiers that she wore strapped to her chest like little square breasts" (39). Deafness in *Hurt Go Happy* is a complex part of Joey, a disability that contributes to cultural and emotional conflicts, especially in her immediate family.

Most influential in teaching Joey, as well as the reader, to accept the realities of being deaf in order to find pride is her new friend and neighbor Charlie, an "old man" and scientist with an adopted chimpanzee named Sukari, "Swahili for sugar" (18, 24). Upon meeting Joey, Charlie explains that his "mother was born deaf, and . . . [his] father lost his hearing . . . [when] he was only two" (32). They both communicated with American Sign Language (ASL), which Charlie and Sukari use to communicate, as well. With great acceptance of Joey's deafness and the social movements surrounding it, Charlie encourages Joey not to hide her deafness or to consider it a detriment—simply a difference. Finding pride in this difference proves quite a challenge, but Joey personally—if not publicly—grows to love that, "being deaf," she has the gift and power to "sit for hours and watch the birds flittering through the woods and *listen with her eyes* to the little waterfall . . . and fill her sight with sound" (17; emphasis in original). Charlie then introduces Joey—somewhat indirectly but also persuasively—to Deaf culture and pride.[1] Charlie's honesty and forthrightness contrast with Ruth's quiet insistence that Joey read lips and *not* "learn to sign" (19). As a gentle representative of the Deaf community, Charlie echoes an understanding of oralism—teaching children only to speak and lip-read rather than sign—as a form of abuse, because "oralism deprived children of linguistic competency and communication," which is an important part of Deaf identity, with ASL seen "as bonding the community together" (Hamill and Stein 395). As Joey's mentor and friend, Charlie teaches her—as well as the reader—the importance of a common and fully shared language. When Ruth tells Charlie that "people will stare" at her daughter if she signs and that "now at least she looks normal," Charlie responds with blunt, persuasive honesty: "'My parents were normal,' he said. 'And staring is just unfamiliarity with the language, like listening closely to someone speak French. It's not pity. It's curiosity'" (115). Though Ruth does apologize for her use of "normal in that sense of the word," she attempts to hold her ground, even when Charlie accuses her of protecting not her daughter, but herself, by preventing the public from noticing Joey's disability and "wonder[ing] how it happened," while simultaneously "cutting [Joey] off from the rest of the world" (116, 117).[2] Charlie finally speaks firmly: "Deafness *is* different, dammit. And for Joey it is normal not to hear. But she's missing so much more because you're trying to pound her deaf ears into hearing holes. She is what she is. Let her be deaf" (117; emphasis in original).[3] Charlie, in his death, leaves "a trust fund so . . . [Joey] can go to the California School for the Deaf" (147). In one of her first iterations of pride, Joey explicitly tells her mother, despite her worry, "'This [school] is where I belong, Mom. Here I won't be different.' Joey laughed. 'Isn't that wonderful?'" (161). While never explicitly acknowledging debates among deaf people and within the Deaf community—including the difference between Deafness as a "linguistic minority" and deafness as a "category of disability"; the uses of cochlear implants and hearing aids, the latter of which Joey can finally afford but often intentionally leaves behind "in an abalone shell on her desk in the dorm"; and the politics involved in both signing and lip-reading—the novel forcefully presents Joey's growing pride as a deaf, if not (yet) Deaf, adolescent in social domains (Lane 80, Rorby 167).

Literary and complex, Rorby's narrative continues beyond simple, stereotypically young adult solutions, and disability falls to the side of new political messages regarding animal rights. Because *Hurt Go Happy* develops other issues, while still following its deaf protagonist, it carries unspoken acceptance of disability, and Joey's actions illustrate her own confidence and pride. In a school for the Deaf and wearing a sweatshirt advertising "DEAF PRIDE," Joey flirts with separatist Deaf politics, but the narrative never engages—perhaps because the focus has changed to animal rights, perhaps because the author chooses not to alienate readers, or perhaps because the overarching message is meant to include deafness in the larger disabled community (169). In *Hurt Go Happy*, deafness is undeniably medicalized and presented as a disability, but the reader is never led to believe that Joey's deafness should be considered "an individual *affliction*" or "a social *problem*," as the Deaf community views the construction of deafness as a disability, rather than a linguistic minority (Lane 80; emphases added). Rather, in *Hurt Go Happy*, a politically effective problem novel, disability is part of the protagonist's identity that is worthy of acceptance and pride. Rorby's text ultimately suggests that Joey does not *need* to change her self-perception from deaf to Deaf, does not *need* to separate herself from (other) people with disabilities, and does not *need* to worry about the political implications of using both hearing aids and ASL. Joey and *Hurt Go Happy* teach greater inclusivity; all primary characters by the novel's end know at least some sign language and also can communicate at least somewhat effectively in spoken English. Rather than dividing communities, Joey—herself frustrated by "the in-between" and at times wishing she were "either totally deaf or not deaf at all"—resists separation, making actual her early wish to "do both," to read lips *and* to sign (Rorby 166, 106). *Hurt Go Happy* leaves the reader with a strong, developed adolescent character who accepts, appreciates, and takes pride in her disabled identity, and who welcomes questioning and other views.

POWERFUL THEMES

Hurt Go Happy, with its strong and developed protagonist Joey, and *Inside Out*, with Zach as a thoughtful and observant narrator, refuse to allow didactic messages to overwhelm or dominate their narratives; Rorby and Trueman break free from the restraints of typical problem novels by developing truly complex characters and by giving stories as much space as didactic lessons.[4]

While disability remains the primary story and concern for Zach in *Inside Out*, his character is developed beyond symptoms of schizophrenia, and his story collides and interacts with the equally compelling story of Alan and Joseph Mender, the adolescents who enter Zach's familiar coffee shop with guns, looking "mad, [and] mean, too" (Trueman 3). Likable, socially awkward, and perceptive, Zach is not a simple character. He is not simply an archetype or stand-in for *anyone* with schizophrenia, as expected in a problem novel. Quirky and easily preoccupied, Zach spends the entire novel—several hours in time and 115 pages in length—focused on getting and eating a maple bar from the coffee shop. He opens the narrative with a simple and observant statement: "All I want is a maple bar; but I don't think these kids with the guns care about what I want" (3). He closes his narrative simply, too: "I take a huge bite of maple bar . . . ummmmm . . . perfect! Time to go home" (115). The maple bar, consequently, becomes an important part of Zach's personality and indicative of his generally optimistic attitude. While the other hostages stumble and bump into each other, Zach "keep[s] thinking how much farther away [he is] from getting a maple bar—Damn [he thinks], I hate that!" (11). Such an obsession—which is not a common symptom of schizophrenia—contributes to Zach's fully realized disabled, adolescent, individual character.

Also complicating the narrative, Alan/Frosty and Joey/Stormy reveal their own history, which intersects directly with Zach's. Alan and Joey show full personalities, revealing their motives and more, with Joey first saying aloud that their mother is "too sick" before Alan cuts him off (45). Emotional about his mother and worried that the police will "just come in and shoot us . . . [so that] Mom's gonna have nobody," Joey *is* a bit stormy, as his nickname suggests, and is willing to share that they are trying to help their mother and "need money" (51). Alan tries to stay strong and "looks pissed" when Joey reveals information about their family, but eventually he trusts Zach, too: "Our mom has cancer. We don't have any medical insurance because Mom had to quit her job. She's really sick from the chemotherapy and radiation treatments, and her medicine costs a fortune. We're down to nothing. We had to get some money, so I came up with this idiotic idea" (51, 71). All three adolescents discuss growing up without fathers and feeling thoroughly devoted to their mothers (71–72). Because the brothers' story takes place simultaneously with Zach's, the characters together gain control over how the day will end. They negotiate with the police and with Zach's Dr. Curtis, and they stick together, unified for reasons Zach clearly spells out for his reader:

> But here's the deal. These two kids [Alan and Joey] aren't so different from me. I mean, I'm sick and messed up and they're messed up now, too. They're probably going to jail, which can't be that different from going to the hospital—all three of us are kind of the same. Plus, neither Alan nor Joey has called me Wasteoid. (81)

Trueman does, of course, include his final chapter that details the brothers' lenient sentence and Zach's "tragic" suicide, but the primary narrative ends with Zach grabbing "three maple bars," one for each of them, and all three hugging their mothers (117, 111). Rather than focusing entirely on the struggles faced by one adolescent with schizophrenia—as a typical problem novel might—*Inside Out* includes the stories of three adolescents, each different from the others but all "kind of the same" (81).

Similarly complicated, *Hurt Go Happy* offers its reader years of Joey's thoughts and memories; Joey is deaf, and she is *also* an adolescent who notes that, in seventh grade, even "worse than being the only deaf student, she was tall for her age and twig-thin, with so much hair that she thought she looked like one of those long-handled brushes her mother used to clear cobwebs from the ceiling" (Rorby 38). Her story includes more than learning ASL and embracing a deaf identity; Joey, a wallflower who narrates to herself, sees the world as a battle between childhood and adulthood, assuming that adults work together "perhaps *because* they were adults, who seemed to enter into conspiracies against kids even when they didn't like each other" (172). While still in public school, a place controlled by those adults, Joey finds joy and excitement when she receives attention from Kenny, a boy whose smiles make "her face [flush] crimson," and she eventually—through coy smiles and genuine conversation—develops a real connection with Kenny, realizing "that she kind of [has] a boyfriend" (40, 100). Joey's development as a sexual adolescent continues at the California School for the Deaf, primarily through the actions of her roommate, who is "so boy-crazy," because Joey sees herself as the opposite and believes she has "better sense" from knowing that "at sixteen, Joey was six months older than her mother had been when she fell in love with her father" (171). Most notably, of course, *Hurt Go Happy* features the complex and compelling stories of Joey's family history of domestic abuse and of Sukari, who becomes Joey's responsibility after Charlie's death.

A survivor of abuse who has never felt safe expressing her anger or actively remembering, Joey grows more confident in herself and decides *not* to give up on Sukari, because, as Joey explains to her mother, "Sukari trusted me, don't you see? . . . She only had me to count on" (Rorby 201). Even though Joey hadn't been able to count on Ruth years earlier, she engages her mother in a crusade to further their individual recoveries and to save Sukari from laboratory testing. This mission to save the chimp quickly becomes a means to teach the reader about animal rights, especially the rights of chimpanzees, humans' "closest relatives" who are frequently used "to test all kinds of things including medicines before they're approved for use on humans" (30).[5] Joey's remarkable journey to save Sukari from a research lab, find her a safe home, and eventually help her die peacefully—years later, when Joey herself is "applying to veterinary schools"—helps Joey connect with another community and to return to the natural world of her "favorite spot[s]" (253, 99). In a complex intertwining of several serious plotlines, Hurt Go Happy gives Joey room to love Sukari and her mother the space to accept herself.

EXEMPLARY ACCIDENTS

Johnson's *Accidents of Nature* works as an exemplary, politically oriented problem novel; the text uses a simple story that offers its characters—along with the reader, whether disabled or nondisabled—the agency to demand acceptance and find pride, without having to reject, ignore, or demean disabilities. Johnson's text is successful in its never-overwhelming didacticism, because it introduces and explains complex theoretical notions through fully developed adolescent characters; *Accidents of Nature* does not solve a problem, but instead inspires its reader to search for solutions and improvements. The text's structure and setting, ten days of summer camp, and its principal characters—inexperienced Jean, looking to put words to her feelings, and intellectual Sara, desperate to explain how the "trappings of privilege" affect people with disabilities and all marginalized groups (Johnson, *Accidents* 42)—provide the skeleton for a typical problem novel with "supposedly thin character and plot development" (Sommers 259). However, the novel succeeds *because* it is a problem novel, *because* it places individual and group identifications centrally; *Accidents of Nature* is *about* education, community, power, and civil rights.

A simple story of narrator-protagonist Jean—an adolescent with cerebral palsy—attending her first summer at a camp for teenagers with disabilities, Johnson's narrative guides the reader through everyday difficulties that arise from living with disabilities in a society controlled by the nondisabled. *Accidents of Nature* teaches quite clearly that disabilities first must be acknowledged as disabilities and then, with acceptance, used as sources of pride; this lesson is unabashedly clear *because* of the novel's focus. *Accidents of Nature* takes advantage of a simple plot to guide its reader; blunt descriptions to emphasize its message; language play to further emphasize that message; complex theory without adult authority to empower adolescents; and actions to create a hopeful future.

By using the problem-novel convention of employing a relatively simple plot, Johnson is able to parallel narrator-Jean's experiences with the assumed-to-be-abled reader's experiences; Jean and the reader learn together. *Accidents of Nature* begins with a simple source of tension: Jean, accustomed to fitting in with normative friends at her public high school who "smile and give . . . [her] pep talks and hugs, but behind . . . [her] back . . . exchange sad looks" of pity, is thrown into an unfamiliar environment where disability never recedes behind characters' backs (Johnson, *Accidents* 157). This narrator-protagonist embarks on a journey to learn to "make all kinds of friends" with disabled fellow campers and nondisabled counselors, all of whom address and illustrate important issues and arguments considered by disability theorists, critics, and activists (8).[6] Both Jean and the reader are candidly introduced to complex ideas through the story of personal awakening; she works hard to understand her place in her new world, while also negotiating how she will return to the mainstream world of her family and high school. In those places, Jean lives with a family that adheres to mainstream views of disability: her parents encourage her to succeed *in spite of* her disability, have "always treated her just like a normal girl," and praise "the treasured place [she has] . . . won in the normal world" (16, 157). Attending Camp Courage places Jean, for the first time, in a community populated primarily by people with disabilities. She can no longer feel "proud to be with a group of healthy, good-looking people" at home, while confidently ignoring her disability, but still, she is "not ready to join the leper colony" as she first sees camp (157). Jean has always assumed that, "for most people it makes sense to try to become as normal as possible," and through most of the text, she continues to try to ignore, hide, and forget about her disabled body (41). However, Johnson's unabashed narrative makes the bodies at Camp Courage—including Jean's—impossible to ignore.

Blunt descriptions, as well as an unrelenting push to refuse the characters shame, allow Johnson's text to illustrate and exemplify characters' differences—the critical beginning to understanding that disability must be acknowledged before becoming a source of pride. Bodies in *Accidents of Nature* exist as they are, free from judgment or narrative sentiment. Johnson presents her characters' disabilities as facts, disabilities that may change but are chronic and would not improve with cures, rather than chosen treatments. Though Jean's parents patronizingly assert that she's "never let cerebral palsy hold her back," Jean herself cannot simply brush aside her disability; the text shows the constant attention she pays to her "spazzo's body" that is "nothing but straight lines and angles" (Johnson, *Accidents* 6, 152). As much as she wants to ignore that hers is not a "normal girl's body," the text refuses to let her, forcing her to confront other disabled campers and to watch her own body, "knees bent, . . . toes curled," in the presence of others (152, 153). Accepting help showering while watching another camper with CP do the same, Jean admits to herself that the facts of her body are not always comfortable or easy to accept, but they are always present:

> I can't clear my mind of the image of that body, of my own body. I cannot stop despising that body. I can't stop thinking that whoever sees my naked body sees those clumsy lines and angles. I've always assumed that I will get married one day. Now I question whether a man will ever want to touch that body—or if he does, whether I could allow it. (153)

Jean's thoughts and feelings solicit neither sympathy nor pity—only acceptance and understanding.

Johnson's careful descriptions force Jean and the reader to see these campers as different, disabled, deformed, and recognized at camp exactly as they are. Jean's intellectual and talkative new friend Sara has muscular dystrophy, and "her head, which looks fairly normal, barely reaches the tabletop" while her "shoulders and arms sprout right from her seat"; Sara's longtime confidant Willie is an "eyesore" whose face is made of "lips stretched like putty over twisted teeth, fish eyes, too far apart on his head, one sticking out, one almost buried by a bulging lump of something, flesh or bone"; Dolly, like Jean, has cerebral palsy, but Jean "can't understand at all" her "geyser of meaningless vocalization [that] shoots from a contorted throat toward the beams overhead"; and when Jean observes the larger group, she sees "eyebrow tappers and babblers and all kinds of strange people" (11, 12, 8, 9, 17). Sara helps Jean identify members of the group: "three wheelchairs, a one-leg amputee, two MRs [intellectually disabled (or mentally retarded) campers], and two walkie-talkies," who "can walk and talk" but are "diabetics, epileptics, crazies, whatever" (142, 141, 21). "Some of them," Sara adds, "are more messed up than we are . . . [but all] want to belong" (21). Jean, too, wants to belong and eventually accept that she is not just a "Norm in Crip's clothing," after having worked so hard to fit in "the normal world" (200, 157):

> Until I came here, I never knew any Crips. I didn't think of myself as a Crip; I always figured that, beneath the surface, I am just like everyone else. A Norm at heart? Okay, maybe. But what's wrong with that? Why worry about it? Why care what Crips think?
>
> Maybe because a Crip is what I am.
>
> The idea almost makes me sick, so I seek another idea.
>
> It's because I care for them. Not Crips as a group, but these particular Crips—Sara and Margie and the rest. It's my caring that gives them the power to hurt me.
>
> They have the power. But no right to judge. (200)

Jean spends the novel judging herself and others, while working to figure out how she wants to identify; she eventually decides that "a Crip is what" she is—and how she *wants* and thinks she *should* identify herself.

Peppered with words such as "Crip" and "spazzo," which may provoke uncomfortable reactions from the reader, *Accidents of Nature* uses language to engage in provocative play, serving not only as a political gesture to reclaim words and labels, but also as a sophisticated rhetorical tool to further enhance the novel's lessons. Sara immediately uses words that are usually derogatory; she says, "Not bad, Spazzo," to Jean, who is able to "throw" her suitcase on her cot

(21). While a nondisabled counselor "gives her a stern look," Jean is not offended; Sara "winks and keeps on talking," welcoming Jean into a community of disability and othering those without disabilities (22). The reclamation of words has proven useful in other civil rights movements, and theorists have suggested using "severe" in reference to disability, letting such a word perform "work similar to the critically queer work performed by *fabulous*" (McRuer 96). As Johnson does, Robert McRuer advocates using words that emphasize "inadequacies" in order to "reverse the able-bodied understanding of severely disabled bodies as the most marginalized, the most excluded from a privileged and always elusive normalcy, and . . . instead suggest that it is precisely those bodies that are best positioned to refuse 'mere toleration' and to call out the inadequacies of compulsory able-bodiedness" (96). Sara, especially, teaches Jean and the reader to reconsider meanings when she describes her best friend Willie as "hideous" and "ugly as sin," because she also describes him as "really a great guy. The best" (47, 48). Just as blunt descriptions of characters' disabilities push Jean to accept and really *see* those differences, Sara's use of language creates a community based on acceptance that others those traditionally in power: "The Crip Nation" (Johnson, *Accidents* 82). Jean embraces the community, because—as she carefully explains during "a full-blown spaz attack": "At home I always try to act normal, and spaz attacks definitely aren't normal. Here, people understand. They know a spaz attack signals that I'm excited. They're excited too" (61). Jean slowly enters a world in which she accepts and grows able to celebrate her nonnormality.

With its simple story, clear focus on disabilities, and deliberate word play, *Accidents of Nature* establishes characters' realities before moving into theoretical conversations on issues within the disability rights movement; ultimately, disability becomes a proud socialized identity. Simultaneously, the novel resists simplifying its "problems" by forcing Jean, like the reader, to develop informed opinions on normative institutions and traditions. The novel's theoretical lessons are delivered without an authoritative, adult presence—instead allowing Jean to wonder about her preconceived notions, and allowing Sara to serve as a fountain of knowledge, for others to absorb or not. No simple answers or solutions are provided, but a desire for change becomes encompassing, and with understanding of sociological theories, the campers are moved to act. Jean becomes a member of the Crip community and spends more time talking and listening to fellow campers, especially Sara; as she surrounds herself in the community, she reconsiders her ideas and understandings of "normal" (41). Jean must "think again of . . . [the normal] romantic fantasy" that she has found in soap operas and assumed she wanted, because she can no longer imagine herself as normal (153). Jean, along with her reader, encounters questions that she had never before thought to ask: "Can a wheelchair be a choice and not a failure? I'm not sure" (41). The text follows Jean's wondering and learning. At times heavy-handed, the narrative asks the reader to understand Jean's growing acceptance of a disabled identity. Through unsentimental and accurate descriptions of characters, Jean indeed wonders *why* she has valued normality, and she is offered some suggestions from Sara.

With explicitly theoretical language and analyses, Sara, Willie, and other campers pull Jean into a compelling belief system of acceptance, of knowing that "normal isn't the only way to be": for her, "an oddly thrilling idea" (41). Sara reads books by "terrific Marxist historian[s]" and lectures her peers on "the idea that politics should reflect the choices of individual people . . . [and] all that shit" (110). Sara keeps attention, as the campers lounge in their cabin, by announcing and paraphrasing Erving Goffman's words from his 1963 text *Stigma: Notes on the Management of Spoiled Identity*: "It's the best thing I've ever read about cripples," she explains. "And homosexuals and prostitutes. . . . This book lays it all out—how stigma marks you as different, takes away the things that give people 'normal' identity" (112). Shifting her weight "from one elbow to the other" with excitement, Sara tells her interested friends about questions Goffman poses: "Like, should we identify with our group or with the Norms? We can say, basically, to hell with the normal world and flaunt our differences like carnival freaks. Or we can accept Norm values" (112–13). These theoretical sections of text still allow the reader to move slowly and to consider Sara's lectures; Jean herself is still somewhat unsure and even somewhat optimistically "convinced that handicapped people can fit into the normal world," but with deeper understanding and help from Sara, Jean learns not to internalize discomfort and not to blame herself (112,

121). For example, Jean understands her discomfort at a camp-run carnival at which *all* disabled contestants win:

> When the games are rigged, does it make everyone a winner—or no one? All I know is that I don't feel much like a winner. But I don't feel like a loser either. That's something. It is better that I didn't get with the program this time. I believe in competition. The program seems to say that handicapped people aren't up to it; we can only pretend to be winners. I don't want to pretend. I want to achieve, really achieve. Or I will take my disappointments just like anyone else. (137)

With her convincing and powerful rhetoric—stating that "it is *better* I didn't get with the program this time" and refusing to "pretend" the way she always has (137; emphasis added)—Jean is losing her desire to fit in with the patronizing Norms, who "act like [people with disabilities] show spirit in just being alive; persistence in not curling up and dying; determination in doing ordinary things; courage in showing [their] faces in public" (207). Jean *experiences* the lessons Sara explains, and the novel's theoretical didacticism continues to broaden questions rather than fix problems with easy lessons.

Always without adult interference or supervision, Sara pushes her peers to push themselves; she makes the abstract theories real. Sharing her own experiences forces campers—and the reader—to think more carefully about supposedly well-intentioned actions: "One year my face wound up in the camp brochure over the caption, 'Smiling through the tears.' That will never happen again!" (32). She makes real the ways in which "Inspirational" advertisements about "courage and determination" are intended to benefit a nondisabled audience, while patronizing the disabled subjects (32, 39). With similar thoughtfulness, Sara discusses therapists' attempts to help Jean walk, and explicitly illustrates the subtle, common, and harmful implicit messages such attempts deliver:

> "They all think walking is such a wonderful thing. And we don't question that. We believe it must be worthwhile, or they wouldn't torture us for it. And then, finally, you get up on your

> feet, take a few halting steps—pardon me, I mean courageous and determined steps—and the cameras flash and everyone's inspired. But then you find out walking is a lousy way to move from place." (39–40)

Sara's analyses of brochures and everyday events push Jean to realize how frequently disabled people *are* used to inspire and to reassert that there is indeed a way to be and look "normal" in Western society. And for a normative, mainstreamed society, Jean learns, it is preferable to help those with disabilities, like Sara and herself, walk and talk more easily so that their disabled identities are less noticeable. Theoretical readings of real events do help Jean understand her past experiences, such as how her childhood attempts to walk produced "proud parents" and local celebrations, while her ultimate inability to walk "has remained in . . . [her] scrapbook as a permanent reminder of . . . failure" (39, 41). After listening to Sara and her cabinmates explain their disregard for society's obsession with "straight legs," physical therapy, and surgeries, Jean is ready to ask, "Can a wheelchair be a choice, and not a failure?" (41).

Similarly, while using the common literary theme of an adolescent finding comfort in a new situation, Johnson's novel takes place at Camp Courage, where disability defines the majority, and the nondisabled staff exist on the margins. The text follows Jean's realization of the critical need for accommodation and inclusion for an incredibly heterogeneous group of disabled campers. While Dolly, "the worst CP . . . [that Jean has] ever seen," talks incoherently, Jean watches "a plump young woman on a stretcher, lying on her stomach, propped up on her elbows like a sunbather" so that she is able to have a conversation with "a blind girl, who gently sways from side to side" (10). These returning campers are comfortable chatting in ways facilitated by simple acceptance and accommodation. Jean watches a quadriplegic camper "[drive] his electric wheelchair with his mouth," while no one seems to notice or pay mind to his need to control all of his movements with his mouth and outside support (10). Just another piece of the scene in the lodge, along with voices, "high rafters, big fans [that] churn the air, folding the smells of sweat and bug spray into sweet odors," a "boy camper and good-looking boy counselor are talking in sign language," while an "eyebrow tapper across the table is still at it" (10). So many accommodations—a wheelchair, a nonverbal language, and an acceptance of what may be considered unusual or different behaviors—draw no more attention from Jean than do the good-looking counselor and her own appearance: no longer the "only crippled student, ever," but still with "blond hair and blue eyes and skin that tans just right" (11). Jean becomes a part of Camp Courage, admittedly imperfect but dedicated to making sure no campers are expected to or ought to hide or ignore their disabilities.

By the end of the novel, Jean feels rage and is compelled to act. She, Sara, and their cabinmates channel their rage into the performance of a public, angry, and proud skit at the camp's Talent Night. Organized mostly by Sara and based largely on Jean's experiences, their skit is a "reverse telethon," the fictional "third annual Telethon to Stamp Out Normalcy" (176). With rage, Jean recalls being "a regional state poster child" and a telethon participant, interviewed only when she "felt good. My parents were proud. I thought I had a posi-tive mes-sage. Then the MC looked into the cam-era" and said, "'Friends, this girl needs speech thera-py.' . . . He said, 'Without your help, she won't get it'" (11, 161). She was presented as being *almost* normal, as "a speech-therapy success story. As good as it gets. . . . Never mind that it's false. And insulting" (162). Consequently, in their skit, Sara plays the passionate MC and Jean the nodding sidekick in "Stamp[ing] Out Normalcy":

> "All of you out there, if you have a normal child or grandchild, you know the importance of this cause. Please call and give what you can.
>
> "And if you have a crippled child, have you ever thought, 'There, but for the grace of God, go I'? It's true. Normalcy can strike any family. You should light up these phone lines in celebration of your good fortune, and thank God for your crippled child! Right, Jean?"
>
> I nod and wish with all my heart that it were true. Thank God for crippled children! (176, 178–79)

Repeated phrases such as "a horrible condition like normalcy" and campers' tongue-in-cheek explanations of how they "focus on . . .

disabilities, not . . . abilities, . . . [in order to] be positive" shock Talent Night's audience (180, 182). When cabinmate Denise poses as someone "terribly afflicted" by being able to "walk, run, even dance" without difficulty, Denise concludes for the audience that she does whatever she can to "feel almost like a Crip," mocking those who strive to help disabled people feel "almost normal" (182). Mocking her own telethon memory, Jean presents Denise to the audience, saying, "That girl needs speech THER-a-py," which creates "uncomfortable silence" until the disabled campers in the audience begin to laugh (183). Ultimately, their cabin is punished for the skit, but they have acted and have shown themselves loudly proud to be disabled.

Through all of these confident realizations, the text still complicates and pushes the reader to keep thinking. Sara gets "a bit tiresome," which makes her human and fallible, allowing Jean and the reader to question her arguments, which prevents the novel from pushing simple solutions (23). While cabinmate Denise engages with Sara about whether or not "passing" is possible—according to Goffman, at least—Jean feels "tired of being lectured at" (113). Johnson does not use an adult character—common in problem novels—to provide solutions, answers, and philosophies, forcing the disabled adolescents to work on understanding for themselves (113). Without a true authority, Jean, like her reader, develops a critical eye and comes to her own conclusions. Jean notices and analyzes how nondisabled staff members illustrate common irritations and problems of being disabled in a normative world: games are rigged so everyone wins, a counselor physically arouses a disabled camper as a joke, and counselors consistently patronize campers in order to "provide freaks with 'normal experiences'" (145, 93–94). Bitter and jaded, Sara and Jean still work to understand the motives behind problematic attitudes and actions; *Accidents of Nature* avoids simple lessons about how to act, and instead encourages figuring out why some people should change. The issues tackled are complex, and even "Sara, who has an answer, an analysis, for everything, doesn't" always (95). She does, however, have hope for future political action. Sara, like the novel itself, is ready to demand greater visibility, accessibility, inclusion, and pride for the disabled community.

A strong case for inclusion, Johnson's novel promotes a connection between all people with disabilities. Even though she criticizes so much about Camp Courage, Sara continues to return, because "I need to be with my people. The Crip Nation" (82). The text allows Sara to connect all disabilities, along with all people, by noting that "*everyone*'s terminally ill" and consequently temporarily able-bodied at best (142; emphasis added). Sara's disabled community comes first, and within that inclusive and supportive group, she finds her own independence and pride by "refusing to be put on the horse," refusing to have her picture taken, refusing to play carnival games, and refusing other activities (82). Sara, like Johnson's text, teaches Jean and the reader to value individuality and self-determination, while finding comfort and power in a larger disabled community that strives for empowerment.

Consequently, unlike presumed-to-be shallow and stereotypical problem novels, *Accidents of Nature* leaves readers with theoretical groundwork and call for political action and empowerment; it also leaves readers wondering and questioning. Accomplished with humor, and sensitivity—as well as with a simple plot, direct descriptions, language play, theoretical ideas without a true authoritarian, and frank discussions of needed accessibility—Johnson's novel follows Jean from her reluctant position as "almost normal" to a much more complex and difficult position. In the end, Jean is a disabled adolescent finding pride in her identity, working to understand how disability is marginalized in society, and trying to foresee a future for herself. Because this social issue surrounding disability is more complex than a problem to be thoroughly handled and solved in simple "books with glaring teens on their covers," Johnson's text begins to transcend "the trappings of the problem novel," but not by using disability artfully enough so that it doesn't overshadow "the story itself" (Feinberg 2; Miskec and McGee 164). *Accidents of Nature* works as an exemplary problem novel: a politicized text with a deliberate structure and well-developed characters that both explain and illustrate the primary "problem" with theoretical ideas and political causes.

Chapter 6

BULLETPROOF FAMILIES

Disability as the Unifier

Surprising viewers when it premiered in 2016, *Speechless*, a weekly TV series on mainstream network television, featured a disabled actor, Micah Fowler, in the starring role and immediately began challenging stereotypes (Broverman). The series' very first scene culminates with J.J. DiMeo—a nonverbal wheelchair-using teenager with cerebral palsy—exiting the family van to stares from laughing onlookers; J.J.'s gesture in response is given voice by his mother, who shouts dramatically that, yes, "that's the finger" he's giving them ("Pilot" 00:02:07). Refusing to minimalize or bury its social messages about adolescent disability, the series follows daily annoyances and larger transgressions that the DiMeos challenge. The first few episodes introduce the series as one that welcomes all viewers, disabled and abled, to join the fight for disability rights and pride—while also laughing and caring for the characters. Episode titles are styled to show how family members, caregivers, and friends read J.J.'s communication board, and the third episode, "B-O-N—BONFIRE," firmly demonstrates dominant themes: the DiMeo family operates with confidence, an explicit rejection of "normal," and a strong *family* identity. Disability in this family, as in the series itself, is never represented as a simple, static, or overwhelming problem; it's not even represented as a part of only one person's identity. Near the end of "B-O-N—BONFIRE," father/husband Jimmy stops driving the van in order to explain to middle-child Ray—as well as to the viewer—why the family's rejection of "normal" and cultivation of solidarity make them who they are:

> **JIMMY:** Buddy, why do you care so much what other people think?

> **RAY:** Why don't you? Seriously, Dad, don't you want to be normal? How can you live like this?
>
> **JIMMY:** You want to know how? Because all this stuff, other people's opinions—it's nothing.
>
> You know what's *not* nothing? A doctor tells you there's something wrong with your kid, all the things he's never gonna do, and it's a nice, long list. But look at your brother. He's great. He's smart, funny. Without naming names, he's apparently cooler than some of my other kids. So now, when something happens, it's like, "What else you got? Bring it on."
>
> I get it. Normal seems good. But guess what? We're *not* normal. We're better. We're bulletproof. (00:15:39)

The DiMeos refuse to abandon their unwavering, bulletproof approach to dealing with a traditional, narrow world.

Beginning in the earliest years of the twenty-first century, traditional analog media faced competition from both transformed-traditional media and digital media. These technology-based labels frequently change, so for this project, I use "traditional media" or "traditional analog media" to refer to "print and art analog broadcast models, such as those of television and radio" (Bigdely et al. 121). "Digital media"—or "computer-based, online media"—refers to forms that use "digital computers, such as the Internet and computer games," along with other online "participatory media" (Bigdely et al. 122; Ellcessor 5). Such digital technologies also "transform" traditional media by making television, films, music, and publications available online or in other digital forms, so I call such formats "transformed-traditional media" (Bigdely et al. 122). Consequently, while *Speechless* aired on traditional network television from 2016 to 2019, its availability online necessarily makes it a text in "transformed-traditional media." Around this time, in-print and other traditional media are left behind, as analog broadcast models maintain their basic structures even while using digital platforms to reach audiences.

As of 2020, digital media platforms offer homes to online cultures, or cybercultures, that dominate popular culture—including online critiques of *all* media. Digital platforms are more widely accessed and are unquestionably *participatory*; they offer the vision of a future "in which increased access to cultural production, political participation, and social collaboration produces more just, egalitarian forms of culture" (Ellcessor 5). Certainly, social media platforms, such as Facebook, Twitter, YouTube, and Instagram, enable participants from nearly any location or culture "to create, evaluate and police content" (Dates and Ramirez 125). Because this digital content is both generated and moderated by participants, rather than a central authority, it "blur[s] the lines between web producers and consumers," making it nearly impossible to know the expertise or qualifications of media creators (Ellcessor 40). These blurred lines and hidden identities also have "fostered the demise of the mediating role between traditional media" and the public, allowing creators to "disseminate their own messages" without filters (Dates and Ramirez 125, 126). Consequently, online communities—epitomized by the tightly knit Black Twitter subculture—find power to challenge mass media biases precisely *because* of their unmediated and "participatory democratic nature" (Lee 2). Following analyses of young adult novels in the earlier chapters of this project, in this chapter I seek to include other narratives: in traditional media other than novels, such as memoirs, short stories, and song lyrics; in transformed-traditional media, including twenty-first-century television series, films, and publications; and in participatory, digital media, which allow for narratives produced in radically different ways.

Importantly, twenty-first-century young adult disability narratives in all media are challenged and praised by often-unidentified participants in unmoderated cybercultures. This online criticism creates expectations that differ greatly from those placed on twentieth-century print novels—which are the narratives that have defined "young adult literature" since its emergence. Twenty-first-century narratives in print and other traditional media generally do little more than illustrate how ill-equipped they are to meet the expectations of digitally based criticism; many transformed-traditional narratives similarly fail to meet cyber-expectations, but occasional texts, such as *Speechless*, exceed them. Digital narratives allow authors/producers to use various creative techniques, which blur and solidify lines shaping both personal identities and communities. Even though narratives in digital media are plagued by accessibility barriers and stunted by disagreements both within and among groups, they exalt the power of young adult disability narratives, when representing family-like unity, to redefine and change cultural norms.

THE STARTLING EFFECTS OF DIGITAL VOICES

Online critical attention attracts large audiences for narratives, but that attention, often from anonymous or unknown sources, places additional expectations—often based on pop-culture and political trends—on literary narratives. In the 2010s, hashtags began to propel these online critical movements, particularly through social media websites. Hashtags find traction, as easily searchable topics to discuss, on Twitter, the social "networking and microblogging service" that was founded in 2006 and that exploded with users in 2009 (Gruzd et al. 1296). On this platform, where participants both create and read "tweets," hashtags enable users to hold public community conversations around single topics. Twitter functions as "a necessary platform for dissent, discussion, and breaking news," and hashtags allow online coalitions to prioritize and publicize issues important to their communities (Dates and Ramirez 127). The hashtag #BlackLivesMatter, "tweeted more than 9 million times in 2015," allowed Black Twitter "to create awareness and share cases of police violence," which ultimately expanded to other platforms, as well as political, mainstream audiences in all media (Lee 9). As the Black Twitter subculture redefined Twitter as *the* online platform to discuss and "alter critical discourse on controversial themes," other cybercultures, including Disability Twitter, have followed suit to solidify communities and produce platforms for discussion—often around media representations (Dates and Ramirez 128).

Appearing around the same time as #BlackLivesMatter, the #OwnVoices hashtag, coined by Corinne Duyvis, popularized the demand that "kidlit about diverse characters [be] written by authors from that same diverse group" (Duyvis). Still in use, as of 2020 at least, #OwnVoices is used and debated primarily by online disability activists, as well as those concerned with diversity, equity, and inclusion in education and literature. Because #OwnVoices advocates generally accept only texts in which "the protagonist and the author share a marginalized identity," authorial identity has grown overwhelmingly important (Duyvis). And because online activists' and participants' levels and areas of expertise are often unknown or presented only vaguely, criticism by and for the #OwnVoices movement differs quite radically from literary criticism, produced by scholars whose academic backgrounds and qualifications are clearly noted. Unfortunately, unmoderated debates held on Twitter often result in important discussions and new ideas, but some end with the acceptance of unproven statements—falsely presented as facts—and demeaning accusations.

Consequently, while online media may increase access to information and allow online communities to grow, digital media forums do little to bridge the already-disparate worlds of scholarship and activism, of the ivory towers and grassroots organizing. An informal Twitter conversation regarding #OwnVoices and disability, for example, may arise from a provocative tweet or response to a tweet that uses a searchable hashtag:

> Your book isn't #ownvoices if you're the able parent of a disabled child. Your book isn't #ownvoices if you're the able spouse of a disabled partner. Your book isn't #ownvoices if you're the able sibling/family member of a disabled person.
>
> I'm so tired. Angry. But tired. (@lillielainoff et al.)

Reminding other "tired" activists how frequently the arguments must be made, the above tweet draws a number of responses, each of which illustrates the way hashtags enable participatory, provocative discussions. While centered around contemporary children's and young adult literature, the arguments noticeably vary from scholarly criticism; like other tweets, the above uses declarative statements without explanation, context, or research to support them. A simple response from prominent activist @DisVisibility (Alice Wong)—"Yup!"—lends some authority to the politically oriented disabled community, and another response, from @AutumnOwl_, again shows the power of hashtags: the participant presumably does not yet know the topic of debate, but is connected by following familiar participants or by finding the searchable hashtag: "Oh god what's happened now. Why are ableds like this 😩" (@lillielainoff et al.) This tweet, indeed, illustrates how easy it is for participants in online forums to confuse or alienate participants or groups—in this case, those who identify as nondisabled, or as part of "the ableds"—perhaps without intending to.

This #OwnVoices Twitter thread branches off into an exchange between participants @lillielainoff and @RJSomer—to address a number of parallel issues related to children's literature, disability studies, and publishing:

> **@lillielainoff:** I'd really like to know when kidlit is going to start centering disabled people in conversations/books about disability. I'm starting to lose my voice from screaming into the void so often, and I need to know how many jumbo-size bags of cough drops I need to buy 🙃🙃🙃
> **@RJSomer:** Seriously. It would be nice to not have it swept under a rug for once.
> **@lillielainoff:** Honestly, I think the key is the industry publishing more #ownvoices disability books, that way there's no excuse for people not to understand.
> **@RJSomer:** It would be a nice step forward. Unfortunately most books with disabled characters are written by abled people 🤦
> (@lillielainoff et al.)

Without a doubt, the above interaction presents the ways in which social-media-based conversations affect the reception of young adult disability narratives *and* related scholarship. However, finding authoritative sources for the expectations and boundaries of movements such as #OwnVoices is difficult, if not impossible; the participatory, online movement intentionally avoids central authorities or fixed definitions. Corinne Duyvis's own website, perhaps the closest to an #OwnVoices authority, offers very little: "It's not my place to decide what counts as diverse/marginalized, nor what counts as 'same group.' I won't police either the hashtag or people's/characters' identities" (Duyvis). #OwnVoices, consequently, may offer more questions than it does answers and systems for evaluation. For instance, the hashtag-based movement does not work for all literary texts. For example, how can a reader know the identity of an author from the past or an author who does not share autobiographical information? What if a character's (disabled) identity is not made explicit in the narrative? Is a text that includes a disabled character automatically "bad" or "inappropriate" if written by an abled—or assumed-to-be abled—author? Is a disabled narrative automatically "good" and "authentic" if written by a disabled author? How close must an author's disability be to the protagonist's? Does it matter if the disabled character is a secondary character, as opposed to a protagonist? At the same time, the broad intention and motivation of #OwnVoices—that disabled characters and stories are created and told by disabled authors, who deserve audiences for their voices—is quite easy to support.

Readers and critics who adhere to #OwnVoices expectations, consequently, assume that all creative texts are at least semi-autobiographical; they expect to know how authors' identities and backgrounds compare with their protagonists', and only if they match can a narrative be accepted as "authentic." With the presence of authentic voices taking hold of the disability community's reception of narratives, attention is also pulled to the roles and identities of editors, publishers, and other mediators. Narratives in print may indeed be autobiographical (or assumed-to-be autobiographical), but even they must pass through several filters before publication, the effects of which do limit potentially authentic voices. Even major publishers that *prioritize* the importance of publishing disabled voices often fail to explain the mediating factors or to treat authors' identities with the importance demanded by twenty-first-century online critics and readers.

RESISTANCE AND HOPE IN TRADITIONAL MEDIA

In most cases, young adult disability narratives in traditional media—novels, print memoirs, short stories, poems, and songs not connected to online media—are simply unable to meet the expectations of digitally based criticism; publishing and production filters lack transparency and generally do not offer authorial identities. These forms, however, do demonstrate the need to add adolescent voices outside of traditional print novels to the category of young adult literature.

If young adult narratives are defined as texts that are thematically centered around adolescence and that often use the prominent "wall-flower" voice, scholars must consider such narratives in any form—and plenty of young adult narratives there are. For instance, early songs by Scottish indie-pop band Belle and Sebastian, released in the second half of the 1990s and with lyrics composed by Stuart Murdoch, are frequently stories of adolescent characters. "Inhabit[ing] a fictional world" of Murdoch's, characters like Lisa, Judy, Jenny, and Jean, exist in seemingly liminal spaces—no longer children and not yet adults—each one fitting Kristeva's "mythical figure" of the adolescent, a kind of "imaginary" existence without a firm superego (Murdoch, Video Interview; Kristeva 135). These characters are often distanced from adults, with "too much history, too much biography between" them, and much like other young adult narrator-protagonists, Murdoch's are a part of a "younger generation . . . [who] grew up fast" ("Me and the Major"). Their adolescent narratives reflect and join the voices of influential young adult wallflowers in print; Murdoch's characters are intelligent, solitary, judgmental, sensitive, looking for truth, and distressed. Isolated, one narrator urges a friend, "Do something pretty while you can / Don't be afraid / Skating a pirouette on ice is cool" ("We Rule the School"). Sung with wistful desperation, this narrator, urgently desiring to act "while you can," echoes Holden Caufield, whose desire to preserve the innocence of childhood dominated *The Catcher in the Rye*. Rather than seeking childhood innocence, though, most of Murdoch's characters work to preserve a tumultuous adolescence and to avoid entering adulthood, which is a world "made for men / Not us" ("We Rule the School").

Living, if not always speaking, as wallflowers, Murdoch's characters inhabit a world too large for just one song, allowing each of Belle and Sebastian's early albums to capture part of Murdoch's longer young adult narrative. In addition to other songs, the band's second record, *If You're Feeling Sinister* (1996), is set almost entirely in that imaginary world, holding an unnamed character "kissing girls in English at the back of the stairs," to Anthony searching for something that's "bound to be less boring than today," to an adolescent writing a diary "like the bible with its verses lost in time" ("The Stars of Track and

Field," "If You're Feeling Sinister," "Mayfly"). Unknown narrators, who speak to directly to adolescent characters, understand the anxious, urgent desires, and the unsettled feelings caused by social- and self-identification; Murdoch explains that "the world of those characters" arose from his "world view, which was unique at the time, [of] looking out at the people around about me," especially during his late-adolescent years (Murdoch, Video Interview). Just as the songs' narrators allow "rain / falling against the lonely tenement" to inspire peering through windows, Murdoch, too, perhaps has seen characters "kissing men like a long walk home" or helping friends who've "got a lot to be mad about" ("Get Me Away from Here, I'm Dying," "Like Dylan in the Movies," "She's Losing It"). Like Holden, Esther, and Charlie—archetypal sensitive characters with symptoms of mental illness—Murdoch's Lisa, among the others in his world, is "only slightly mental / beautiful, only temperamental" ("Beautiful").

Perhaps most interestingly, Murdoch's young adult characters inhabit a world that challenges common representations of both disabled and adolescent characters. While Bildungsromane force adolescents into adulthood and narratives of disability often end with deaths and cures, Belle and Sebastian's characters—speaking in voices that suggest forms of depression or other illnesses—remain existentially trapped in unstable, tumultuous states. Adolescent characters called Belle and Sebastian find themselves the focus of two 1997 songs: "Belle & Sebastian" and "Put the Book Back on the Shelf."[1] Weighted down by existence and "in a mess" from the beginning, "poor Sebastian is heading for a fall," while Belle is simply occupied by the boys she's got "queueing up to tell her she's a star" ("Belle & Sebastian"). Wallflower Sebastian "wants to love and he wants to care," which separates him from classmates and defines him as one of those sensitive, intellectual loners ("Belle & Sebastian"). He keeps a diary to bemoan that "he would never be young again"—no longer a child, but certainly not an adult ("Belle & Sebastian"). When an outside narrator finally finds Sebastian's ear, it's to tell him, "Fellow, you are ill," and that he must not anticipate some kind of magical, life-changing end or cure, but rather, he must accept his position, make the best of it, and grow in order to find some comfort:

> You'd better take a weight off of your mind and listen
> To what other people say
> 'Cause things are going wrong your own way ("Belle & Sebastian")

Still preoccupied by sex, death, and truth, Sebastian is again left "all alone" in the second song of his narrative; right away, he "came to dance, but there's no poignancy" when "standing alone" ("Put the Book"). Just as Charlie's teacher in *The Perks of Being a Wallflower* suggests Charlie may want to "participate in life," Sebastian knows that he will "have to pay / for looking at the floor / when people talk to him" (Chbosky 24; "Put the Book"). Unable to "leave [his] troubles home," Sebastian is so absorbed in existential angst that he fails to notice or care about "the wider issues of the day" ("Put the Book"). Sebastian stays where he is—firmly planted in adolescence.

While distinctly young adult in voice and subject matter—adolescence and possible illness—Murdoch's early narratives do not offer any evidence of "authenticity" or adherence to #OwnVoices. In the 1990s, Belle and Sebastian—led by Murdoch—refused interviews, avoided photographs, and offered very little of themselves to the public, leaving the songwriter's life as mythical as his characters'. Like most narratives in traditional media—especially those published before the growth of digital media—Murdoch's narratives, as released in traditional media, fail to meet the demands of twenty-first-century online critics.

Similar failures to assure audiences of authenticity arise, and are nearly exaggerated, in the publication of *The Reason I Jump: The Inner Voice of a Thirteen-Year-Old Boy with Autism* (2013). The back cover of the memoir's 2016 trade paperback edition champions the importance of reading the book because it is "written by Naoki Higashida, a very smart, very self-aware, and very charming thirteen-year-old boy with autism." However, the front cover begins to reveal filters through which the book has passed in order to reach a mass English-speaking audience: underneath the book's title are credits for the introduction and the translation from Japanese—neither of which involves Higashida. Regardless of intent, editors, translators, and writers (of introductions, prefaces, cover designs, and other paratexts) function as mediators between unpublished manuscripts and published books. *The Reason I Jump* includes no explanation or description of *publishing* filters, even while novelist David Mitchell, in his introduction, draws attention to *autism*-based filters in Higashida's narrative. Mitchell asks the assumed-to-be-abled reader to imagine life without a "mind-editor," as a metaphor for autistic adolescents' difficulties communicating (vii); "for those people born onto the autistic spectrum," he writes, "this unedited, unfiltered and scary-as-all-hell reality is home . . . [and communication] is an intellectual and emotional task of Herculean, Sisyphean and Titanic proportions, and if the autistic people who undertake it aren't heroes, then I don't know what heroism is" (ix). Higashida, the author and one of Mitchell's autistic "heroes," of course, is *not* able to use his memoir as a means to communicate in an "unedited, unfiltered and scary-as-all-hell" way, which is exactly what the book claims to provide. Rather, Higashida's "inner voice" has necessarily been altered for readers, most of whom are assumed by Mitchell (in his introduction) to be parents of disabled children. Consequently, he considers the book important because it forces him, like other parents, "to stop feeling sorry for myself, and start thinking how much tougher life was for my son, and what I could do to make it less tough" (xvi). Riddled with patronizing assumptions and stereotypes of disability, and addressed directly to parents, Mitchell's introduction *must* color the experience of reading the text itself. The disabled adolescent author may even disagree with much of the introduction, but the reader does not—and cannot—know.

Translated by Mitchell and his wife K. A. Yoshida, Higashida's autobiographical narrative *noticeably* reflects Mitchell's opinions, but no paratexts or notes explain whether the translation was influenced by the introduction, or whether the introduction was influenced by the translated text. For example, Higashida's preface, like Mitchell's introduction, welcomes a neurotypical, abled reader, "a friend of someone with autism," into an autistic brain in order to help the reader grow (Higashida 4):

> During my frustrating, miserable, helpless days, I've started imagining what it would be like if everyone was autistic. If autism was regarded as a personality type, things would be

> much easier and happier for us than they are now. For sure there are bad times when we cause a lot of hassle for other people, but what we really want is to be able to look toward a brighter future. . . . So my big hope is that I can help a bit by explaining, in my own way, what's going on in the minds of people with autism. I also hope that, by reading this book, you might become a better friend of someone with autism. (3–4)

The "inner" thoughts and words that appear in print, by necessity, are not the originals; first, Higashida "communicate[d] by pointing to the letters . . . [on an alphabet grid], which a helper at his side then transcribe[d]," and then Yoshida created "an informal translation . . . so other carers and tutors could read it, as well as a few friends who also have sons and daughters with autism" (Mitchell xiii, xvi). Mitchell does not specify how much influence the other readers may have in translating, editing, or presenting the text. He does, however, inform the reader that "the author is not a guru," but does not explain what he means or how his own judgements may have influenced the translation or editorial process (xvi). Consequently, the reader must simply trust that Higashida's powerful words describing thoughts and memories—which, he writes, are "like a jigsaw puzzle, where if even one piece is misinserted, the entire puzzle becomes impossible to complete" (Higashada 56)—are indeed the author's own.

Other in-print young adult disability narratives acquired by mainstream publishers are available with similar opacity concerning authors and editing processes. *Unbroken: 13 Stories Starring Disabled Teens*, published in 2018 by Farrar Straus Giroux, begins with a dedication *from* the disabled community *to* the disabled community (made clear with the use of "we" and "us"):

> *To every disabled reader, dreamer, storyteller—*
> *We can be heroes.*
> *This one's for us.* (v)

Additionally, paratextual language on the book's dust jacket—about "bestselling author Marieke Nijkamp team[ing] up with fellow disabled authors to create fictional stories"—suggests the stories are written entirely by disabled authors. However, in the "About the Authors" section at the end of the book, not one author is identified as disabled or abled. Authors have founded, cofounded, and created online movements, including "We Need Diverse Books," "Disability in Kidlit," the #DisabledAndCute hashtag, and contributor Corinne Duyvis's #OwnVoices hashtag. Undoubtedly, this team takes *seriously* authorial identities of those writing about disability, but whether disabled editor Nijkamp teamed up *only* with "fellow disabled authors" or with a team *including* "fellow disabled authors" is left unknown. Without further research, a reader only knows for sure that the stories are all "starring disabled teens," and because the stories are labeled as "fictional" on the dust jacket, characters' identities reveal nothing about the authors' (iii). Even if biographical information is found, questions then arise over how similar the author's and protagonist's identities must be in order to meet the expectations of #OwnVoices.

Another collection of disability narratives—though not explicitly young adult—*Resistance & Hope: Essays by Disabled People: Crip Wisdom for the People* (2018) offers authorial information right in its title. Indeed, this clarity *may* be because the collection's traditional book format has "been transformed through the application of [digital] technologies" and not put through the filters of in-print publishing (Bigdely et al. 121). Available only as an e-book, *Resistance & Hope* is edited and published by Alice Wong, founder and director of the Disability Visibility Project. Consequently, this digitally transformed-traditional book, edited and published independently, is actually able to function as "a powerful collection of essays by disabled writers, artists, activists, and dreamers" (Wong, *Resistance & Hope*). Additionally, the e-book's production was made possible with the "resilience and interdependence" of the disabled community, and the final lines of Wong's introduction provide guidance to the reader: "It is my intention for you, dear reader, to soak up crip wisdom from these writers and our ancestors. Think about your privilege, get angry, and become involved in your various communities" (Wong, *Resistance & Hope*). While not a collection of specifically young adult disability narratives, *Resistance & Hope* does illustrate possibilities for reducing the filters imposed on traditional texts in order to reach audiences; the transparency desired by #OwnVoices just may be possible with the help of transforming technology.

SPEECHLESS COMMUNICATION IN TRANSFORMED-TRADITIONAL MEDIA

Introduced by the digitally published *Resistance & Hope*, most other transformed-traditional disability narratives—including the film adaptation of R. J. Palacio's novel *Wonder* (2017) and the Netflix series *Atypical* (2017)—display differences from narratives in traditional media. But unlike *Resistance & Hope*, published by the disability community, they fail to present authorial authenticity, even when possible. Consequently, these narratives are still not very well received by online audiences, who place political effects over literary readings; texts only sometimes demonstrate the possibilities of transforming technology. For instance, *Atypical*, an online series created by Robia Rashid, immediately disappointed critics who called the autistic protagonist, Sam, "a human whiteboard illustrating" the most "obvious autistic behaviors," and also characterized Sam's narration as insightful, "but in a surface sort of way" (Felperin, Genzlinger). A reviewer for *The Atlantic* reveals that Rashid was "inspired to write *Atypical* by her own personal experiences with a person on the spectrum, and that she hired a consultant and relied on feedback from others familiar with the disorder" (Gilbert). However, in the first season of the online series, a real connection with the #ActuallyAutistic community rarely comes through in the narrative, and other consultants are unreported; Elsa and Doug's parents' support group—an unchallenged authoritative voice in the season—requires "people-first language," even though the autistic community generally encourages *identity-first* language—"autistic person," rather than "person with autism"—because autism is "such a strong part of who they are" ("A Nice Neutral Smell" 00:09:20, Thorpe).

Also opaque about including disabled people in its adaptation or production, *Wonder* (the 2017 film adaptation of Palacio's novel) immediately drew negative reviews from the disability community.

Online participant Ariel Henley, who has a craniofacial disorder, objects to the film's marketing strategies, such as sending "Real-Life Auggies" to schools—which further objectifies those with any kind of "facial difference" and has "real consequences for real people" (Henley):

> I've experienced these consequences firsthand. . . . I'm frequently compared to Auggie and told to read *Wonder*. But *Wonder* is a fictional story, written by an author who has zero personal experience with the subject matter. . . . To have my experience and my insight come second to an author with no personal experience on the issue is appalling. (Henley)

Rather clearly and appallingly, the creative teams of both *Wonder* (2017) and *Atypical* (2017) fail to illustrate any involvement with or respect for the disability community—or with disabled individuals able to offer their #OwnVoices.

However, at least one narrative in transformed-traditional media, *Speechless* (2016), succeeds in satisfying this need for transparency and perceived authenticity; additionally, the show is able to play with narrative conventions to create a kind of young adult literature not found in other media. Before the show premiered, the creative team openly and immediately explained online their intentions, as well as their connections to issues surrounding cerebral palsy and disability more generally. The series, heavily marketed online, was quickly welcomed by online communities as "a triumph for media representation" and recognized for partnering with experts at the Cerebral Palsy Foundation (Alston). Creator Scott Silveri—whose brother had CP, similar to but more severe than character J.J.'s and actor Micah Fowler's—asserts the creative team's commitment to present "a character with CP in a way that is informed, respectful and authentic" (Silveri quoted in "CPF JOINS SPEECHLESS!"). An abled brother to someone with CP, Silveri actively encourages feedback from other contributors; unlike "some showrunners [who] want no creative suggestions from their actors," Silveri relies particularly on Fowler and writer/actor Zach Anner, both of whom have CP and insist on stories—always aware of how CP affects experiences—about "what any 17-, 18-year-old wants to talk about," mainly relationships and "growing independence" (Sepinwall, Saclao).

With dedication to including the disabled community in its production and a commitment to engage with issues that are often ignored, the series succeeds as the narrative of a disabled family. It manages to push the narrative possibilities of young adult disability narratives. Rather than starting its story with a family's search for acceptance and pride, *Speechless*'s narrative begins right where the most effective problem novels end. The exceptional *Accidents of Nature* politicizes the disabled identity for individuals and closes with a strong message to cultivate a larger community, a "Crip Nation" (Johnson, *Accidents* 82). While Johnson's *Accidents of Nature* culminates with acceptance, *Speechless* does not celebrate, or even reinvent, these journeys; it avoids them. When Silveri considered a learning-to-walk plotline for J.J., disabled consultants warned against the familiar story of "overcoming . . . disability," and suggested a story "thriving with" cerebral palsy; Silveri dropped the idea immediately (Sepinwall). Just by using the storyline, as "real" as it may be—Micah Fowler himself was working on walking at the time—a narrative could portray the desire to "overcome" disabilities as an acceptable goal. Even *Accidents*' Jean understands that it is a goal in mainstream society. *Speechless*, however, forbids the viewer from wanting J.J.'s life to be "better"; instead, the problem tackled in *this* problem narrative is how that *desire* for normality is what pushes nonnormative people to the margins. Most often, *Speechless* does not even consider the possibility of changing people; instead, inaccessible objects and institutions are the ones forced to change. For instance, when J.J.'s wheelchair gets stuck in a doorway, trapping the whole family in the bathroom, the *doorframe* must change—not J.J. They may "die in [there]," but at least they'll be "together," Jimmy adds with a smile ("I-N-S—INSPIRATIONS" 00:00:57). With a collaborative identity, the DiMeo family delivers lessons about important disability-related "problems," but with high expectations for the viewer and online-based critics; the series features complex, developed characters and refuses to let disability overshadow the DiMeos' other traits and stories.

In direct contrast to *Wonder* and *Atypical*, *Speechless* uses its DiMeo family to quietly challenge narratives that use disability as a damaging family burden to provoke pity for disabled kids—and especially their caregivers. Caregiving mothers, typified by *Wonder*'s Isabel and *Atypical*'s Elsa, are often so "thinly drawn" and "defined by that [caregiver] role," that their characters' pitiful "moments of emotional distress" result in the "treacliness" of *Wonder* and the "pandering" confidence of *Atypical* (Gilbert, Bradshaw, Hugar). In *Wonder*, Isabel's daughter explicitly pities her mother for having to sacrifice her own life:

> My mother put her life on hold for my brother. She always wanted to be a children's book illustrator and teach art. She was one thesis shy of getting her master's when Auggie was born. Then she stopped writing it. She stopped a lot of things when Auggie was born, but she is still great at drawing. I don't know if she even realizes that she makes Auggie the center of every universe she draws. (*Wonder* 00:31:30)

Portrayed as weeping with worry and exhibiting no regret over her quiet martyrdom, Isabel holds, for the viewer, the weight of the family's burden: Auggie. In *Atypical*, Elsa also worries, but unlike Isabel, she craves praise for the unrelenting responsibility she feels for her eighteen-year-old, autistic son Sam. "Do you know that every time the phone rings I jump? Every time. I think he's crossed the street again with his eyes closed, or he had a freak-out in a store, or he's hit a police officer" ("Antarctica" 00:08:10). Shown lifelessly doing chores—with extra time for laundry because of special soaps—Elsa's character, through scenes she's given, stresses her need to "escape . . . [her] real life," even by enjoying an extramarital affair, in order to understandably feel human and appreciated (00:26:19). When she finally receives praise and attention, Elsa will not accept it; she flees when her lover calls her "the best," later agonizing that, because of her family responsibilities, she just can't be for him the person "that cares about . . . [him] and can be with" him ("I Lost My Poor Meatball" 10:00, "A Nice Neutral Smell" 30:15). A martyr, Elsa also blames herself when her husband uses the wrong terms at a support group, because she, much like Isabel, bears the largest burden; narratives like *Atypical* and *Wonder* often use disabled adolescent protagonists to illustrate the suffering of others.

In *Speechless*, of course, Maya serves as an outrageously flashy foil to both Elsa and Isabel. Beyond her genuine love of advocating for J.J. and all special-needs families, Maya never sacrifices herself or her passions, but instead cultivates them and *uses* them to her advantage. Because the DiMeo family acts as a collaborative unit in *Speechless*, and because the series refuses to simplify complexities—especially of emotions—Maya cannot play such an impressive role entirely on her own, without the help and collaboration of the others. Led by Dylan, who was forced to "read a psychology textbook to give her [mother] free therapy," the family openly discuss Maya's "deep-seated issues of guilt," particularly ones that are "unhealthy-slash-inappropriate," as dutifully recited by Maya ("I-N-S—INSPIRATIONS" 00:06:28, 00:08:09). When Ray and Dylan also express guilt for complaining, Jimmy takes over the narrative; the kids don't believe that they "can have fun without . . . [their] brother" precisely because their "mom never does," so he drags them all to an ice-skating rink, where Maya skates peacefully while the others watch (00:14:44). "She's not feeling guilty," he tells them pointedly and simply. "Neither should you" (18:58). Jimmy is also the one to remind his kids that passions change, and rather sacrificing their own lives to care for a disabled child, he and Maya have let their lives change in order to have a family—and everything that comes with it. Ray's worries about career options prompt Jimmy to show his son windows he'd designed as an architecture student before his current career as a baggage-handler. Jimmy loved architecture, he tells Ray, and "then, you know, your mom and I had a baby, and I needed insurance *now*, something solid *now*, not something great later. So, you know, family beat windows" ("C-H—CHEATER!" 17:54). In the lessons they deliver to their kids—as well as to the viewer—Jimmy and Maya rarely single out J.J. as a particular source of problems, and they never voice regret over the choices; regardless of disability, the DiMeos support each other with love.

Because *Speechless* has already assured the viewer that feelings of guilt and regret are understandable, and because the DiMeos operate with "brutal honesty" and laughter "to celebrate the bonds they share," Silveri and his writing team give Maya the freedom to exaggerate her world-changing efforts (Silveri quoted in Sepinwall). Beyond educating authorities and demanding necessary accommodations at school, Maya spends time dealing with insurance companies and bemoaning healthcare costs—generally and egregiously ignored by other narratives. When J.J. needs a new wheelchair and receives a faulty used one, Maya tells Kenneth that "you have to" have connections in insurance companies in order to receive what's needed ("H-E-R—HERO" 00:01:23). When Jimmy adds that "having a disability's expensive—it's almost not even worth it," *Speechless* helps viewers by turning the camera to a laughing J.J.; the joke is safe, and the humor is for those (being welcomed) in the disabled community (00:01:30). When forced to deal with a "tough" new insurance representative, Maya—confident and direct, rather than manipulative—doesn't worry and instead says, "I like a challenge"; with her "mom powers," she—with Jimmy's assistance—dupes the agent to get what her family needs (00:04:05, 00:08:04). Less publicly but just as meaningfully, Maya and the DiMeos show their dedication and shameless confidence by orchestrating potential first-kiss for J.J. Failing extravagantly, Maya takes responsibility but is able to laugh at herself; "I'm sorry," she tells J.J. "I went a bit overboard. I don't know if you've noticed—I sometimes do that" ("R-A-Y-C—RAY-CATION" 00:15:12). Go overboard she does, and even when needing a break, she does not collapse or fall apart as Isabel, Elsa, and other caregivers are prone to do. Rather, Maya receives a jury-duty notice as an incredible gift, rather than an additional responsibility; she glows in a spotlight and sings her own version of "(I've Got A) Golden Ticket" (from *Willy Wonka & the Chocolate Factory*, 1971).

> I thought that all my life would be
> Fighting insurance companies
> But suddenly I begin to see court-ordered time off for me
> 'Cause I've got a golden ticket,
> A special-needs mum's excuse to do jack squat ("One
> A-N—Angry M—Maya" 00:00:29)

With smiles and laughs, Maya celebrates her temporary freedom—without *feeling* sympathy, and without *earning* sympathy. While *Speechless* relies on humor, Maya does show vulnerability and concern in other situations; she admits to J.J. when she "doesn't know how to do" something they haven't yet experienced; still, Maya remains a supportive parent and assures her independence-claiming adolescent, "We'll figure it out together—separately" ("B-O-N—BONFIRE" 00:18:10).

Demonstrating that her passion for "righting the world" is a source of pride and also central to her character, Maya is admirable and, at times, annoying—but always loving and ready to stand up for a cause, not always related to disability (00:06:50). When Kenneth brings over the wrong kind of pizza, Sal's, the DiMeos provide a whole list of businesses and cultural trends that are "dead to Maya" and forbidden in their household ("H-A-L—HALLOWEEN" 00:01:46). While some *are* institutions that have harmed or actually insulted the family, the list really just demonstrates Maya's passion for objection and hyperbole; among the "dead" are energy drinks, human pyramids, nineties ska music, cologne, puns, fun shoes, bowling, mayonnaise, and more ("H-A—HALLOWEEN"). When school budget restrictions pit Maya against a new friend—whose son was on the fencing team until funds were shifted to upgrade the (accessible) elevator—she battles passionately, before realizing that other families have needs, too. While she would never back away from an elevator upgrade to improve daily life for J.J., she does figure out a compromise by standing before a large group of parents at a fundraiser and announcing, with acknowledgment of her powers, "I've got a lot of fight in me, and I've had to do much practice. So anyway, that's what I'm offering: me fighting for anything you desire. One hundred bucks a pop. Proceeds go to the Lafayette fencing team" ("The H-U-S—Hustle" 00:18:26). *Because* she has unwavering support from family and an over-the-top personality, Maya and *Speechless* avoid drawing sympathy or pity from viewers and online critics.

In addition to making savvy political statements and challenging harmful disability representations—and consequently aligning itself with online disability movements—*Speechless* cements its position as a young adult narrative by reflecting the wallflower voice only to disrupt and revamp it completely; the DiMeo family—with multiple voices—adopts the position of a single protagonist. While *Speechless* does not feature first-person narration, the voices of all three teenaged characters, J.J., Ray, and Dylan, exhibit wallflower qualities, including preoccupations with sex, death, and truth. Dylan explores not-yet-stable sexual desires, from a crush on Ray's bully to a more serious interest in "the hot new kid in . . . [her] class," Kai, whom she's invited over to study; certainly not a potential friend, Kai has her attention because of "his face" and because "all three queen bees in . . . [her] class like him" ("S-P—SPECIAL B—BOY T-I—TIME" 00:01:17, 00:15:05). Just as J.J.'s romantic goals and interests drive many plotlines, Ray's inability to attract a girl is a running joke that lasts the entire series. When he finally does find a girlfriend, J.J. must explain to the incredulous family that, "in a lot of movies, the pretty girl dates the dork for a bet" ("J-J's D-R—Dream" 00:00:28); while not the case with pretty-yet-equally-dorky Taylor, Ray's luck does run out. He remains clueless until the final episode, when the girls in his class help him see that he has "been chasing a feeling, not a person," to which one girl responds, "You don't know us. And you're so busy trying to get us to notice you, we don't get to know you ("U-N-R—Unrealistic" 00:13:43). Preoccupied by questions about the future and desiring the truth, Ray and Dylan repeatedly express concern about how they will care for their currently eighteen-year-old disabled brother, who, just as realistically, is working to gain independence from the family unit. Maya and Jimmy suggest, without J.J. visibly in the room, that even though they don't know exactly "what kind of help he will need," they do know that J.J. will "probably not" be able to live on his own, and they simply hope Ray and Dylan will there offer some help ("C-H—CHEATER!" 20:13). Concerns and preoccupations continue—J.J. is "upset" by the conversation he overheard and tells Dylan that they think he's a burden, "a 'H-O—Hot potato' to pass around"—but worries remain, as *Speechless* offers no neat conclusions ("R-U-N—RUNAWAY" 00:03:16, 00:04:38).

Also like narrator-protagonists in young adult novels, the DiMeos are concerned by issues of identity—but without a single narrator-protagonist or first-person narration, both common in narratives in traditional media. In *Speechless*, that narrative voice buckles under the much louder voice of the DiMeo family, able to speak as one through television and online technologies. Embracing a united identity, the DiMeos accept that individuals cannot function, or thrive, alone. Maya, for instance, both leads and relies on her "special-needs moms' group," which offers support through shared experiences, sometimes life-changing and difficult, and sometimes as simple as understanding messy houses and constant late arrivals ("O-S—OSCAR P-A—PARTY" 00:02:30). The DiMeos host the group, along with their families, for their annual Oscar Party, but when the TV malfunctions, Maya takes a stand, refuses to end the party, and advocates for her fellow moms: "These women's self-esteem is on the line. They need this party to prove that the way they live their lives—the way that we live our lives—is nothing to apologize for" (00:09:27). The families stay put, and the episode reinforces the importance of group solidarity. Kenneth and J.J. allow the other special-needs kids to join their movie trivia game, already modified to require both of them to point with a laser (00:05:00). Studying the group, Kenneth identifies "visual impairment, hearing impairment, Down syndrome, autism, and a walker," and announces the pressing task of "how to make this game fair for these beautiful kids" (00:09:49). They figure it out, and with all participants competitive and adept at movie trivia, the intense game finally sparks "a brawl." Dedicated to inclusivity, Kenneth devises even more accommodations "to allow these gorgeous youths an equal-opportunity death-match" (00:13:28). When parents find the brawl, however, they are horrified to see their kids fighting, blindfolded, with newly designed weapons, as Kenneth watches. The episode, of course, ends with light humor, but the viewer is left with the solidarity found in battle—competitors united, with quite different skills and needs.

Aware that they cannot understand all of J.J.'s questions because they do *not* have CP, Maya and the family are eager to connect with and welcome others. When she cannot further or restrict J.J.'s attempt to run away, Maya stumbles upon a "pretty girl [with a] wheelchair badass," played by Zach Anner, a consultant and writer with cerebral palsy ("R-U-N—RUNAWAY" 00:14:59). With her usual brash persistence, Maya convinces Lee, the not-quite-as-young adult with CP, to talk with J.J. By offering a mentor who actually has cerebral palsy, *Speechless* gives J.J. a friend who makes him laugh by telling him to "get as many girls on your lap as possible" as his most important piece of advice (00:19:18). Later, Lee gives J.J. his phone number and says that he's "really glad" Maya got them together; even though they both have passionate, caring mothers, Lee tells J.J., "It kind of kept me from doing things for myself . . . [and] you're gonna have to make some space for yourself, if you ever want to live your life" (00:19:38). Maya and J.J. smile at each other, acknowledging the importance of Maya's support, and allow their family dynamics to evolve, making sure to leave space for each individual voice.

The DiMeo family does indeed live as one unit, in the kind of "tumultuous" existence considered a "developmental norm" of adolescence (Kidd 149). A quick introduction to the second season even hints that, regardless of age, each DiMeo feels that adolescent tumult and change: "As a result of J.J.'s growing independence, Maya . . . [has the] opportunity to re-discover herself" (Silveri quoted in Saclao). Even as their collaborative identity evolves, the DiMeos do not expect or receive radical "cures" or "ends" to their situations, which allows the *Speechless* narrative to offer a refreshing celebration of adolescence, complementing its celebration of a disabled family. The DiMeos, of course, do find methods to discover and rediscover parts of themselves, sometimes switching roles within the family, and always asking questions and growing from answers. The family acts together in pushing boundaries and rules; in "T-H—THE C-L—CLUB," they sneak into a private club to swim, hiding from staff members and creating fictional personas. In a similarly reckless move, they drop everything to travel to the Grand Canyon in "W-E—WE'RE B-A—BACK!" just to help J.J. achieve his first kiss, because "this family doesn't split apart . . . [but rather] come together to do things that are awesome and stupid" (00:13:41). In "D-I—DING," when Ray accuses his mother of leaving a ding on a car, the entire family, unusually at odds, works through disagreements in a grocery store; they hide from staff, argue loudly, and enjoy messy disasters.

With deliberate chaos in "R-O—ROAD T-R—TRIP," Maya and Jimmy announce the family's annual road trip with a guitar and microphone, finishing their song with "Ray objects every year!" (00:00:47). The family brazenly skips school for their unplanned trip—the kind of adventure associated with adolescence—which results in typical DiMeo chaos. Secretly and self-righteously, Ray has hijacked the tradition and curated this year's road trip, so the other DiMeos, led by a goofily furious Maya, trick Ray into losing his agenda, so that they can continue on their unplanned way. *Speechless*, however, does not let its adolescent family last an episode without realism and acts of love. They save Ray from painful appendicitis more efficiently than seems possible, simply because it's "not . . . [their] first emergency room," visit; Maya rattles off answers to the doctors' questions before they're asked, pulls Ray's complete medical records from her bag, and joins the others in sending Ray into surgery with composure and confidence (00:15:13). When Ray awakes, the tricks and fights have ended—as has the road trip—but Maya is by his side with thoughtful offerings, and Ray sincerely tells her, "You were so good back there" (00:19:16). Surprised by his mother's organization, a trait he assumes he bears for the entire family, Ray listens as Maya teaches her son to rediscover both of their characters: "Where do you think you get it? I'm that way for the stuff that matters, and I have a lot that matters, which is why I have to let go and have fun with the rest of it" (00:19:25). With echoes of Jimmy's words from "B-O-N—BONFIRE"—"We're *not* normal. We're better. We're bulletproof"—Maya reinforces the family's inconsistent, yet organized, character (00:16:27). *Speechless* is a narrative that finds success when multi-voiced, united, and delivered in transformed-traditional media; acting a bit like the DiMeos, activist and marginalized communities may grow powerful, embrace tumult, and become bulletproof.

SINGING ALONG IN DIGITAL MEDIA

With widespread praise for its empowering portrayal of a disabled teenager—played by a disabled actor—*Speechless* and its messages reach critics on mainstream websites, who reinforce the series' strong political challenges to harmful types of representation. Participants in the disabled cybercommunity reinforce—with authenticity and authority—exactly why the series' representations are so noteworthy and important for all viewers to recognize. These politically motivated online reviews—along with articles, posts, and hashtag-based conversations and movements like #OwnVoices—usually are not literary works themselves. However, digital, online young adult disability narratives, some of which suggest political or critical motivation, arise from reviews and reflections of other literary narratives. Appearing parallel to online criticism, these online literary narratives are assumed to be autobiographical, which may remove questions of authenticity, but may also cause more questions about accuracy and authority. To identify the roles of participants in online, digital communities, I try to use the digital-media terms "producers" and "consumers," modified versions of "writers" or "creators" and "readers" or viewers." Additionally, the disabled online community is generally most active on Twitter—with prominent hashtags, brief and immediate communication forms (tweets), and real-time chats and conversations. While participants do take advantage of other digital media services, including blogs, microblogs, vlogs, and podcasts, to attract and accommodate additional users, Twitter remains the central hub of activity—as of 2020—and participants often use Twitter to announce and share links to activity in other places. While not entirely precise, I intend to accept as young adult disability narratives all digital works with narrative qualities—stories, connected events, character-based descriptions, and more—that are also thematically focused on disability and adolescence. Just as online platforms provide space for debating interpretations and reactions without traditional publishing filters, they provide space for the creation of narratives without traditional restrictions or acknowledged sources of authority.

Such narratives are produced by a number of different people and groups, most of whom are unrestricted by publishing filters. Prominent disabled activist and one of the first to take advantage of digital media platforms stories of disability, Alice Wong uses her *Disability Visibility Project* website to collect personal narratives; uses Twitter to share experiences and create participatory conversations/chats that often take narrative form; produces a podcast—available on several digital media; and publishes her own stories more formally in online journals and newspapers (*Disability Visibility Project*). Emerging online from a creative background, rather than from activism, Stuart Murdoch, Belle and Sebastian's lyricist of young adult narratives, uses digital media to advocate for those, including himself, living with myalgic encephalomyelitis, or chronic fatigue syndrome (ME/CFS). On Twitter, Murdoch shares narratives, creates online conversations, and shares links to narrative vlogs (video blogs) that he produces for his "ME people" (Murdoch, Video Interview). Both Murdoch and Wong—one an invisibly disabled songwriter and the other a visibly disabled sociologist and activist—find common space online, where members of the heterogenous disability community connect more easily. In these malleable and participatory spaces, Wong, Murdoch, and others produce narratives that further political messages introduced in problem novels and narratives, and they fundamentally alter the forms, voices, and applications of disabled young adult narratives. Ultimately, these narratives both blur and separate literary genres, as well as individual and group identities; this complexity results in a participatory community of political and authorial chaos, brimming with energy and power.

With digital media, participants in the disabled community, like those in other cybercultures, often adopt literary forms of incredibly brief narratives that are immediately available to potentially enormous audiences. In a thorough analysis of the prominent cyberculture Black Twitter, sociologist Latoya A. Lee offers explanation of the potentially mammoth impacts these communities may have.

> Digital homespaces serve to (re)create and (re)define individuals' sense of self by exposing bias [*sic*] news coverage, and through the sharing of testimonies, obstacles, struggles, and triumphs that oppressed folks on the margins face on a day-to-day basis, while building coalitions and communities. (Lee 6)

Without a doubt, the online disabled community takes advantage of these strategies, often with parallel purposes; most importantly to this project, the narratives shared, including "testimonies, obstacles, struggles, and triumphs," are quite frequently narratives about adolescence, about finding personal and social identities as disabled people (Lee 6). They are young adult disability narratives produced and consumed on digital media.

A previously disparate group, disabled people are able to find each other and to become a part of something larger—often accomplished through radically altered forms of literary narrative. On Twitter, the disability community began to take shape around 2016, when hashtags and introductions allowed leaders to emerge and their followers to grow, and personal narratives have always played important roles in the community. One of the earliest hashtag movements to unite participants, #CripTheVote gained traction before the 2016 American presidential election; created by online activists Alice Wong, Andrew Pulrang, and Gregg Beratan, the #CripTheVote movement encourages solidarity: "Every day there's something to read, and all are invited to contribute to the ongoing #CripTheVote discussion of disability, politics, policy, identity, and voting" ("Frequently Asked Questions"). Perhaps stemming from the popularity of #CripTheVote, disability narratives, movements, and activist leaders gather participants through social media. With informal participation in Disability Twitter, @coffeespoonie, a self-identified "elephant-loving disabled jewess with ink-stained hands," has over fifty-one thousand followers as of 2021 and consequently tweets with accepted authority: "I just started tweeting about my experiences, really," she explains, "and made connections with spoonie [chronically ill] friends. I was rly lonely at the time and the spoonie community on here was a huge support for me" (@crabbyeabbye et al.). By participating in "SpoonieChat," @coffeespoonie relays that she was able to make connections, both established and emerging, with members of the disability community, including Alice Wong (@SFdirewolf), @fromsarahlex, @punny samosa, and Dawn M. Gibson (@DawnMGibson).

With short narratives about disability—often as disabled adolescents—participants enter and introduce themselves to the online community, which proves "extremely helpful," notes @Phoebe92987793: "Very few we interact with in our daily lives, face to face, are able to comprehend the reality of our experiences, thoughts and feelings, leaving us feeling invalidated and silenced. #DisabilityTwitter" (@mssinenomine et al.). Interactions and conversations begin, at times, with provocative mini-narratives: "Just realized something. If not for Twitter I would feel like there is not a single person on earth who understands. Today especially I feel alone in this city and today especially so grateful for Disability Twitter" (@mssinenomine et al.). Perhaps intended simply as a remark on the Disability Twitter community, this tweet is composed in the first-person present-tense narration of a wallflower narrator, with a palpable tone of dreariness, loneliness in a crowded city, to express the struggle of finding community and to offer gratitude—while remaining existentially "alone." On the first day of March 2019, @mssinenomine (G Peters), undoubtedly, produced a young adult disability narrative that was consumed and "liked" by almost two hundred readers. In order to collect, promote, and prioritize such narratives, Wong initiated her website, *Disability Visibility Project* even earlier, in 2014. The *Disability Visibility Project*, founded and directed by Wong, "believes that disabled narratives matter and that they belong to us . . . encourages people with disabilities to . . . record their oral histories," and "creates disabled media from collected oral histories in the form of tweets, podcast episodes, radio stories, audio clips, images, blog posts, etc." (*Disability Visibility Project*). As accessible as possible, Wong's *Project* collects and shares personal disability narratives in all literary forms.

Also using a brief, audio/visual narrative form in digital media, Murdoch's group Belle and Sebastian released—initially available, in late 2014, only as an online video—"Nobody's Empire" (2014). Revelatory for Murdoch, the song's narrative worked as a "kind of full-disclosure . . . personal announcement" of "how big of a role ME play[s]" in his life (Murdoch, Video Interview). Through digital media, Murdoch brought his and his band's fans and audiences into disability-based movements, while also introducing himself to the growing online disability community. Perhaps even more importantly, with his rich storytelling background, Murdoch *demonstrates* the political importance of personal narratives, like the ones Wong works to collect. Similar to his earlier songs of quirky adolescents, "Nobody's Empire" must be read, or heard, as a young adult disability narrative specific to chronic illness. Right away, the narrator introduces himself from a "hiding place," returning to a childlike existence and receiving care from a parent:

> I was like a child, I was light as straw
> And my father lifted me up there
> Took me to a place where they checked my body
> My soul was floating in thin air
> I clung to the bed and I clung to the past

> I clung to the welcome darkness
> But at the end of the night there's a green, green light
> It's the quiet before the madness ("Nobody's Empire")

In an undefined existence, where both a "welcome" past and a future "madness" occur at once, leaving the narrator "floating in thin air," the song—like Murdoch's earlier songs—reflects Kristeva's "mythical figure" of the adolescent ("Nobody's Empire"; Kristeva 135). These theoretical readings of "Nobody's Empire," along with direct commentary from Murdoch himself, offer insight into the importance of writing and sharing brief narratives about disability and adolescence:

> The reasons to do art or to write songs are, I think, quite different from what people expect. So often, the reason to do something like that is consolation; you're trying to console yourself. . . . At that time when the second big wave of ME had hit me, I was looking back to the old days of twenty-five years before, for comfort, because . . . looking with rose-tinted glasses, it suddenly seemed like there was something cozy about my experience of ME before. It seemed much easier and simpler. Also, it was wrapped up in adolescence, and I knew the outcome was pretty successful and hopeful, you know, so it felt good (Murdoch, Video Interview)

Articulating perhaps what Wong encourages disabled participants to find by sharing stories, Murdoch allows and encourages others with ME/CFS to share feelings—of pride, frustration, anger, and acceptance—by consuming and responding to songs, tweets, and vlogs. His own online narratives include efforts "to stay positive . . . but it's tricky . . . suddenly things that were easy, you know, like I've got to record with the band next week, instead of that seeming like a nice thing, suddenly it's a bit of a cloud" (Murdoch, "Stuart Murdoch on ME/CFS . . ."). Demonstrating that life with a chronic illness, like other disabilities, is rarely consistent or static, he also shares "experiences of the first few years of having ME. . . . When I was younger . . . I was never angry about it as such. . . . Our attitude was that, in a sense, you had to give into it . . . you had to accept what was happening to you . . . you can fight it, and we were fighting it . . . we weren't just giving into it" (Murdoch, Video Interview). With his online presence, Murdoch brings a more personal connection to the characters in earlier songs, which he created following his first wave of ME. In "Nobody's Empire," he shares his own story of "dangl[ing] a while in this waiting room" and uses the narrative to publically introduce himself as someone with ME/CFS (Belle and Sebastian, "Nobody's Empire").[2]

Participants in the online disability community, quite frequently, express deep gratitude—sometimes in literary narratives—to the cyberculture, simply for existing. In response to a question about finding community "leaders," community participant and leader Gregg Beratan (@GreggBeratan) shares his story of becoming part of Disability Twitter. His response—produced in a Twitter thread of connected tweets—arguably forms a narrative on its own with a strong voice and the beginnings of a plotline. By responding in such a way, Beratan illustrates the kinds of narratives—especially very brief ones—made possible through digital media:

> I signed up pretty early on, but it took a couple years and encountering the above folk [@Imani_Barbarin and @Dis Visibility] to really start to get the power of the platform and the community I found here. I was very slow on the uptake.
>
> Oh finding the Disability Community both online and off has been one of the best things that has ever happened to me. It has made such a difference in my life to finally feel I was a part of a community, to have that connection to the world.
>
> . . . I can't overstate how much I have benefitted from the acceptance, knowledge, strength and compassion of the Disability Community. I am grateful for it every day. (@GreggBeratan)

In addition to the impact of producing and consuming very brief narratives, the immediacy of sharing alters literary forms by allowing for real-time interaction between participants. Twitter, seemingly quite simple and generally the platform used for chats, allows brief personal narratives to get lost in flurries of activity, but at the same time, Twitter chats—as well as immediate comments left on blogs, vlogs, and other digital media—become yet another literary narrative form. Understood and consumed as chronological and longer narratives, chats emerge as multi-voiced narratives. In some ways akin to the DiMeos' united, multi-voiced-yet-single character, Twitter chats feature more disagreement, plots, and themes than individual tweets. With assumed-to-be-autobiographical contributions from known disabled participants, chats produce narratives that offer inherent authorial authenticity, but with so many unidentified participants, chats are composed with almost no control and without central authorities.

One such chat from 2019, #AccessIsLove, hosted by "the co-partners of Access is Love, Sandy Ho, Mia Mingus, and Alice Wong . . . [encourage discussions on] access and solidarity in the form of love" (Wong, "Recap"). As a single narrative, compiled by Wong, with multiple voices and contributors, the Twitter chat works as a literary narrative made up almost entirely by dialogue. Introductions, short narratives, and interactions between participants develop into a longer, wider story that branches off into sub-threads, or subplots:

> **@DisVisibility:** Q1: Please introduce yourself and what brought you to today's #AccessIsLove chat. If you are willing, share anything about your life, advocacy, or work. Feel free to include links about yourself!
> **@IntersectedCrip:** A1: I just got home from presenting @lasell college about Practicing Allyship to a group of students, faculty, and staff. I used memes from Schitt's Creek and cat memes. So. that sums up my professional life. #AccessIsLove
> **@RebeccaCokley:** A1. I'm Rebecca. I work at @amprog and run the @CAPDisability. It's been a long week and it's only tuesday. The idea of hanging with @DisVisibility @miamingus and @IntersectedCrip has been what I've been looking forward to all day. #AccessIsLove
> **@miamingus:** hahaha love you, @RebeccaCokley! #AccessIs Love (Wong, "Recap")

Open to all, especially those who are already a part of the disability cyberculture, moderators produce the searchable hashtag #Access IsLove in order for any participant to join at any time. Not only does Twitter unite voices from multiple sources, it blurs the line between producers and consumers; responses carry the narrative as much as the questions do. Certainly, the above response from @RebeccaCokley (Rebecca Cokley), Director for the Disability Justice Initiative, not only welcomes her nearly twenty thousand followers to the narratives, it sets the tone of the chat, a rather informal "hanging with" the community, which hosts cyber-events worth "looking forward to" (Wong, "Recap"). And the response—"hahaha love you"—from @miamingus (Mia Mingus), activist and moderator, continues the casual, welcoming tone of the community's stories. The moderators, too, are reading responses and are willing to respond, and a reader of the entire "Recap" may suspect that Cokley and Mingus know each other, at least online—which may be an important relationship to note, both narratively and politically. Much later in the conversation, a tweet from @dasoultoucha (Keith Jones), a new character presented to an outside reader, offers a view of access based on "the intersection of racism ableism and stupidity"; when @SFdirewolf (Alice Wong) responds, the outside reader recognizes the casual friendliness, but does not know the relationship between the two and may feel literary tension: "Hey Keith! Welcome! Looking forward to your stories and thoughts about access . . . especially since I've seen some of your Tweets about flying #AccessIsLove" (Wong, "Recap"). Simultaneously, Wong's referencing another narrative from Jones, his "tweets about flying," which may or not focus on disability, directs participants to another now-connected narrative, and it also furthers the welcoming and growing community allowed by digital media.

Whether or not the #AccessIsLove chat could be classified as a young adult narrative is unclear and unknowable, since most participants write about themselves; however, participants and consumers do quickly learn that co-moderator @IntersectedCrip (Sandy Ho) has just returned from teaching college students, so adolescents are certainly not irrelevant. Other hashtag-based conversations that result in collaborative narratives provoke explicit adolescent memories, even if not necessarily from adolescent participants. The #AbledsAreWeird chat, also from 2019, begins with a memory from writer and disabled activist @Imani_Barbarin (Imani Barbarin): "I think about the time an abled random stranger threw my crutch into the pool "to help me swim" a lot. #AbledsAreWeird" (@Imani_Barbarin et al.). Popular enough to be "trending" on Twitter and to earn stories on *National Public Radio's* website, the *Daily Dot*, and *Romper*, #AbledsAreWeird ultimately grows into a narrative (with many producers) within a narrative (produced by those who began as consumers). The original tweets were created by and perhaps intended for disabled participants, but coverage of the collective narrative by mainstream websites suggests abled audiences. The story in *Romper* even begins by explaining to an assumed-to-be-able-bodied reader that "the trending hashtag #AbledsAreWeird shines a light on the uncomfortable experiences nondisabled individuals create for people with disabilities and serves as a reality check" (Modan). Produced online, disabled personal narratives, both brief and long, and often about adolescence, create narratives in a form quite different from those possible in traditional media; they also allow for narrators with multiple voices.

Because they provide space for brief, participatory literary forms and collaborative voices, digital media platforms are home to young adult disability narratives with a number of applications, produced for different purposes and different consumers. Though most online narratives created by the disability community include, at the very least, political undertones, commentary does not dominate. Some political posts, however, *do* include mini-memoirs. In 2019, when an elected member of the United States federal government turned to Twitter to ask, "Now: who are your favorite disability advocates to follow? Share below ⬇," some participants answered only with names and Twitter handles, while others offered stories (@AOC, et al.):

> **@dave_pitsch:** I'm disabled with multiple sclerosis. I can't move my right leg I can't even hold a pencil with my right hand. I use a wheelchair to get around, I can't take my 4 year-old out to play, but I'm in nobody so nobody cares about me, I just don't make a big enough splash.
> **@SFdirewolf:** I didn't make too much of a splash when I first started on Twitter. I tried to find and connect with folks. I told my own story as best I could. We're all doing the best we can with what we have. (@AOC, et al.)

Such responses, even if not necessarily young adult, become a collective disability narrative that introduces and examines the workings of the disability cybercommunity.

Other online narratives are similarly purposed for political activism, but as literary narratives, they are presented much more explicitly as personal stories. Problem narratives in digital media, autobiographical stories, interviews, and discussions appear more often on platforms that encourage longer posts; podcasts, blogs, vlogs, and online articles offer the space for more traditionally styled narratives, while nearly always accompanied by participatory platforms. Quite a number of narratives, which at least sometimes focus on disability, appeal specifically to adolescent audiences, such as the popular-in-2019 *Geek Girl Riot*, a podcast on which "hosts take turns on the mic to discuss all the things close to our geeky hearts, topped off with fresh and far-out segments, and special guest appearances for talks and spotlights"; and *Sickboy Podcast*, described as "hilarious, ridiculously insightful and absolutely determined to break down the stigma associated with illness and disease!" (*Geek Girl Riot*; *Sickboy Podcast*). A number of blogs, vlogs, podcasts, and other media that hold disability narratives are explicitly intended to offer support to disabled people who spend most time alone, or without in-person communities. *The Mighty*, a 2019 participatory website, encourages participants to "Find Your Community: Once you follow what matters to you, your community will be right here. Start with our most helpful posts" (*The Mighty*). Offering spaces to post personal experiences, including current thoughts and feelings, as well as space to respond to posts, the website is meant to provide community with support, conversations, and share narratives. However, *The Mighty*—like other community-based websites—whether intentionally or not, prompts and produces multi-voiced narratives. The site also sends emails to subscribers with simple questions and ideas, along with political and social news: all with the potential to produce narratives and all to fit the mission of providing a "digital health community created to empower and connect people facing health challenges and disabilities" (*The Mighty*).

Other disability-focused blogs, vlogs, and podcasts are directed at a more specific audiences but with similar purposes. Stuart Murdoch's vlogs, for instance, specifically address those with ME/CFS to create community and offer support. These digital media, Murdoch says, alter narrative structure and authenticity; they are what allow his audiences to "feel that they are getting [information] from the horse's mouth," and "it's completely unedited, so you get the subtext and pretext and everything all at once. You know, there's no hiding—you get to see how a person feels at the present time, and I think that can be especially helpful" (Murdoch, Video Interview). Revealing his personality through unedited conversations—or monologues—Murdoch is the narrator-protagonist of the stories he tells of chronic illness, and he becomes a character, or personality, to whom consumers return. Murdoch also speaks quite openly about the isolation of chronic illness, using vlogs to reduce shame and to offer immediate connection for members of the ME/CFS community:

> I know a lot of you will be stuck in your houses and things like that, and not be as lucky as me to get out, so that's why it's quite nice to film when I'm out. You see the cows? They're just hanging out, having a late lunch. It's so nice to be outside. I tend just to walk. I walk really slowly, and I always walk in the direction that the wind is going, although there's not much wind today. So, you know, I've got really good shoes. (Murdoch, "Stuart Murdoch: ME/CFS . . . ")

Simultaneously, Murdoch considers his earlier narrative songs with adolescent characters—in "a fictional world" and about whom he couldn't "have written . . . unless [he'd] had those experiences"—to be quite separate from his autobiographical, ME/CFS-focused vlogs (Murdoch, Video Interview). Regardless, Murdoch's digitally delivered, autobiographical words of the 2010s respond to characters from his mid-1990s fictional world, especially regarding solitude and needs for connection. In one song from the fictional world, the narrator spots a solitary girl and wonders, "Girl in the snow, where will you go / To find someone that will do? / To tell someone all the truth before it kills you?" (Belle and Sebastian, "The Fox in the Snow"). Also in search of connection and peace, an unnamed boy rides alone on a bus, "dying" and doubting that he'll ever find "love in everything and everyone," so he begs, "Play me a song to set me free" ("Get Me Away from Here, I'm Dying"). Elsewhere in that world, waiting "in the queue for lunch," a girl who's been "used" and feels "confused," survives her days as the strange and queer one at school, while the consoling voice of a narrator tells her, "Write a song. I'll sing along" ("Expectations"). In yet another song, another solitary figure—this time a boy who has "done wrong again"—hangs his head in shame and cries, "All I wanted was to sing the saddest song / And if you would sing along I will be happy now" ("The Boy Done Wrong Again"). More often than not, Murdoch's adolescent characters are outsiders, usually alone but hoping for connection to soften their loneliness; they want to tell "all the truth" to kindred spirits through sharing stories—quite often in song ("The Fox in the Snow"). Indeed, while some characters long to hear a song, others receive comfort from narrators, who offer to sing along.

"Couched in metaphor," as Murdoch says, 2014's autobiographical "Nobody's Empire" certainly finds a familiar one, perhaps as a response to his earlier characters' pleas for someone to "sing along" (Murdoch, Video Interview; Belle and Sebastian, "The Boy Done Wrong Again"). In need of community during an earlier wave of ME/CFS, Murdoch, as the song's narrator, finds support in the ethereal way that his characters once suspected they would:

> There was a girl that sang like the chime of a bell
> And she put out her arm, she touched me when I was in hell
> When I was in hell
> Someone sang a song and I sang along
> 'Cause I knew the words from my childhood"
> ("Nobody's Empire")

Perhaps the words in his vlogs, sometimes intentionally filmed when "really feeling rubbish again—just weak, dizzy," provide the same connection for his "ME people" that narrator-Murdoch seems to have found when "someone sang a song" with him (Murdoch, "Stuart Murdoch on ME/CFS"; "Nobody's Empire"). Murdoch's digital narratives may also prompt online audiences to return to or find his earlier songs that, perhaps due to digitally available authorial authenticity, may resonate for those with chronic illnesses, who see themselves in adolescents like Judy, who "wrote the saddest song":

> With a star upon your shoulder lighting up the path that you walk
> With a parrot on your shoulder, saying everything when you talk
> If you're ever feeling blue
> Then write another song about your dream of horses ("Judy and the Dream of Horses")

Even if not ready to share or to announce herself, Judy—identified in another song as "a mastermind" on a "rollercoaster ride" of troubles—has already prepared her song of connection, which she can share if and when she is willing and able ("The Rollercoaster Ride"). In the meantime, listening to Judy's stories may relieve the pressure some may feel to share their own stories; though active with participants, digital media do keep that participation optional.

Certainly, digital platforms offer space to so many types of literary forms, voices, and purposes that they destabilize and blur definitions of familiar genres. Not only are creative personal narratives sometimes indistinguishable from critical commentaries, voices are sometimes single and other times combined; narratives are used for entertainment, literature, art, information, and community. With such literary space, narratives in digital media often blur both personal and group identities. Categories that divide are sometimes reinforced, and at other times those categories spill into each other, creating varied, undefined, and confusing groups. The line between producer (or creator or writer) and consumer (or audience or reader) nearly vanishes in participatory media; conversations on social media sites, as well as comments made on narratives posted online, allow those asking questions to join those responding, removing mediating filters and accepted authorities. On digital media, teachers become students, and students teachers; leaders are also followers, just as followers become leaders. Because participants can control how much information about themselves to provide, the already-imprecise distinctions between children, adolescents, young adults, and older adults are unclear—or even left unknown. Consequently, identifying a narrative as being intended for adolescents or consumed by adolescents becomes impossible, and traditional, marketing-based definitions of young adult literature are irrelevant. Even literature, as a broad name for creative expression, is difficult to distinguish from haphazard comments, critical commentaries, news updates, and more.

UNITED, MULTI-VOICED FAMILIES

Blurred divisions between groups of people create grey areas, with unlimited possibilities, as well as unlimited confusions. In a 2018 online piece, "Living in the Grey Area between Disabled and Able-Bodied," Becca R, a contributor to *The Mighty*, explains, "The majority of the times I disclose my disability, I get the response of 'I'd never have known if you didn't tell me,' or even the 'you don't really, do you?' Sometimes they don't believe me at all. For that reason, I rarely disclose the fact that I have CP" ("Living in the Grey . . . "). Her cerebral palsy is mild enough to be considered "'invisible' by outsiders," and when she temporarily used a wheelchair as an adolescent, "the kids called me a faker. I must have been 'faking' everything since I could get up and walk a little, but used a wheelchair to navigate the halls at school the rest of the day. To this day, I still feel a lot of shame regarding my cerebral palsy, and it's really tough to talk about" ("Living in the Grey . . . "). This brief young adult disability narrative, if nothing else, brings to the fore the distress any set lines dividing identities may cause. The narrative also approaches passing, and divisions between those who can and do pass as nondisabled and those who proudly embrace disabled identities; those with invisible disabilities may pass without intention, which points to the problems of relying on any assumptions. Among the general blurring of identities over digital media, some dividing lines grow even stronger—more solidified. Those who identify with different groups may grow alienated.

Even a lighthearted, community-building hashtag-based collection of mini-narratives, such as 2019's #AbledsAreWeird, has the potential to fracture solidarities and strengthen separations. The disabled community being built—or made visible—by the hashtag, however, is not homogenous, but disagreements rarely receive the same media coverage. Blogger mirandaleeoakley asks in response to the hashtag, "Ableds Are Weird but Aren't Blind People?" (miranda leeoakley). In her blog post, she addresses the way such hashtags may reinforce notions that disabled people and nondisabled people are inherently different. Also questioning the use of the term "ableds," mirandaleeoakley writes, "Yes, people can be mean. Yes, people can be nice, too. I know plenty of great 'Ableds' as they are lately being called. I believe though, when we call them, 'Weird,' we are potentially pushing them away" (mirandaleeoakley). Blogger and activist Imani Barbarin—creator of #AbledsAreWeird—points out the many ways that nondisabled people prevent equity and unity. In "Disabled People Have an Ally Problem: They Need to Stop Talking for Us," Barbarin begins by describing a time she and her mother were in the store and ran into an acquaintance. Once the conversation turned to kids, the acquaintance asked Barbarin's mother what subject her daughter liked most in school:

> Despite standing right beside my mother, despite having been introduced to me by my mother, despite the fact I had nodded quite attentively to what she had yammered on about, she decided to ignore my presence and address the question to my mother. For most abled people, this may seem like a momentary slip up in decorum, but for disabled people this is all too familiar: proximity to disabled bodies are confused with authority over them. (Barbarin)

Writing in more detail about how, in the creation of policies and spaces for inclusion, the voices of able-bodied allies override the voices of disabled people, and "where feminists see all-male panels on women's inclusion in executive spaces, the same happens with disabled people and their able-bodied allies" (Barbarin). When allies take "up space in advocacy . . . for a marginalized group" in order to center themselves, rather than to "make the public sphere more inclusive," they further infantilize and reinforce stereotypes around those with disabilities (Barbarin). Raising questions for and about those in the "grey space" between disabled and abled, or by other members of the heterogeneous disabled community, Barbarin's statements could begin conversations; however, the blog post ends with a firm declaration, seemingly without space for discussion: "No matter how close you are to a disabled person, you cannot completely know what it means to be disabled or experience the world and its people in a disabled body" (Barbarin).

In finding spaces and voices for their own voices, participants in the disabled community generally pay little attention to those existing in the grey areas, and at times, risk "potentially pushing . . . away" nondisabled allies (mirandaleeoakley). Online, democratic conversations—often forming digital disability narratives, at least in the second decade of the twenty-first century—build strength and visibility for a rather narrowly, yet imprecisely, defined group of disabled people. However, just by functioning as a heterogeneous community that allows multiple opinions to be expressed and considered, even if imperfectly, the online disability community is functioning as one that includes voices of nondisabled people, caregivers, parents, ableds who may be weird, and others. Many voices share similar goals of eliminating harmful representations of disability and advocating for civil rights, while disagreements and divisions separate groups within that larger community. Participants in the online disability community may not realize that they are beginning to form a multi-voiced community, with the potential to stand as proudly and strongly as the DiMeos' bulletproof one. By demonstrating and engaging in collaboration, visibility, and even debate and alienation, the community *is* functioning as a family—perhaps as an even more realistic, though dysfunctional, one. As the disability activist movement continues to grow and as identities continue to blur—or separate in ways that allow for careful collaboration—allies and caregivers may learn the ways in which they can work to empower those with disabilities. And disabled writers, actors, and activists will be able to both rely on allies, as well as function as allies themselves, widening the entrances to the community, rather than narrowing them.

Whereas #OwnVoices makes great progress in emphasizing the need for disabled people to share their own stories—and for disabled actors to play disabled characters—*Speechless*, with its welcoming family filled mostly with allies, promotes finding solidarity wherever possible. The creator, Scott Silveri, was not disabled, but instead the brother of someone with cerebral palsy; similarly, most of the creative team—whether or not they identified as disabled in some way—did not have cerebral palsy. But just as Maya turns to Zach Anner's disabled character to offer advice that she cannot, Silveri relied on consultants, disabled writers, and also allies and family members. With the DiMeo family acting as a multi-voiced protagonist, *Speechless* presents an authentic portrayal of one disabled family—with all of its voices able to speak, listen and learn, never ignoring or diminishing J.J.'s personal experiences. *Speechless* demonstrates how one family welcomes grace and chaos in order to function, thrive, and strengthen their familial connections. With multiple voices, the *Speechless* family reflects more accurately a slogan coined well before #OwnVoices: "Nothing About Us Without Us." First heard in 1993 by activist—and author of *Nothing About Us Without Us: Disability Oppression and Empowerment* (2000)—James I. Charlton, the slogan has become ubiquitous, generally used in regard to the disability community's right to participate in policy-making that affects them; a primary goal is to reduce or eliminate oppression that is internalized when disabled people are told who they are and what they need (3). Embracing "Nothing About Us Without Us," members of the disabled community must feel capable of participating in policy making and confident in "influencing political and social trends" (71).

Applying the slogan to narratives, published in both traditional and digital media, encourages multi-voiced groups; as long as disabled contributors are prominently involved, able-bodied creative partners may also participate. In other words, following the message of "Nothing About Us Without Us," the identities of individual contributors to collections like *Unbroken: 13 Stories Starring Disabled Teens* and of individual collaborators involved in a television series like *Speechless* may not be so important; relative to other narratives, *Speechless* may have found its success because of its multi-voiced, collaborative, creative team. In one of the series' final episodes, "P-R-O-M-P—PROMPOSAL," the three DiMeo siblings ride to prom with an abled-bodied actor seeking "insight" on how to play a disabled character—without provoking "all the super-angry people, uh, protesting every day in wheelchairs" (00:09:00). Appropriately, the group encounters a mass of "super-angry people" chanting, "Nothing about us without us! Nothing about us without us!" (00:10:05). For the DiMeos, for the creators of and contributors to *Speechless*, and for the viewers and reviewers of the show, individual identities matter less than the collection of individuals. The *Speechless* family offers implicit lessons to the community it represents; they act with confidence, pride, and power that can arise from the celebration of a community with multiple voices that challenge and support each other.

The DiMeos celebrate their collective identity with humor and lightheartedness, rather than earning pity with tear-jerking sentiments. An early episode of *Speechless* allows the DiMeos to explain to a horrified Kenneth why they rely on J.J.'s disability as their own "personal get-out-of-jail free card":

> **MAYA:** Don't judge us. Having an excuse to get out of stuff is one of the, like, three benefits of being a special-needs family.
> **J.J.:** There's skipping lines at amusement parks.
> **DYLAN:** Good parking spots.
> **MAYA:** And it's taught us lots about human dignity, patience, and compassion—blah blah blah. ("T-H-A—THANKSGIVING" 00:02:44)

Without ignoring reality, the family has fun with and feels pride in their collective identity. Pity is not the only response to disabled characters. Similarly, Murdoch's young adult characters receive encouragement rather than pity. Even a "mousy girl," who is "much too tall for a boyfriend . . . [with a] buck tooth and split ends," finds admiration. The song's narrator sings with celebration, coaxing a submission "to the allure of *[The] Catcher in the Rye*," and reassuring the girl that:

> Like the books you've read
> You're the heroine
> You'll be doing fine . . .
> And you love like nobody around you
> How you love, and a halo surrounds you (Belle and Sebastian, "Le Pastie")

Nonnormative, as least compared to the "heartless swine" who avoid her, this mousy girl is a connection for Murdoch's online followers and collaborators ("Le Pastie"). Much like the DiMeos, his characters too crave connection, along with "the chaos of trouble / 'cause anything's better than posh isolation" ("The Boy with the Arab Strap"). Neither Murdoch's narrators nor *Speechless*'s characters promote patronizing or alienating messages like "See the Ability, Not Disability"; rather than erasing nonnormative characteristics, the characters (and narratives) celebrate "the acceptance and love for one's own body" (Barbarin). Tumultuous families with united voices indeed find joy in each other's disabilities and differences, even with the acknowledgment of difficult realities; as Imani Barbain reminds her online community, "You can dislike your disability and still like you" (@Imani_Barbarin).

Chapter 7

CONCLUSION

Solidarity in Expression and Action

With a revolutionary and "participatory democratic nature," digital media are reshaping and redefining young adult disability narratives, while also allowing digitally based criticism to affect the reception of earlier narratives (Lee 2). The resulting unstable mess of literary forms, narrative techniques, authorial identities, inconsistent expectations, unknown audiences, and forceful political messages suggests that the reshaping and redefining is only beginning. Consequently, this project concludes, I hope, with some of the "radical work," engaging disability studies with scholarship of children's literature, that Scott Pollard imagined in 2013, combined with anticipation of not-yet-produced (as of 2019) work that will surely arise from the chaos, brimming with energy and literary experimentation (Pollard 265).

Much as Marah Gubar has developed a "kinship model" for understanding children's literature, with more attention and respect paid to children, young adult disability narratives are sounding a similar call for kinship (451). The narratives, especially those published in the early twenty-first century, are modeling the literary success found in a familial uniting of voices. Gubar's model, while focused on children, fits almost perfectly what *Speechless* and other young adult disability narratives suggest about disabled people and adolescents:

> This model is premised on the idea that children and adults are akin to one another, which means they are neither exactly the same nor radically dissimilar. The concept of kinship indicates relatedness, connection, and similarity without implying homogeneity, uniformity, and equality.

> Regarding similarity, kinship-model theories emphasize that children, like adults, are human beings. It is dehumanizing and potentially disabling to say that a human being has no voice, or no agency. (453)

Adolescent and disabled people, too, are human beings frequently dehumanized in literature and scholarship—even in unintentionally problematic uses of words, like Gubar's "disabling" (above). Metaphorical dehumanization—caused both by complex literary metaphors and by simple words, carry meaning only by relying on mainstream assumptions: "child" means "powerless and voiceless," when "adolescent" refers to "bad attitudes and emotional tumult," and when "disabled" implies "broken and unwanted." Gubar's use of "kinship" to mean "relatedness, connection, and similarity without implying homogeneity, uniformity, and equality," is itself akin to the united, multi-voiced family hoped for in *Accidents of Nature* (in traditional media), represented in *Speechless* (in transformed-traditional media), and performed by participatory narratives (in digital media). Exemplified by the familial strength portrayed in *Speechless*, young adult disability narratives are calling for increased solidarity and community: voices that are united, collaborative, and linked. Like *Speechless*'s DiMeos, who increase their strength by bringing others into their bulletproof family, the disability community, too, can grow. While the *Speechless* narrative portrays just one family, it addresses issues that arise frequently in the heterogeneous disabled community. In an early episode, "D-A-T-E—DATE?" Kenneth is excited to see a new accessible van at school, while J.J. shakes his head at the red parking pass that identifies a temporarily disabled passenger. Illustrating a common—and often accurate—stereotype, Claire emerges from the van and immediately complains:

> **CLAIRE:** Why me? Why do I have to be in a stupid wheelchair for three whole weeks? What did I do to deserve this? I'm a freak. Great. People are already staring. What? Never seen someone in a wheelchair before?
> **J.J.:** [Uses his communication board.]
> **KENNETH:** Mm hmm. Tourists. (00:00:40)

With levity and seriousness, *Speechless* introduces this temporarily disabled character as one who will leave the community after visiting, and who sees herself through already-held assumptions. Claire is embarrassed, and J.J.—who will always use a wheelchair and who celebrates it as part of his identity—cringes and shakes his head.

J.J.'s always-loyal brother Ray offers viewers another approach to working with the heterogeneity of the disabled community. While he has always joined his family in chastising those who use "the word," Ray reacts differently—and very uncomfortably—when a girl at prom shockingly shows interest but then tells him, "I'm so sorry. I'm such a retard!" ("P-R—PROM" 00:00:16, 00:07:07). His description of the girl's "self-deprecating" use of the word as simply "one tiny thing" nearly drives Dylan to violence, so Ray promises to demand an apology; the girl refuses, so Dylan turns to J.J., who gives Ray permission to kiss the girl (00:07:37).

When he approaches the girl, however Ray's thoughts stop him:

> No. It's not about J.J. . . . [Or about] that not being an accurate description of him. What about people who *do* think a different way or at a different pace? Should we reference them in a nasty way when we do something dumb because we think it's cute? (00:16:20)

Emphasizing both respect for and complexities caused by the community's heterogeneity, the DiMeo adolescents allow viewers to learn along with them; as usual, *Speechless* makes confusing and complex issues and situations accessible—and even funny.

Suggesting a bit more subtly that the disability community may increase its power by joining other marginalized groups in solidarity, *Speechless* uses a season-two episode, "S-H—SHIPPING," for another learning experience. Kenneth explains "shipping"—a word for "when people are dying to get a couple together"—to J.J. to describe his classmates' desire for him to date a new wheelchair-using student. When J.J. wonders why they've chosen that specific classmate, Kenneth tells him, "Because you've both got CP. It's like when people always try to get me to date their only black friend. . . . That's shipping for you—horny profiling" (00:02:10). Kenneth links, but never equates, his experiences as a black man to J.J.'s as a disabled adolescent. Similarly, J.J. teaches Kenneth how to take advantage of sympathy because, as a pair, they are a kid in a wheelchair and a "big, manly guy . . . [who] treat[s] him with such tenderness" ("I-N-S—INSPIRATIONS" 00:04:55). Assumptions about race and gender, *Speechless* illustrates, can produce social effects similar to those about disability.

Speechless may echo, with a bit of accessibility, scholarly understandings of disability as a political identity. Notably, Lennard J. Davis has suggested that "disability may turn out to be the identity that links other identities" (233). As most identity categories have been exposed as nonbinary or even purely socialized, Davis urges an emphasis on disability as "itself an unstable category" (237). Narratives and characters considered in this project—from the wallflower narrators who conflate adolescence and disability, to the multi-voiced narrators who question all individual identities—certainly project such instability in representation. Davis delves into the effects of embracing instability in much more depth, but ultimately he argues that postmodernism relies on the acceptance of a "normal" subject in order to separate nonnormative identities—which vary from the norm in a number of ways—and to encourage "making all identities equal" in comparison to that norm (240). Davis, however, challenges that "normal" identity, revealing that "*all* humans are seen as wounded" (241).

The idea of linking all identities, especially by acknowledging unavoidable wounds, uses "disability" metaphorically to emphasize the ways in which societal norms "disable" anyone who does not fit. However, if *everyone* is disabled, then *no one* is disabled, and the disabled community loses its power; disabled activists, as of 2019, are still fighting for visibility, acceptance, and civil rights, goals that require a distinguishing label. Consequently, while young adult disability narratives are pushing political movements further in destabilizing categories, they must *use* traditional tropes of disability in order to challenge them. The novels in "Chapter Two: Wallflowers" redefine both disability and adolescence as inseparable identities, and they claim respect and narrative spaces for both. "Chapter Three: Fruits," "Chapter Four: Freaks," and "Chapter Five: Accidents" demonstrate how young adult disability narratives expose common literary tropes of using disability: as a metaphor for abstract problems, to create a simple secondary character to help others grow, and to create lessons for adolescent readers to learn. Young adult narratives in these chapters *use* those tropes of disability, as well as representations of adolescence, to disrupt and destabilize them: metaphor, especially with fantastical elements, can force readers to question the meaning of character traits; with experimental narrative techniques disabled characters, expected to elicit pity, can force readers to find the complex nature of all (wounded) humans and their relationships; proud, political, disabled identities demand recognition of the humanity of disabled characters and the variety of stories they tell. Narratives in "Chapter Six: Bulletproof Families," of course, use all of these assumptions about disability and adolescence to further destabilize literary representations, political roles and movements, notions of authors and audiences, and even identities themselves.

Readings of young adult disability narratives point to the power that already exists, with unimaginable potential. Without question, when inseparably linked to disability and adolescence, these narratives demonstrate both *how* certain representations are harmful and *how* young adult literary texts force new understandings; they demonstrate *how* these literary elements work to push social movements further, and *how* the alternate messages affect social norms; and they demonstrate the overwhelming power of instability, chaos, and confusion. Maybe disability, when conflated with adolescence, really is the identity that links other identities.

Most simply, young adult disability narratives suggest collaboration, honest communication, and solidarity in expression and action. As Stuart Murdoch suggests, "Humanitiy is a broad spectrum: some people struggle sometimes or some people are just a bit different," and that maybe "the state of adolescence . . . is a [necessary] form of madness" all its own (Murdoch, Video Interview). Perhaps a willingness to approach identity categories differently in recognition of their power is the lasting message. Perhaps the quiet solidarity built by the #AccessIsLove project—in donating all proceeds to a center "solely dedicated to Transgender and Gender Noncomforming people in the

US"—is the lasting message (*Disability Visibility Project*). Regardless, with messages like these, narratives thematically focused on both disability and adolescence, especially when inseparably linked, offer the power needed to radicalize literature and to unite people through love and solidarity.

NOTES

CHAPTER ONE

1. To label medical procedures and innovations "genocidal" may seem overly dramatic, but theorists such as Robert McRuer and Harriet McBryde Johnson address the problematic nature of cures with passion and bluntness. McRuer reveals how even seemingly innocent questions simply reiterate and affirm ableist perspectives and suggest that eliminating otherness is preferable:

> I can imagine that answers [to the question: "In the end, aren't you disappointed to have a retarded child?"] might be incredibly varied to similar questions—"In the end, wouldn't you rather be hearing?" and "In the end, wouldn't you rather not be HIV positive?" would seem, after all, to be very different questions, the first (with its thinly veiled desire for Deafness not to exist) more obviously genocidal than the second. But they are not really different questions, in that their constant repetition (or their presence as ongoing subtexts) reveals more about the able-bodied culture doing the asking than about the bodies being interrogated. The culture asking such questions assumes in advance that we all agree: able-bodied identities, able-bodied perspectives are preferable and what we all, collectively, are aiming for. A system of compulsory able-bodiedness repeatedly demands that people with disabilities embody for others an affirmative answer to the unspoken question, Yes, but in the end, wouldn't you rather be more like me? (92–93)

With the same force, Johnson, who lived with muscular dystrophy, finds similar ableist assumptions in arguments for selection abortion and infanticide, procedures that would "have given my parents the option of killing the baby I once was, and to let other parents kill similar babies as they come along, and thereby avoid the suffering that comes with lives like mine and satisfy the reasonable preferences of parents for a different kind of child" (Johnson, "Unspeakable"

201). However, Johnson argues that the assumption of suffering is unwarranted, that "disability shapes all we are" and that we "take constraints that no one would choose and build rich and satisfying lives within them" (208).

CHAPTER TWO

1. Using mental illness to speak as adolescence, challenging scholarly discussions surrounding the beginning of young adult literature, and returning focus to two specific narratives that were not aimed at teenagers, this project challenges other scholarship. Roberta Seelinger Trites and Kenneth Kidd offer extensive histories of the literary form, but their histories define young adult literature in terms of other genres and theories, rather than allowing young adult literature to stand as its own phenomenon. Trites's focus of study in *Twain, Alcott, and the Birth of the Adolescent Reform Novel* is the notion of rebellion and the use of "adolescents as metaphors for reform" (Trites, *Twain* xiv); Kidd's focus in *Freud in Oz: At the Intersections of Psychoanalysis and Children's Literature* is the notion that out of turn-of-the-century theories of psychology and adolescence was born the American literary genre of young adult literature. While Kidd acknowledges *The Catcher in the Rye* as an important contribution, he chooses to mark Maureen Daly's *Seventeenth Summer* (1942) and Carson McCullers's *The Member of the Wedding* (1946) as "legitimate beginning point[s] for adolescent literature" (Kidd 159). Kidd's definitions of the genre rely on subjects tackled by authors, such as identity and sexuality, but most often, young adult narrators also include something else: a specific, urgent, intelligent, anxious first-person narrative. While *The Member of the Wedding* quite simply reads differently because of third-person narration, *Seventeenth Summer* possesses intimate first-person narration, but without urgency. As narrator Angie recounts her summer romance with the flair of someone telling an old story for entertainment and for remembering: "We walked out to the lake, he and I. It was about half-past seven in the evening and the summer sky was still brushed red with the sun" (Daly 12). Kidd even notes that the narrators of both novels are ultimately "not traumatized by [their] experiences" (Kidd 163). Such a keen observation, however, gives weight to marking young adult literature's beginning a bit later, with *The Catcher in the Rye* (1951) and *The Bell Jar* (1963)—archetypal young adult literary novels *do* feature traumatic events and signs of mental illness.

Much has been written about trauma in children's and young adult literature. As Kidd notes, young readers are able and forced to "witness trauma," especially through first-person narratives and often about cultural traumas such as the Holocaust and American slavery (191). Personal trauma frequently triggers mental illness, including post-traumatic stress disorder, anxiety, and depression, a reminder that mental illness can be influenced by experience. In all but *Nick and Norah's Infinite Playlist*, the novels considered in this chapter contain trauma: a younger brother's death in *The Catcher in the Rye*; a father's death; incorrectly performed electroconvulsive therapy, and sexual assaults in *The Bell Jar*; a friend's death, an aunt's death, and memories of sexual abuse in *The Perks of Being a Wallflower*; and a father's death in *King Dork*. While Nick and Norah are not traumatized, they use the language of despair and anxiety in the same way the other narrators do: narrative voices in young adult literature show signs of mental illness, even when not explicitly shown or when absent altogether. The voice of literary adolescence has been shaped by two narrators, Holden and Esther, who experienced traumas and lived with mental illness, and that voice has remained constant.

2. Readers may question the absences of John Knowles's *A Separate Peace* (1959). While frequently lumped together with *The Catcher in the Rye* and *The Bell Jar*, *A Separate Peace* is narratively different: narrator Gene emphasizes quite heavily that he is an *adult* remembering his story, a quirk that necessarily removes urgency and immediacy from the text. The opening line of the novel, for instance, is the narrator's memory: "I went back to the Devon School not long ago, and found it looking oddly newer than when I was a student there fifteen years before" (Knowles 9). Holden, on the other hand, tells his story as a seventeen-year-old narrator just after the events in his tale, and while Esther subtly notes in just one place in her text that she is an adult looking back at her late adolescent years—telling her reader, "I still have them [free fashion gifts] around the house. I use the lipsticks now and then, and last week I cut the plastic starfish off the sunglasses case for the baby to play with"—the reader has no choice but to return to the immediately presented details of adolescence (Plath 3). Furthermore, *A Separate Peace* is the story of adult nostalgia, centered around the mystery of a memory couched in a specific wartime setting and refusing to dwell on the nature of adolescence.

While earlier novels such as Alcott's *Little Women* (1868) and Twain's *The Adventures of Huckleberry Finn* (1885) are sometimes understood as precursors to young adult literature or as early members of a larger group of adolescent literature, the former is made up of didactic tales aimed at young readers, while the latter is understood as a political comment on tensions in the United States rather than a study of adolescence. Similarly, *Seventeenth Summer* (1942), though written with rather urgent first-person narration, as noted by Kidd and Trites, lacks the fraught and distinctively adolescent themes that define young adult literature; Daly's novel must be considered an early romance novel, regardless of the characters' ages.

3. For the sake of this discussion, mental illness may be defined largely by the American Psychiatric Association's *Diagnostic and Statistical Manual of Mental Disorders, Fifth Edition* (2013): "A mental disorder is a syndrome characterized

by clinically significant disturbance in an individual's cognition, emotion regulation, or behavior that reflects a dysfunction in the psychological, biological, or developmental processes underlying mental functioning" (20). The mental illnesses relevant to these adolescent narrators are generally forms of depressive disorders, and the American Psychiatric Association even notes that bipolar, depressive, and anxiety disorders all "commonly manifest in adolescence and young adulthood" (13).

4. While Holden cannot stay put—having "left schools and places" so frequently by age sixteen because "if it's a sad good-by or a bad good-by," he likes to know he's leaving—he spends the duration of the novel attempting to connect both sexually and emotionally with old flames Jane Gallagher and Sally Hayes, a prostitute called Sunny, and his younger sister Phoebe, who as a child is "someone with sense and all" (Salinger 4, 66). At the same time, Holden repeatedly alienates himself from those closest to him. Esther, quite similarly, has isolated herself with intimidating intellect and unusual choices; she interacts with others on a superficial level, and she both contemplates and attempts suicide. Perhaps more severely depressed and more reluctant to seek connections than the other narrators, Esther obsesses over sexuality as a kind of connection, attempts to have romantic relationships with men, and even reluctantly hints that she envies the desire for "tenderness" that women may find in another woman (Plath 219).

5. The initial premise of *King Dork*, with a cover featuring *The Catcher in the Rye* with the title scratched out and replaced by its own, is of a narrator who despises *Catcher* but at the same time needs it to solve mysteries of his family's past. Tom even considers himself quite "Holden-y," a trait he describes as "troubled and intense, yet with a certain quiet dignity," which makes living among "the psychopathic normal people" quite difficult (13). Consequently, Tom puts himself in a rather impossible situation: he hates *Catcher* but sets himself up to be the Holden of his own story, and he hates "High School Hell," especially Advanced Placement classes, which are the only places safe for "Holden-y" kids (10, 13). He insults the teachers who love *Catcher* but admits early in the novel that he's able to open his "backpack and [pull] out [his] *Catcher*" on command, and he eventually declares that *Catcher* is "not even that bad of a book," though only with one sentence about his ability to empathize—finally—with Holden (33, 322).

6. Famously, of course, Holden's strongest emotions surface when talking with his sister Phoebe, especially near the end of the novel, when he sneaks into his parents' home to see her. Acutely aware of her actions and reactions, Holden observes with amusement, "Boy, was she wide-awake. She gets very excited when she tells you that stuff [about school activities]" (Salinger 162). He delights in her mannerisms and enthusiasms; "Then she hit me on the leg with her fist. She gets very feisty when she feels like it," he describes. "Then she flopped on her

stomach on the bed and put the goddam pillow over her head. She does that quite frequently. She's a true madman sometimes" (165). Phoebe, of course, shows affectionate dismay over her brother's faltering, and Holden accepts her worry with the same affection and respect: "'I suppose you failed in every single subject again,' she said—very snotty. It was sort of funny, too, in a way. She sounds like a goddam school teacher sometimes, and she's only a little child" (167). A little child she may be, but when Phoebe listens, asks questions that probe for truth, and attempts to comfort him with a hug, Holden creates distance and leaves, worried that he "scared the hell out of poor old Phoebe" (179).

Holden trusts and loves his sister as she is, but he also seeks to *protect* her from the upcoming emotions of adolescence. Always self-aware, he even attempts to describe his protective impulses to Phoebe with the novel's central metaphor; if he could be anything, if he "had [his] goddam choice," he would save the "little kids playing some game in this big field of rye" from falling off a cliff (173). Holden's famous desire to save children from falling into adulthood, inspired by misremembered lines from a Robert Burns poem, may actually build on both his capability for feeling intense emotions as an adolescent and his desire and reluctance for connection—all exemplified in his relationship with Phoebe.

7. While her diagnoses are never given, Esther—much like Holden—shows symptoms common in major depressive episodes and manic or hypomanic episodes. "I hadn't slept for twenty-one nights," she claims, and she also describes an inability to think and write clearly: "my hand made big, jerky letters like those of a child, and the lines sloped down the page from left to right almost diagonally, as if they were loops of string lying on the paper, and someone had come along and blown them askew" (147, 130). Unable to write a letter, Esther may demonstrate "disorganized thinking" or "grossly disorganized or abnormal motor behavior," both symptoms of psychosis (American Psychiatric Association 87). She identifies herself as "incurable" and believes her "symptoms tallied with the most hopeless cases" (Plath 159).

8. Both "depressed mood" and "recurrent suicidal ideation" are classic symptoms of major depressive episodes, single or recurrent; major depressive disorder; and bipolar disorders (American Psychiatric Association 125). Holden also shows signs of mania or psychosis, when he does not feel tired, stays awake until witnessing "daylight outside," and doesn't "sleep too long" (Salinger 98, 105). Real hours of sleep are tough to locate in the novel, as Holden does not go to sleep until after daylight and rarely sleeps later than nine or ten o'clock (105, 194). Such a lack of rest, combined with his inability to "concentrate too hot" and his being told that he "jump[s] from one" thing to another, suggest the "decreased need for sleep" and "flight of ideas or subjective experience that thoughts are racing" that mark both manic and hypomanic episodes (Salinger 169, 131; American Psychiatric Association 124). Holden describes himself as "crazy" and "a madman,"

and while these self-identifying labels cannot be trusted as medical diagnoses, he also sees hallucinations, which "are vivid and clear, with the full force and impact of normal perceptions, and not under voluntary control" (Salinger 125, 134; American Psychiatric Association 87):

> Anyway, I kept walking and walking up Fifth Avenue, without any tie on or anything. Then all of a sudden, something very spooky started happening. Every time I came to the end of a block and stepped off the goddam curb, I had this feeling that I'd never get to the other side of the street. I thought I'd just go down, down, down, and nobody'd ever see me again. Boy, did it scare me. You can't imagine. I started sweating like a bastard—my whole shirt and underwear and everything. Then I started doing something else. Every time I'd get to the end of a block I'd make believe I was talking to my brother Allie. (Salinger 197–98)

Of course, these hallucinations—or even delusions—may also be a product of Holden's lack of sleep and intensely emotional few days.

CHAPTER THREE

1. *The Secret Fruit of Peter Paddington* (2005) was originally published as *Fruit* (2004), with more explicit clues that it takes place in Canada; the renamed paperback removed these Canadian references.

2. In many ways, fatness functions in *The Secret Fruit* as a political identity, discussed in "Chapter Five: Accidents." The fat acceptance movement, part of disability rights movements, questions the representations of fatness in literature, as well as the assumptions made about those with nonnormative bodies (Murray 153–56). Focusing on the social effects of disability, Susanne Gervay emphasizes "the influence of social attitudes on disabled persons [*sic*] capacity for independence, social integration, equality and pride in their uniqueness" (Gervay). This approach is crucial to fat activists such as April Herndon because the accepted use of medical frameworks resists "seeing fatness as a disability and fat people as a politicized group" (Herndon 123). Herndon attributes mainstream viewpoints to fatphobia, expressed in "familiar narratives of fatness as a voluntary condition resulting from poor eating habits and sedentary lifestyle and of disabled people as dangerous to the American purse because accommodation must be suffered by the public writ large" (124). Not only does Herndon dismiss medical constructions of fatness (that categorize fat people as "ill," regardless of their lifestyles, and that offer faulty treatments to the condition) as "fueled more by the drive toward normative bodies than by solid medical evidence," she considers the social stigma

that arises from these medical constructions as being even more disabling than the fat body itself (126). In *The Secret Fruit*, Peter and his family members are confronted by social stigmas attached to fatness and to medical models of fatness as a problem to correct. Peter serves as a representative of fat adolescents, and his desire to change himself to "[become] thin and normal" provide insight into the effects of social and medical fears of fatness (Francis 1). The pressures Peter feels to change his body come from his sisters, who deride his habits, and from his doctor, who tells his parents, "If you don't change his eating habits, I guarantee you there [will] be health problems in the future" (98). With a list of "all the things [he] need[s] to change" about himself that includes losing weight (listed twice), Peter is forced to suffer under unrealistic expectations put upon him (100).

CHAPTER FOUR

1. Certainly, Hamilton's use of porphyria in *Sweet Whispers, Brother Rush* must be considered in connection to the novels discussed in "Chapter Three: Fruits"; if nothing else, the continued presence of porphyria in an African American family, traced back to the American slave trade, is a metaphorical paralleling of actual illness with societal ills. However, the most dominant literary function of disability in this complex novel remains the use of Dab as a freak to inspire growth and teach lessons.

2. To Jack and other students, suicide is seen as preferable to physical disability or deformity, which is what hurts Auggie so badly; certainly, the text didactically suggests, *nothing* could or should be worse than suicide. The implied suggestion that *nothing* is as bad as suicide loosely suggests that *nothing* is as bad as (a common symptom of) severe mental illness. Small suggestions about other disabilities in texts such as *Wonder* alienate members of the heterogeneous disabled community.

3. While critic Elizabeth A. Wheeler argues that *Wonder* has made monumental strides in disability rights, "stag[ing] a revolution in the portrayal of kids with disabilities," it simply hasn't; Wheeler argues, "*Wonder* shows how the public presence of people with disabilities benefits a whole society," but she fails to acknowledge that using freaks—like other nonnormative characters—unfairly posits responsibility on those characters to teach and benefit their communities (Wheeler 335). Wheeler's effusive praise of *Wonder* perhaps prevents asking how those *with* disabilities could benefit from what she considers "a larger revolution in US middle grade chapter books" (336). *Wonder*, she argues, creates a "vision of a community transforming itself" but at the expense of its disabled hero, used as a spectacle for the community's transformation (338). Wheeler suggests that the novel functions as a "fairy tale of inclusion, to show the benefits for *everyone*

when a child with a disability enters a previously segregated school for the first time" (338; emphasis added). Jack, like the other nondisabled characters, "realizes that a life with a disability is well worth living, even if the disability has profound repercussions," because "August's community gets both bigger and better" when nondisabled peers accept him (347, 349). *Wonder*, above all else, is still the story of a freak who teaches others about acceptance, inclusion, and kindness. The message that disabled life is "worth living" is hardly revolutionary.

4. Notably, Ben's character is not overshadowed by disability like the other underdeveloped freak characters. *Stoner & Spaz* uses the wallflower narration, and that Ben's symptoms of depression are not addressed while Colleen's *are* illustrates again that depressive qualities are standard in young adult narrators.

CHAPTER FIVE

1. Charlie's own political views grow apparent in a letter he writes to Joey after learning about Ruth's reservations:

> My mother was born deaf and never heard a single word, she never spoke, though oddly she had a wonderful laugh that I still miss. When she was young, the traditional thinking was to make the deaf learn to speak, but luckily, her parents quickly gave up that notion. They wanted to be able to communicate with her themselves so they sent her to a school that taught American Sign Language and they learned it, too.
>
> My father was a baby, just learning to talk, when he lost his hearing. His parents were caught up in the same debate, but they chose the other path. It was a terrible handicap. Because it took so long to teach him to approximate the sound of each word, the rest of his education had to wait. What little speech he learned, no one could understand. The frustration finally drove him to quit school in the eighth grade and take the only job he could find—a janitor. The good news is that the job was at a school for the deaf. That's where he met my mother and where he learned to sign. Eventually, he found his life's work as a printing press operator (the perfect fit for him; presses make a "deafening" racket). He made a good living and they were happy. We were happy.
>
> Don't get me wrong. Both arguments have valid points. But if I had to decide for a child of mine, I would choose sign language. If we hadn't all signed, I would not have been able to talk to my own parents. (83–84)

With only a bit of knowledge of Charlie's way of embracing deafness and of ASL, Joey quickly decides that, "in spite of her mother, she was going to learn to sign. She felt as if her world had doubled in size" simply by meeting Charlie and Sukari (35). For Charlie and the characters in *Hurt Go Happy*, deafness is accepted as a disability while also regarded proudly—with a distinctive push to "choose sign language" (Rorby 84). Rorby's uses of language and capitalization let the novel advocate pride in a political identity without engaging in the more separatist notion that, within the Deaf community, "deafness is not a disability," because disability is simply a social construction (Lane 84). *Hurt Go Happy* follows adolescent Joey's somewhat naïve wish to "do both" signing and speaking—remaining a part of both worlds (Rorby 106).

2. Rorby's protagonist does not occupy a stereotypically problem-novel-like role, in which her disability would be represented much more simply in order to facilitate learning. Joey specifically lost her hearing from being physically abused. Ruth's story on its own, however, warrants attention because her history has affected Joey so strongly while also depicting commonly felt guilt among parents of disabled children. Yet Ruth presents another important lesson about surviving abuse to Joey and to the reader. Portrayed critically—which helps to reaffirm Charlie's pro-ASL sentiments—Ruth is not a simple villain or misunderstanding parent. Even when Joey feels frustrated, angry, and isolated, she still catches glimpses of her mother's love and compassion; while Sukari and Joey play, for example, Ruth "stopped to watch. In the instant before she went inside and closed the door, Joey thought she saw her smile" (90). Without a doubt, Ruth loves and is aggressively protective of her daughter, partly as a response to physical abuse from the man she thought she loved. Before the novel's present, she and Joey "had lived in their car, eaten one meal a day of handouts from local restaurants and depended, for their safety, on the community of other homeless people" (14–15). Ruth's job, which "had seemed like a miracle then," as a waitress at the Old Dock Café, is how she met Ray, a husband and stepfather with whom Joey has always "felt an odd kinship" and "really liked" (15, 34).

Rorby's narration—while sometimes pitying Ruth as a martyr who cries when "an old song" reminds her "of all the things she wanted to do with . . . [her] life"—eventually allows Ruth to grow and to reveal herself as a strong survivor (155, 116). When she and Joey lived in their car, Ruth "had tried to make their homelessness an adventure," protecting her daughter from pain by taking time to explore beaches and take trips (51). Ruth ultimately learns to support and respect Joey, as much as she does herself. For example, at their neighbors' annual potluck, when musicians play after dinner, Ruth initially "shake[s] her head" and stops Joey from "drumm[ing] randomly on her thighs," but after some reflection and thought, Ruth "tap[s Joey's] shoulder," smiles, and encourages Joey's clapping until her daughter's "hands . . . smacked in time with her mother's" (154, 156). With good intentions, Ruth eventually writes to Joey—once she has left for the California School for the Deaf—that she "wallowed in self-pity," and continues,

"I've spent the last seven years of your life unable to face the fact of your deafness by ignoring your drive to learn to sign. I believed all along that I was making the right decisions for you, just like I'd believed it was the right choice to marry your father" (163). In the latter half of the novel, Rorby also reveals through Joey's flashbacks the extent of the abuse that she and Ruth survived:

> "Run," her mother screamed, blood streaming from where the kitchen stool had split her eyebrow in half. She saw her father turn his fiery red eyes on her. "Run, Joey. Run," her mother screamed again. She did, out the trailer door, past her father's car with the door still open, the key's in the ignition, dinging. She crouched behind the car. He stood on the top step looking for her. When she peeked over the trunk, he saw her. "I'm going to fix you this time," he roared. Her mother had his ankle. When he turned to kick her off, Joey ran for the woodshed, scrunched into a dark corner, and watched the shadow coming for her, swelling to blot out the light, then the stool leg coming down. . . .
>
> Joey felt as if she were shrinking, like in the old movie where a man shriveled until he was forced to fight a spider with a straight pin. She pulled her head down between her shoulders and closed her eyes. Her mother, her forehead split and bleeding, her arm up to protect herself from another blow, kicked out at the legs standing over her. Joey wanted to bite one again, to feel the lump of flesh between her teeth, and hear her father howl, but she couldn't move. Instead, she waited for the smell of cut, dry firewood, and the darkness that always ended this nightmare. (194–95)

Near the novel's conclusion, Joey realizes and explains to her mother that she is "afraid of most men," so together, they confront the lingering effects of the abuse (202). After being followed by a "dirty, smelly man" in San Francisco, Joey tells her mother that, once she was finally able to calm her "terror" and to see the man clearly as "little and kind of shriveled," she was able to "quit running" (202, 203). Through her hurt—beyond "the stark white scar that split . . . [Ruth's] left eyebrow into two halves"—and her learned habit of "giv[ing] in rather than fight[ing]," Ruth recognizes the strength of her now-sixteen-year-old daughter: "I wish I knew what that felt like [to quit running]," Ruth tells her (203). Having accepted that seeing Joey "signing would [always] remind her" of a painful past, Ruth is able to stop feeling so much shame over those family "secrets" and to admit that "Charlie was right" (121, 93, 157). By connecting Ruth's healing to her philosophical change regarding deafness, the text suggests again that deafness is a fact to accept it and celebrate. Without explicitly acknowledging Deaf culture, *Hurt Go Happy* reinforces Charlie's lesson: "Deafness [like other disabilities] *is* different, dammit. And for Joey it is normal not to hear. . . . She is what she is. Let her be deaf [and proud]" (117; emphasis in original).

3. Charlie's passionate argument that, by "trying to pound her deaf ears into hearing holes," Ruth is forcing her daughter to hide her identity (Rorby 117), echoes one of Sara's strongest statements in *Accidents of Nature*:

> The cripple is a square peg [in an advertisement for Goodwill]. Then rehab rounds off his corners and he's a happy face. But in the real world, our corners are permanent and incurable. If we could get over false consciousness, we might start changing the shape of the holes. (Johnson 111)

Like pegs desperately being pounded into differently shaped holes, Sara explains, "We come to accept the views of our oppressors [until we] think there's something wrong with ourselves" (Johnson 111). Both *Accidents of Nature* and *Hurt Go Happy*, like *Inside Out*, directly explain that disabled people must not be expected to change, and instead *society* should change to accommodate them.

4. Both *Hurt Go Happy* and *Inside Out* demonstrate strategies that unquestionably define the texts as *literary* fiction. In *Hurt Go Happy*, Rorby uses Joey's deafness as a means to provide artfully detailed descriptions, underscoring the "gift" Joey finds in deafness that lets her "[watch] the music" of the natural world around her (Rorby 13, 12):

> Just outside the front door, Joey slipped into Ray's rubber boots, then headed across the yard and down the hill to the creek. A chain girdled the bent trunk of an old tan oak tree. In summer, a rope chair-swing hung there. This was a favorite spot of Joey's. She would sit for hours and watch the birds flitting through the woods and listen with her eyes to the little waterfall. If she took a book, she could completely lose herself in its pages, then look at the waterfall and the leaves trembling in a breeze and fill her sight with sound. She loved that about being deaf; Smiley had been right, that was its gift.
>
> Joey stopped beneath the tan oak to watch the silty, butterscotch-pudding-colored water tumble over the rocks as if it were on the boil. The creek was still high from the storm, too swollen to cross. She walked the high bank instead, scanning the thick brush for chanterelles, her personal favorite [mushrooms]. (17)

Joey's connection with the natural world not only offers the author a chance to play with phrasing and imagery—with "silence [that] gave her the creeps, especially in the dim light with anger in the air" and with "sunlight [that] played with the wind-stirred shadows on the deck, rolling and flickering"—it offers Joey safe places and "favorite spot[s]," where she is able to feel secure and able "just . . . to be alone" (56, 177, 97, 55).

Along with artful descriptions that amplify Joey's emotions, *Hurt Go Happy* uses distinct metaphors—unlike sustained metaphors that often result in problematic interpretations—in order to enhance the stories and themes. When Joey describes her mother turning away "so Joey couldn't see what she said . . . [feeling] as if a lid had been clamped down on the jar she lived in, and twisted shut, airtight" (95), she is referring to a childhood experience that represents a fear of isolation. When Joey sees hermit crabs collected in a jar, "circling and circling, their tiny pincers feeling for a way out," leaving her "scream[ing] and kick[ing], pleading for the crabs" because "they can't hear in there," Joey uses the crabs as a metaphor for herself (52). Subtly achieved by the narration, Joey's signing is repeatedly portrayed as silently musical, as she "learn[s] to sing with her hands," "listens with her eyes" to the "birds singing," and is connected to "grin[s]," "twirl[ing]," and warm with happiness (164, 11, 64, 61). The enormous importance of first meeting Charlie and Sukari is warmly described as Joey feeling "as if her insides were roasting" (25). Almost always in relation to the natural world, metaphors strengthen Joey's and Ruth's fears and convictions about protection and loyalty. During the summer of Joey's ASL class, her stepfather rescues "two newly hatched, nearly dead Canada geese"; while one dies quickly, the other grows close to both households, and "where Sukari went, the goose named Gilbert followed" (125, 126). Wrapped together, snuggling, playing, and tickling, Sukari and Gilbert live almost as humans, and as Sukari grows attached to "BIRD," Ruth simultaneously grows "attached to Sukari" (128, 130). Sukari mourns Gilbert's eventual release to a twenty-acre pond with "five other tame Canada geese," and Ruth eventually wonders "*why [she]* had *decided to let . . . [Joey] go*," feeling both love and loss (128, 163). Joey, too, falls apart with feelings of loss on her first evening alone at school when she stumbles upon a "lawn [that] was full of Canada geese, hundreds of them. . . . The sight of them was almost more than she could bear," remembering Gilbert, Sukari, and her human friends and family (162). Images of geese reappear again when Joey spends her afternoons on that lawn, worrying about Sukari's increasingly unstable situation and location, while sitting in "the same swing each time" and "let[ting] her own weight drag her backward over and over until she had created trenches in the sand with her heels" (180).

With emotional and often metaphorical descriptions, *Hurt Go Happy* takes advantage of language—even sign language—in its paratexts: each chapter is marked with a drawing of hands signing the chapter number. Similarly, *Inside Out* takes advantage of language and paratextual material by including the easily recognizable words of Zach's aggressive, violent voices—called Dirtbag and

Rat—in the bottom margins of many pages; these unpredictable appearances of words and phrases, such as "Yes, yes, yes . . . end it all!! Long gone . . . ," "Squish-wish," "gong is a wong," " . . . long gone . . . long," "wing-wong," and " . . . end it all," allow the reader to experience visually the chaos of Zach's voices, some of which make sense and some of which do not (Trueman 1, 13, 19, 27, 107, 117). Trueman uses several voices in creating a rich narrative: Zach's first-person narration provides the principal text, and an untitled prologue written in third-person narration ends with Zach responding to the voices' commands to "DIE!" by "cock[ing] the weapon and lift[ing] it up, taking the muzzle into his mouth"—either foreshadowing the novel's end or providing further information about Zach's first encounter with "suicidal impulses" (1, 92).

In another play with language and paratextual elements, Trueman begins short chapters, save the first and last, with notes presented in different typefaces to differentiate between Dr. Curtis's notes, transcripts of sessions, and letters. With more complexity than is generally expected of problem novels, the notes and letters reveal a backstory that provides a more complete picture of schizophrenia, in general, and a story that is Zach's alone; Zach's prognosis "is not good" because "schizophrenia is incurable," and after these notes and letters have shown that Zach cannot be left alone without risking behavior such as putting "the barrel of . . . [a] rifle in his mouth," a note from Dr. Curtis explains that this character "shows a severe psychosis" and will become extraordinarily dangerous when "stress and/or interruptions to his regular medication regimen occur" (99, 83, 92). While these notes may quite literally place the novel's "problem" of schizophrenia before the narrative, they also increase the stakes of Zach's story. Once aware that Zach has been and could become "extraordinarily dangerous" in situations like the one in which he's trapped, the reader must realize the possibility of several endings (92). These excerpts of writing by Dr. Curtis and Zach's mother, as well as the newspaper article that concludes the novel, allow other characters to speak in their own voices, and they help the narrative function as a longer story of Zach's history with schizophrenia, told nonchronologically.

5. Perhaps even more central to *Hurt Go Happy* is the message that animals must not be abused. Charlie's and Joey's loving relationships with Sukari, a chimp who "has learned, better than some people, what it is to be human," along with Joey's experiences at a research laboratory make the forceful "Afterword"—in which Rorby urges her reader to engage in efforts to protect chimps (261)—completely unsurprising (190, 261). Indeed, the reader has already experienced, through Joey, the melodrama of walking through a research lab, through "the stench of fear" and into a room filled with bare cages, each holding a chimpanzee, some of whom run "to the bars and [hold] out their hands with pleading looks," while accompanied by a smiling and emotionless care-tech (221, 223):

> Joey felt as if she'd lost all sensation; a numbness moved from her head to her feet and she thought she might faint. She bit down as hard as she could stand on her bottom lip, so that she'd have a physical pain to focus on. She moved forward, concentrating on one foot, then the other. When the tech stopped again, Joey stared straight ahead. . . .
>
> Joey's knees were weak and offered no resistance as she sank to the floor. The chimp sat in the corner, staring blankly and rocking. (224)

At first unable to respond, Sukari finally recognizes Joey and signs, "HELP ME, PLEASE" (223). As the humanized, emotional, and pitiful chimp "walk[s] across the barred cage floor . . . [and comes] out unsteadily on all fours," the reader cannot help but hope, as Joey does, that Sukari can "forgive being deserted" by her loved ones and that research labs like this one in which Sukari suffered will be closed (226, 229, 234).

6. Harriet McBryde Johnson, who lived with muscular dystrophy and went "to a cross-disability summer camp until age seventeen," and then continued her education through law school to fight for civil rights, was a well-known activist for disability rights until her death in 2008 (233). As of the novel's publication, Johnson held "the world endurance record (fifteen years without interruption) for protesting the Jerry Lewis telethon for the Muscular Dystrophy Association" (233). Johnson also published a collection of essays, *Too Late to Die Young: Nearly True Tales from a Life* (2005), that explore both her own autobiography and her critical, theoretical readings of disability in Western society.

CHAPTER SIX

1. While Belle and Sebastian are both characters in Stuart Murdoch's imaginary world, they also name the band. Explained in the liner notes of *The Boy with the Arab Strap* (1998), "Belle et Sébastien is the title of a novel and a filmed series by Mme Cécile Aubry; the artists would like to thank Mme Cécile Aubry for having given them permission to take on this name." The band's name, "Belle and Sebastian," is sometimes stylized as "Belle & Sebastian," but in this project, I use the original "and," rather than the ampersand.

2. Stuart Murdoch's public statement of his disabled identity in the 2010s maybe allows those mid-1990s songs to retrospectively gain the authorial authenticity expected by the #OwnVoices movement. But in those songs—filled with narrators and protagonists symptomatic of illnesses that keep them isolated, separated from others—Murdoch offers no diagnoses. If a character *seems* to have a mental illness or chronic illness, and if the author identifies as having a specific chronic illness, does that allow the text to be a part of #OwnVoices?

The transparency possible through digital media does reinforce the barriers of traditional media *as well as* the failure of #OwnVoices to evaluate most literary texts—regardless of publication date or media. Not all authors disclose their experiences and identities, and not all authors are able or willing to do so. Again, criticism made on digital media cannot remain separate from narratives themselves or from literary scholarship; narratives produced in the digitally dominated 2000s and 2010s are inherently different from the traditional-media narratives of the twentieth century.

BIBLIOGRAPHY

"About the Author." *Accidents of Nature*. New York: Henry Holt and Co., 2006. 233.

Alexie, Sherman. *The Absolutely True Diary of a Part-Time Indian*. Ill. Ellen Forney. New York: Little, Brown, and Co., 2007.

Allen, Marjorie N. *What Are Little Girls Made Of? A Guide to Female Role Models in Children's Books*. New York: Facts on File, Inc., 1999.

Alston, Joshua. "*Speechless* Is a Delightful Addition to ABC's Stable of Family Sitcoms." *AV/TV CLUB*, 21 Sep. 2016, tv.avclub.com/speechless-is-a-delightful-addition-to-abc-s-stable-of-1798188829.

American Psychiatric Association. *Diagnostic and Statistical Manual of Mental Disorders, Fifth Edition*. Arlington, VA: American Psychiatric Association, 2013.

Anderson, M. T. *Feed*. Cambridge, MA: Candlewick Press, 2004.

@AOC (Alexandria Ocasio-Cortez), et al. "I see . . . " *Twitter*, 27 Mar. 2019, twitter.com/AOC/status/1111064929195487232

Barbarin, Imani. "Disabled People Have an Ally Problem: They Need to Stop Talking for Us." Crutches & Spice, 15 May 2018, https://crutchesandspice.com/2018/05/15/disabled-people-have-an-ally-problem-they-need-to-stop-talking-for-us/

Bigdely, Mahdi, et al. "Effective Digital Technologies and New Media on Increasing the Size of the Sports Audience." *2011 International Conference on Environmental, Biomedical and Biotechnology*. IPCBEE vol. 16 (2011): 121–27.

Bloor, Edward. *Tangerine*. Orlando, FL: Harcourt, 1997.

Bradshaw, Peter. "Wonder Review—Manipulative Feelgood Drama Comes with Hefty Dollop of Treacle." *The Guardian*, 12 Nov. 2017, www.theguardian.com/film/2017/nov/12/wonder-review-owen-wilson-julia-roberts

Broverman, Aaron. "Micah Fowler of New Sitcom Speechless Speaks." *New Mobility: Life Beyond Wheels*, 1 Sep. 2016, www.newmobility.com/2016/09/micah-fowler-speechless/.

Cadden, Mike. "The Irony of Narration in the Young Adult Novel." *Children's Literature Association Quarterly* 25.3 (Fall 2000): 146–54.

Carey, Allison C. *On the Margins of Citizenship: Intellectual Disability and Civil Rights in Twentieth-Century America*. Philadelphia: Temple University Press, 2009.

"CPF JOINS SPEECHLESS!" *Cerebral Palsy Foundation*, 2016. www.yourcpf.org/press-releases/cpf-joins-speechless/.

Charlton, James I. *Nothing About Us Without Us: Disability Oppression and Empowerment.* Berkeley: University of California Press, 2000.

Chbosky, Stephen. *The Perks of Being a Wallflower*. New York: MTV Books/Pocket Books, 1999.

Coats, Karen. *Looking Glasses and Neverlands: Lacan, Desire, and Subjectivity in Children's Literature*. Iowa City: University of Iowa Press, 2004.

Cohn, Rachel, and David Levithan. *Nick and Norah's Infinite Playlist*. New York: Knopf, 2006.

Cox, Peta. "Passing as Sane, or How to Get People to Sit Next to You on the Bus." *Disability and Passing: Blurring the Lines of Identity*. Edited by Jeffrey A. Brune and Daniel J. Wilson. Philadelphia: Temple University Press, 2013.

@crabbyeabbye (Abbye Meyer) et al. "thank you! . . . " *Twitter*, 2–3 Apr 2019, twitter.com/ crabbyeabbye/status/1113542789021696006.

Crowe, Chris. "Young Adult Literature: What Is Young Adult Literature?" *English Journal* 88.1 (Sept. 1998): 120–22.

Daly, Maureen. *Seventeenth Summer*. New York; Simon Pulse, 1942.

Dates, Jannette L., and Mia Moody Ramirez. *From Blackface to Black Twitter: Reflections on Black Humor, Race, Politics, & Gender*. New York: Peter Lang Publishing, 2018.

Davis, Lennard J. "Bodies of Difference: Politics, Disability, and Representation." *Disability Studies: Enabling the Humanities*. Edited by Sharon L. Snyder, Brenda Jo Brueggemann, and Rosemarie Garland-Thomson. New York: MLA, 2002. 100–106.

Davis, Lennard J. "The End of Identity Politics and the Beginning of Dismodernism." *The Disability Studies Reader*. Edited by Lennard J. Davis. New York: Routledge, 2006. 231–42.

Disability in Kidlit. disabilityinkidlit.com/.

Disability Visibility Project. disabilityvisibilityproject.com/.

Donaldson, Elizabeth J. "Revisiting the Corpus of the Madwoman: Further Notes toward a Feminist Disability Studies Theory of Mental Illness." *Feminist Disability Studies*. Edited by Kim Q. Hall. Bloomington; Indiana University Press, 2011.

Duke, Charles R. "Judy Blume's *Tiger Eyes*: A Perspective on Fear and Death." *Censored Books II: Critical Viewpoints, 1985–2000*. Edited by Nicholas J. Karolides. Lanham, MD: Scarecrow Press, 2002. 414–18.

Dunn, Patricia A. *Disabling Characters: Representations of Disability in Young Adult Literature*. New York: Peter Lang Publishing,

Duyvis, Corinne. *Corinne Duyvis: Sci-Fi & Fantasy in MG & YA*, www.corinneduyvis.net/.

Ellcessor, Elizabeth. *Restricted Access: Media, Disability, and the Politics of Participation*. New York: New York University Press, 2016.

Erikson, Erik H. *Identity: Youth and Crisis*. New York: W. W. Norton, 1994.

Eugenides, Jeffrey. *The Virgin Suicides*. New York: Warner Books, 1999.

Feinberg, Barbara. "Reflections on the 'Problem Novel': Do These Calamity-Filled Books Serve Up Too Much, Too Often, Too Early?" *American Educator (Quarterly Magazine of the American Federation of Teachers)* 28.4 (2004–2005): 1–7. Aft.org. 7 April 2014.

Faulkner, William. "The Text of *The Sound and the Fury*." *The Sound and the Fury: A Norton Critical Edition*. Edited by David Minter. New York: W. W. Norton, 1994. 1–199.

Faulkner, William. "Appendix: Compson 1699–1945." *The Sound and the Fury: A Norton Critical Edition*. Edited by David Minter. New York: W. W. Norton, 1994. 203–15.

Felperin, Leslie. "What Netflix Comedy Atypical Gets Right and Wrong about Autism." *The Guardian*, 14 Aug. 2017, www.theguardian.com/tv-and-radio/2017/aug/14/atypical-netflix-autism-spectrum-depiction-cliches.

Francis, Brian. *The Secret Fruit of Peter Paddington*. New York: Harper Perennial, 2005.

"Frequently Asked Questions." *#CripTheVote*, 2018, cripthevote.blogspot.com/2018/03/frequently-asked-questions.html

Gervay, Susanne. "*Butterflies*: Youth Literature as a Powerful Tool in Understanding Disability." *Disability Studies Quarterly* 24.1 (2004): 7 Apr. 2007, www.dsq-sds.org/_articles_html/2004/winter/dsq_w04_gervay.html.

Garland-Thomson, Rosemarie. *Extraordinary Bodies: Figuring Physical Disability in American Culture and Literature*. New York: Columbia University Press, 1997.

Garland-Thomson, Rosemarie. "Integrating Disability, Transforming Feminist Theory." *Gendering Disability*. Edited by Bonnie G. Smith and Beth Hutchinson. New Brunswick: Rutgers University Press, 2004. 73–103.

Garland-Thomson, Rosemarie. "Introduction: From Wonder to Error—A Geneology of Freak Discourse in Modernity." *Freakery: Cultural Spectacles of the Extraordinary Body*. Edited by Rosemarie Garland-Thomson. New York: New York University Press, 1996. 1–19.

Garland-Thomson, Rosemarie. *Staring: How We Look*. Oxford: Oxford University Press, 2009.

Geek Girl Riot. *iTunes* app, *Idobi Network*, 2016.

Genzlinger, Neil. "Review: Autism, Hormones and Family in Netflix's 'Atypical.'" *New York Times*, 10 Aug. 2017, www.nytimes.com/2017/08/10/arts/television/atypical-tv-review-netflix.html.

Gilbert, Sophie. "*Atypical* Is So Close to Great." *The Atlantic*, 13 Aug. 2017, www.theatlantic.com/entertainment/archive/2017/08/atypical-review-netflix/536538/.

Graves, Caroline. "I'm Disabled (and Not Some Other Word)." *Medium*, 1 Mar. 2019, medium.com/@ccgraves/im-disabled-and-not-some-other-word-ab70e54aefd5.

@GreggBeratan (Gregg Beratan) et al. "Just that I can't overstate . . ." *Twitter*, 19 Feb 2021, https://twitter.com/GreggBeratan/status/1362847564496838656.

Gruzd, Anatoliy, et al. "Imagining Twitter as an Imagined Community." *American Behavioral Scientist* 55 (10), 2011: 1294–1318.

Gubar, Marah. "Risky Business: Talking about Children in Children's Literature Criticism." *Children's Literature Association Quarterly* 38.4 (Winter 2013): 450–57.

Gurza, Andrew, host. *Disability After Dark*, *iTunes* app, *Podcast Jukebox*, 2016–19.

Hall, Alice. *Literature and Disability*. New York: Routledge, 2016.

Hall, Kim Q. "Feminism, Disability, and Embodiment." *NWSA Journal* 14.3 (2002): vii–xiii.

Hamill, Alexis C., and Catherine H. Stein. "Culture and Empowerment in the Deaf Community: An Analysis of Internet Weblogs." *Journal of Community & Applied Social Psychology* 21 (2011): 388–406.

Hamilton, Virginia. *Sweet Whispers, Brother Rush*. New York: Harper Trophy, 2001.

Henley, Ariel. "How the Film 'Wonder' is Commercializing Facial Difference." *Rooted in Rights*. 20 Sep. 2017, rootedinrights.org/how-the-film-wonder-is-commercializing-facial-difference/.

Herndon, April. "Disparate but Disabled: Fat Embodiment and Disability Studies." *NWSA Journal* 14.3 (2002): 120–37.

Higashida, Naoki. *The Reason I Jump*. Translated by K. A. Yoshida and David Mitchell, New York: Random House, 2016.

Hugar, John. "The More *Atypical* Tries to Get Autism 'Right,' the More Things Go Wrong." *AV/TV CLUB*, 11 Aug. 2017, tv.avclub.com/the-more-atypical-tries-to-get-autism-right-the-more-1798191910.

@Imani_Barbarin (Imani Barbarin). "You can dislike . . ." Twitter, 20 Mar. 2019, https://twitter.com/Imani_Barbarin/status/1108550626122829824

@Imani_Barbarin (Imani Barbarin) et al. "I think about the time . . ." *Twitter*, 15 Mar. 2019, twitter.com/Imani_Barbarin/status/1106680185548619777.

Johnson, Harriet McBryde. *Accidents of Nature*. New York: Henry Holt and Co., 2006.

Johnson, Harriet McBryde. "Unspeakable Conversations." *Too Late to Die Young: Nearly True Tales from a Life*. New York: Henry Holt and Co., 2005: 201–28.

Kidd, Kenneth B. *Freud in Oz: At the Intersections of Psychoanalysis and Children's Literature*. Minneapolis: University of Minnesota Press, 2011.

@Kirstie_Schultz, et al. "There are a few pieces . . ." Twitter, 3 Mar. 2019, twitter.com/Kirstie_Schultz/status/1102221582284582914

Knowles, John. *A Separate Peace*. New York: Scribner, 1996.

Koertge, Ron. *Stoner & Spaz*. Cambridge, MA: Candlewick Press, 2004.

Kristeva, Julia. *New Maladies of the Soul*. Translated by Ross Guberman. New York: Columbia University Press, 1995.

Lainoff, Lillie. "TV: Why I Love Speechless, but I Won't be Watching Atypical." *Today's Parent*. 11 Aug. 2017, www.todaysparent.com/family/special-needs/tv-why-i-love-speechless-but-i-wont-be-watching-atypical/.

@lillielainoff (Lillie Lainoff), et al. "Your book isn't #ownvoices if . . ." *Twitter*, 5–6 Apr. 2019, twitter.com/lillielainoff/status/1114209003310125057.

Lane, Harlan. "Construction of Deafness." *The Disability Studies Reader*. Edited by Lennard J. Davis. New York: Routledge, 2006. 79–92.

Lee, Latoya A. "Black Twitter: A Response to Bias in Mainstream Media." *Social Sciences*. 6, 26 (2017): 1–17.

Lewis, Bradley. "A Mad Fight: Psychiatry and Disability Activism." *The Disability Studies Reader*. Edited by Davis, Lennard J. New York: Routledge, 1997.

Marks, Deborah. *Disability: Controversial Debates and Psychosocial Perspectives*. New York: Routledge, 1999.

McCullough, Frances. "Foreword." *The Bell Jar*. New York: Harper Perennial, 2005.

McRuer, Robert. "Compulsory Able-Bodiedness and Queer/Disabled Existence." *Disability Studies: Enabling the Humanities*. Edited by Sharon L. Snyder, Brenda Jo Brueggemann, and Rosemarie Garland Thomson. New York: MLA, 2002. 88–99.

Meyer, Abbye E. "'But She's Not Retarded': Contemporary Adolescent Literature Humanizes Disability but Marginalizes Intellectual Disability." *Children's Literature Association Quarterly* 38.3 (Fall 2013): 267–83.

Meyer, Abbye, and Emily Wender. "Teaching and Reading *Wonder* and *Marcelo in the Real World* with Critical Eyes." *Lessons in Disability: Essays on Teaching with Young Adult Literature*. Edited by Jacob Stratman. McFarland & Company: Jefferson, NC, 2016.

@mia.mingus. "This is one small thing you can do when you're posting hashtags . . ." Instagram, 27 Mar. 2019, www.instagram.com/p/BvhoQ82hv4c/.

Miskec, Jennifer, and Chris McGee. "My Scars Tell a Story: Self-Mutilation in Young Adult Literature." *Children's Literature Association Quarterly* 32.2 (2007): 163–78.

Mitchell, David. "Introduction." *The Reason I Jump*. New York: Random House, 2016.

Modan, Naaz. "Twitter's #AbledsAreWeird Shines a Light on the Things Said to People with Disabilities." *Romper*, Mar. 2019, www.romper.com/p/twitters-abledsareweird-shines-a-light-on-the-things-said-to-people-with-disabilities-16962363.

Mollow, Anna, and Robert McRuer. "Introduction." *Sex and Disability*. Edited by Anna Mollow and Robert McRuer. Durham: Duke University Press, 2012. 1–34.

@mssinenomine (G Peters) et al. "Just realized something . . ." *Twitter*, 1 Mar. 2019, twitter.com/mssinenomine/status/1101649582159650816.

Murdoch, Stuart. Video Interview. By Abbye Meyer. 12 Apr. 2019.

Murdoch, Stuart. "Stuart Murdoch: ME/CFS update, 27 December 2018." *Vimeo*, 27 Dec. 2018, https://vimeo.com/308932752.

Murdoch, Stuart. "Stuart Murdoch on ME/CFS 4th Jan, 19." *Vimeo*, 4 Jan. 2019, vimeo.com/309560853.

Murray, Samantha. "(Un/Be)Coming Out? Rethinking Fat Politics." *Social Semiotics* 15.2 (2005): 153–63.

Nijkamp, Marieke, ed. *Unbroken: 13 Stories Starring Disabled Teens*. New York: Farrar Straus Giroux, 2018.

Nodelman, Perry. "The Other: Orientalism, Colonialism, and Children's Literature." *Children's Literature Association Quarterly* 17.1 (1992): 29–35.

Palacio, R. J. *Wonder*. New York: Knopf, 2012.

Philbrick, Rodman. *Freak the Mighty*. New York: Scholastic, 1993.

Plath, Sylvia. *The Bell Jar*. New York: Harper Perennial, 2005.

Pollard, Scott. "Introduction: The Art of Our Art, the Quirkiness of Our Forms." *Children's Literature Association Quarterly* 38.3 (Fall 2013): 263–66.

Porter, Roy. *Madness: A Brief History*. Oxford: Oxford University Press, 2002.

Portman, Frank. *King Dork*. New York: Delacorte, 2006.

Price, Margaret. "Mental Disability and Other Terms of Art." *Profession* (2010): 117–23.

Quayson, Ato. *Aesthetic Nervousness: Disability and the Crisis of Representation*. New York: Columbia University Press, 2007.

Ranere, Dianna. "SPEECHLESS Creator Scott Silveri on Staying True to His Family Story and a Visit to the Set #Speechless #ABCTVEvent." *FSM Media*, 30 Nov. 2016, www.fsm-media.com/abc-speechless/.

Rorby, Ginny. *Hurt Go Happy*. New York: Starscape, 2007.

Ryan, Pam Muñoz. *Becoming Naomi León*. New York: Scholastic, 2005.

Saclao, Christian. "'Speechless': Zack Anner Talks Writing for Season 2 of the ABC Comedy." *International Business Times*, 27 Sep. 2017, www.ibtimes.com/speechless-zack-anner-talks-writing-season-2-abc-comedy-2594486.

Salinger, J. D. *The Catcher in the Rye*. New York: Little, Brown and Co., 1991.

Savage, Dan, host. *Savage Lovecast*. *iTunes* app, *2010*.

Savage, Dan. "P.S. Insights, Interviews & More." *The Secret Fruit of Peter Paddington*. New York: Harper Perennial, 2005. 1–16.

"Schneider Family Book Award." *ALA*. American Library Association (ALA), 1 July 2014, www.ala.org/awardsgrants/schneider-family-book-award.

Sepinwall, Alan. "Hitting the Bullseyes: Behind the Scenes of ABC's Remarkable 'Speechless.'" *Uproxx*, 20 Sep. 2017, uproxx.com/sepinwall/speechless-great-family-comedy-season-2-preview/.

Sickboy Podcast. iTunes app, 2015.

Sommers, Joseph Michael. "Are You There, Reader? It's Me, Margaret: A Reconsideration of Judy Blume's Prose as Sororal Dialogism." *Children's Literature Association Quarterly* 33.3 (2008): 258–79.

The Mighty. themighty.com/.

The Smiths. "Asleep." *Louder Than Bombs*. Warner Bros, 1987. CD.

Thorpe, J. R. "What Is Identity-First Language, & Should You Use It?" *Bustle*, 9 Aug. 2017, www.bustle.com/p/what-is-identity-first-language-should-you-use-it-74901.

Trites, Roberta Seelinger. *Disturbing the Universe: Power and Repression in Adolescent Literature*. Iowa City: University of Iowa Press, 2000.

Trites, Roberta Seelinger. "Theories and Possibilities of Adolescent Literature." *Children's Literature Association Quarterly* 21.1 (Spring 1996): 2–3.

Trites, Roberta Seelinger. *Twain, Alcott, and the Birth of the Adolescent Reform Novel*. Iowa City: University of Iowa Press, 2007

Trueman, Terry. *Inside Out*. New York: Harper Collins, 2003.

We Need Diverse Books, diversebooks.org/.

Wheeler, Elizabeth A. "No Monsters in This Fairy Tale: *Wonder* and the New Children's Literature." *Children's Literature Association Quarterly* 38.3 (Fall 2013): 335–50.

Wonder, Directed by Stephen Chbosky, Lionsgate, 2017.

Wong, Alice, editor and publisher. *Resistance and Hope: Essays by Disabled People: Crip Wisdom for the People*. Kindle Edition, 2018.

Wong, Alice. "Recap of #AccessIsLove Twitter chat cohosted by Mia Mingus, Sandy Ho, and Alice Wong with guest host House of GG." *Disability Project*, 27 Mar. 2019, disabilityvisibilityproject.com/2019/03/13/3-26-accessislove-twitter-chat/.

BELLE AND SEBASTIAN SONGS

"Beautiful." *3.. 6.. 9 Seconds of Light*, Jeepster, 1997.

"Belle & Sebastian." *Dog On Wheels*, Jeepster, 1997.

"Expectations." *Tigermilk*, Electric Honey, 1996 (Jeepster, 1999).

"Fox in the Snow." *If You're Feeling Sinister*, Jeepster, 1996.

"Get Me Away from Here, I'm Dying." *If You're Feeling Sinister*, Jeepster, 1996.

"If You're Feeling Sinister." *If You're Feeling Sinister*, Jeepster, 1996.

"Judy and the Dream of Horses." *If You're Feeling Sinister*, Jeepster, 1996.

"Le Pastie De La Bourgeoisie." *3.. 6.. 9 Seconds of Light*, Jeepster, 1997.

"Like Dylan in the Movies." *If You're Feeling Sinister*, Jeepster, 1996.

"Mayfly." *If You're Feeling Sinister*, Jeepster, 1996.

"Me and the Major." *If You're Feeling Sinister*, Jeepster, 1996.
"Nobody's Empire." *Girls in Peacetime Want to Dance*, Matador, 2014.
"Put the Book Back on the Shelf." *3.. 6.. 9 Seconds of Light*, Jeepster, 1997.
"She's Losing It." *Tigermilk*, Jeepster, 1999.
"The Boy Done Wrong Again." *If You're Feeling Sinister*, Jeepster, 1996.
"The Boy with the Arab Strap." *The Boy with the Arab Strap*, Jeepster, 1998.
"The Rollercoaster Ride." *The Boy with the Arab Strap*, Jeepster, 1998.
"The Stars of Track and Field." *If You're Feeling Sinister*, Jeepster, 1996.
"We Rule the School." *Tigermilk*, Electric Honey, 1996 (Jeepster, 1999).

ATYPICAL EPISODES

"A Nice Neutral Smell." *Atypical*, created by Robia Rashid, season 1, episode 4, *Sony Pictures Television*, 11 Aug. 2017. *Netflix*, *www.netflix.com*.
"Antarctica." *Atypical*, created by Robia Rashid, season 1, episode 1, *Sony Pictures Television*, 11 Aug. 2017. *Netflix*, *www.netflix.com*.
"I Lost My Poor Meatball." *Atypical*, created by Robia Rashid, season 1, episode 7, *Sony Pictures Television*, 11 Aug. 2017. *Netflix*, *www.netflix.com*.

SPEECHLESS EPISODES

"B-O-N—BONFIRE." *Speechless*, created by Scott Silveri, season 1, episode 3, *ABC Studios*, 5 Oct. 2016.
"C-H—CHEATER!." *Speechless*, created by Scott Silveri, season 1, episode 19, *ABC Studios*, 5 Apr. 2017.
"D-I—DING." *Speechless*, created by Scott Silveri, season 1, episode 18, *ABC Studios*, 15 Mar. 2017.
"H-A-L—HALLOWEEN." *Speechless*, created by Scott Silveri, season 1, episode 5, *ABC Studios*, 26 Oct. 2016.
"H-E-R—ERO." *Speechless*, created by Scott Silveri, season 1, episode 12, *ABC Studios*, 11 Jan. 2017.
"I-N-S—INSPIRATIONS." *Speechless*, created by Scott Silveri, season 1, episode 4, *ABC Studios*, 12 Oct. 2016.
"J-J's D-R—Dream." *Speechless*, created by Scott Silveri, season 2, episode 3, *ABC Studios*, 11 Oct. 2017.
"N-E—NEW A-I—AIDE." *Speechless*, created by Scott Silveri, season 1, episode 2, *ABC Studios*, 28 Sep. 2016.
"O-S—OSCAR P-A—PARTY." *Speechless*, created by Scott Silveri, season 1, episode 16, *ABC Studios*, 22 Feb. 2017.

"ONE A-N—ANGRY M—MAYA." *Speechless*, created by Scott Silveri, season 2, episode 17, *ABC Studios*, 14 Mar. 2018.

"Pilot." *Speechless*, created by Scott Silveri, season 1, episode 1, *ABC Studios*, 21 Sep. 2016.

"P-R-O-M-P—PROMPOSAL." *Speechless*, created by Scott Silveri, season 3, episode 19, *ABC Studios*, 22 Mar. 2016.

"P-R—PROM." *Speechless*, created by Scott Silveri, season 1, episode 21, *ABC Studios*, 3 May 2017.

"R-A-Y-C—RAY-CATION." *Speechless*, created by Scott Silveri, season 1, episode 8, *ABC Studios*, 30 Nov. 2016.

"R-O—ROAD T-R—TRIP." *Speechless*, created by Scott Silveri, season 1, episode 11, *ABC Studios*, 4 Jan. 2017.

"R-U-N—RUNAWAY." *Speechless*, created by Scott Silveri, season 1, episode 20, *ABC Studios*, 26 Apr. 2017.

"S-H—SHIPPING." *Speechless*, created by Scott Silveri, season 2, episode 6, *ABC Studios*, 1 Nov. 2017.

"S-P—SPECIAL B—BOY T-I—TIME." *Speechless*, created by Scott Silveri, season 3, episode 17, *ABC Studios*, 8 Mar. 2019.

"T-H-A—THANKSGIVING." *Speechless*, created by Scott Silveri, season 1, episode 7, *ABC Studios*, 16 Nov. 2016.

"THE H-U-S—HUSTLE." *Speechless*, created by Scott Silveri, season 2, episode 12, *ABC Studios*, 10 Jan. 2018.

"T-H—THE C-L—CLUB." *Speechless*, created by Scott Silveri, season 1, episode 15, *ABC Studios*, 15 Feb. 2017.

"T-R—TRAINING D-A—DAY." *Speechless*, created by Scott Silveri, season 2, episode 4, *ABC Studios*, 18 Oct. 2017.

"U-N-R—UNREALISTIC." *Speechless*, created by Scott Silveri, season 3, episode 22, *ABC Studios*, 12 Apr. 2019.

"W-E—WE'RE B-A—BACK!." *Speechless*, created by Scott Silveri, season 2, episode 1, *ABC Studios*, 27 Sep. 2017.

CREDITS

Quotations from "Expectations" and "We Rule the School," written by Belle and Sebastian, Copyright © 1996 Electric Honey (© 1999 Jeepster Recordings). Used by permission from Belle and Sebastian.

Quotations from "The Stars of Track and Field," "Me and the Major," "Like Dylan in the Movies," "The Fox in the Snow," "Get Me Away from Here, I'm Dying," "If You're Feeling Sinister," "Mayfly," "The Boy Done Wrong Again," and "Judy and the Dream of Horses," written by Belle and Sebastian, Copyright © 1996 Jeepster Recordings. Used by permission from Belle and Sebastian.

Quotations from "Beautiful," "Belle & Sebastian," "Le Pastie de la Bourgeoisie," and "Put the Book Back on the Shelf," written by Belle and Sebastian, Copyright © 1997 Jeepster Recordings. Used by permission from Belle and Sebastian.

Quotations from "The Boy with the Arab Strap" and "The Rollercoaster Ride," written by Belle and Sebastian, Copyright © 1998 Jeepster Recordings. Used by permission from Belle and Sebastian.

Quotations from "Nobody's Empire," written by Belle and Sebastian, Copyright © 2014 Matador Records. Used by permission from Belle and Sebastian.

INDEX

@AutumnOwl_, 111
@coffeespoonie, 133
@crabbyeabbye, 133
@DisVisibility, 111, 136–37
@fromsarahlex, 133
@IntersectedCrip, 137
@lillielainoff, 112
@Phoebe92987793, 133
@RJSomer, 112
#AbledsAreWeird, 138–39, 144–45
#AccessIsLove, 137–38, 154–55
#ActuallyAustistic, 120
#BlackLivesMatter, 110
#CripTheVote, 133
#DisabilityTwitter, 133
#DisabledandCute, 119
#OwnVoices, 110–13, 116, 119–21, 130, 146, 170–71n2

Accidents of Nature (Johnson), 85–86, 122, 151; Camp Courage, 97–106; cerebral palsy, 96, 98–99, 103; cultural identity in, 100–101, 103–6; Denise, 105; descriptions of campers, 98–99, 100, 103–4; Dolly, 99, 103; Jean, 96–106, 122; Jean's parents, 97–98, 104; mainstream views of disability in, 97–98, 102–6, 122; muscular dystrophy, 98; nondisabled counselors, 100, 105; as political treatise, 86, 96, 102, 106; reclamation of words in, 99–100; Sara, 96, 98–104, 106, 167n3; self-acceptance in, 100–103, 106, 122; talent night, 104–5; trees in, 85; Willie, 98–101
adolescence: authentic voice of, 16, 36; definition of, 5–6; disability as young adult voice, 16–36, 109–10, 113–14, 153–54; disabling effects, 38; existentially distressed by, 29–32; history of, 11; lack of stability, 7; narratives, 11–12; overlap with disability, 4, 5, 12–13, 17–18, 36, 158n1; sexuality, 38
Adventures of Huckleberry Finn, The (Twain), 159n2
Aesthetic Nervousness: Disability and the Crisis of Representation (Quayson), 3
Alcott, Louisa May, 159n2
American Library Association, 3
American Psychiatric Association, 8, 40, 159–60n3; on suicide, 40
American Sign Language (ASL), 91–92, 95
Anderson, M. T., 37, 60
Anner, Zach, 121–22, 128, 147
"Asleep" (Smiths), 28
Atlantic, The, 120
Atypical, 120–22; autism in, 120; Doug, 120, 123; Elsa, 120, 123; martyrdom in, 123; parent support group, 120, 123; Sam, 120, 123
Aubry, Cécile, 170n1

Barbarin, Imani, 136, 138–39, 145, 149
Barnum, P.T., 67–68

Becoming Naomi León (Ryan), 63; disability in, 64–66; mother in, 66; Naomi, 65–66; Owen, 65–66
Bell Jar, The (Plath), 12, 16, 158n1; death in, 30, 159n1; desire to connect, 19; Esther Greenwood, 16–26, 28, 31–33, 35–36, 115, 159n1, 159n2, 160n4, 161n7; Esther's father, 30, 159n1; humor in, 23; implied audience, 18; Irwin, 27; judgmental nature of narrator, 22–23, 33; loneliness in, 18–19, 22–23, 30; loss of childhood, 30; mental illness in, 16–17, 32–33, 36, 159n1, 161n7; narrative voice, 16–17, 22; nostalgia in, 30; psychiatric hospital in, 33, 35, 159n1; publication of, 16; sexuality in, 27–28, 159n1, 160n4; suicide in, 27, 33, 160n4
Belle and Sebastian, 114, 131, 134–35, 170n1; "Beautiful," 115; "Belle & Sebastian," 115–16; "The Boy Done Wrong Again," 142; "The Boy with the Arab Strap," 149, 170n1; characters in songs, 114–16, 141–42, 148; "Expectations," 142; "The Fox in the Snow," 141–42; "Get Me Away from Here, I'm Dying," 115, 141–42; "If You're Feeling Sinister," 115; *If You're Feeling Sinister*, 114–15; "Judy and the Dream of Horses," 143; "Le Pastie," 148–49; "Like Dylan in the Movies," 115; "Mayfly," 115; "Me and the Major," 114; "Nobody's Empire,"134–36, 142; "Put the Book Back on the Shelf," 115–16; "The Rollercoaster Ride," 143; "She's Losing It," 115; "The Stars of Track and Field," 114–15; "We Rule the School," 114
Beratan, Gregg, 133, 136
Brown, Christy, 77

Carey, Alison C., 62–63
Catcher in the Rye, The (Salinger), 12, 16–17, 22, 148, 158n1; alienation, 19; childhood in, 29, 32, 114, 161n6; death in, 26, 29, 32, 159n1; desire to connect, 19, 22, 160n4; Holden Caulfield, 16–18, 21–26, 28–29, 31–33, 35–36, 114–15, 159n2, 160n4, 160–62nn6–8; judgmental nature of narrator, 22, 26–27; loneliness in, 30, 160n4; mental illness in, 16–17, 32–33, 36, 159n1, 160–62nn6–8; narrative voice, 16, 22; nostalgia in, 29; opening, 18; Phoebe, 35, 160n4, 160–61n6; psychiatrist in, 33; Sally, 29–30, 160n4; sexuality in, 26–28, 160n4
Cerebral Palsy Foundation, 121
Children's Literature Association Quarterly, 3
Chbosky, Stephen, 16
Cohn, Rachel, 16
Cokley, Rebecca, 137–38

Daily Dot, 139
Daly, Maureen, 158n1, 159n2
Davis, Lennard J., 7, 8, 61
Deaf community, 10; as ethnolinguistic community, 10; pride movements, 10
Diagnostic and Statistical Manual of Mental Disorders, Fifth Edition (APA), 159–60n3
"Disabled People Have An Ally Problem . . ." (Barbarin), 145
disability/disabled people, 7; allies, 145–46; assumptions regarding, 157–58n1; authentic voice of, 16, 111, 113, 116–17, 119–21; as catalyst for growth, 62–84; "cures" for, 7, 157n1; definition of, 5–6; digital, online narratives, 130–31; early views of, 7; as "freaks," 62–94; inclusive definitions of, 9–10; linking, 150–56; as literary metaphor, 37–61; literary representations of, 10–12; medically-based

understandings, 7; normalizing, 7; online community, 110–12, 131–44; overlap with adolescence, 4, 5, 12–13, 17–18, 36, 158n1; as political identity, 84–106, 153; pride, 8; self-definition, 5; as social construction, 7–9, 153; social model of, 7–9; as unifier, 107–49
disability, invisible: chronic illness, 8; "cures," 9; inclusive definitions of, 9–10; intellectual disabilities, 8; madness, 8–9; medically-based model, 9; melancholia, 8; mental disorders, 8; mental illness, 8, 9, 159–60n3; as rebellion, 8–9; treatments for, 8; understanding of, 8; Victorian era, 8
disability community, 10; inclusivity within, 10, 61, 106, 150–56
Disability Justice Initiative, 138
disability studies scholarship, 3, 7, 9
Disability Visibility Project, 119, 131, 134, 155
Disabling Characters: Representations of Disability in Young Adult Literature (Dunn), 3
dismodernism, 8
Donaldson, Elizabeth J., 9
Dunn, Patricia A., 3
Duyvis, Corrine, 110, 112, 119

electroconvulsive therapy, 8
Enlightenment, 8
Eugenides, Jeffrey, 38, 39, 40, 44
Extraordinary Bodies: Figuring Physical Disability in American Culture and Literature (Garland-Thomas), 3

fabulous (McRuer), 100
Facebook, 109
Farrar Straux Giroux, 118
Faulkner, William, 4
Feed (Anderson), 37, 47, 60; Calista, 37–38; lesions in, 37–38; mental illness in, 37; Quendy, 37–38; self-injury in, 37, 38
feminism/women's rights movement, 7, 9
Flowers for Algernon (Daniel Keyes), 4
Foucault, Michel, 8
Fowler, Micah, 107, 121–22
Francis, Brian, 38, 45–49, 51
freak(s), 62–94; developed, 66–76; revolutionary, 76–84; shows, 63, 67–68, 71; simple, 64–66; traditional literary, 77
Freak the Mighty (Philbrick), 63, 74, 76; "cure" of change in, 76; death in, 67, 70, 74, 76, 84; Gran, 69; humor in, 66, 68–69, 78; Kevin "Freak", 66, 68–72, 74–76, 78, 81, 84; learning disabilities in, 75; Max, 67–70, 72, 74–75; role of freak in, 63, 66–67, 70–72, 75; self-acceptance in, 75
Freud, Sigmund, 8, 11
Freud in Oz . . . (Kidd), 158n1

Garland-Thomson, Rosemarie, 3, 7, 12, 66–68
Geek Girl Riot, 140
Gervay, Susanne, 162n2
Gibson, Dawn W., 133
Goffman, Erving, 101
Gubar, Marah, 150–51

Hall, Alice, 3
Hall, G. Stanley, 8, 11
Hamilton, Virginia, 63–64, 163n1
Henley, Ariel, 121
Herndon, April, 162n2
Higashida, Naoki, 116–18
Ho, Sandy, 137
Hurt Go Happy (Rorby), 86; abuse in, 95, 165–66n2; animal rights in, 92, 95–96, 169–70n5; Charlie, 91, 92, 95, 164–65n1, 166–67n2, 169n5;

cultural identity in, 90–93; Deaf community, 90–92; deafness in, 90–92, 95, 165n2–67n5; death in, 92, 95; Joey, 90–92, 95–96, 164n1–67n5, 169–70n5; oralism, 91–93; reality-based narrative of, 86–87; Ruth, 91–92, 95–96, 164n1–65n2; self-acceptance in, 92–93, 96, 167n3; sexuality in, 95; signing in, 91–93, 95, 164n1, 166n2, 168n4; Sukari, 91–92, 95–96, 169–70n5

Inside Out (Trueman), 86; Alan "Frosty" Mender, 88, 93, 94; death, 89, 94; ending, 86, 89; Dirtbag, 87, 168n4; disability in, 87; Dr. Curtis, 87, 89, 94, 169n4; hostages in, 88, 93; Joey "Stormy" Mender, 88, 93, 94; Kenny, 95; maple bar in, 93–94; nonnormative behaviors in, 87; Rat, 87, 168n4; reality-based narrative of, 86; schizophrenia, 87, 89, 90, 93, 94, 169n4; socially marginalized identities in, 87, 88, 167n3; self-acceptance in, 87, 89, 90; suicide in, 89, 94; Zach Wahsted, 87, 88, 89, 90, 93, 94, 168–69n4

Instagram, 109

Jerry Lewis telethon, 170n6

Johnson, Harriet McBryde, 85, 86, 96, 97, 98, 106, 122, 157–58n1, 170n6

Jones, Keith, 138

Keller, Helen, 4

Kidd, Kenneth B., 11, 16–17, 158n1, 159n2

King Dork (Portman), 16; back cover, 21; *The Catcher in the Rye* references, 21, 31, 32, 160n5; change or "cure" in, 35; death in, 26, 28–29, 32, 34–35, 159n1; Fiona, 28–29; implied audience, 21; judgmental nature of narrator, 25–26; loneliness, 21, 31–32, 34; mental illness in, 34; Mr. Teone, 28; narrative, 25–26; peace in, 36; psychiatrist, 35; quest for truth, 29; Sam, 34; self-consciousness in, 21, 35; "A Sex Alliance Against Society," 32; sexuality, 28–29; suicide in, 29, 35; Tom, 21, 31–32, 34–36, 160n5; Tom's father, 26, 28–29, 32, 34–35, 159n1; Tom's intellect, 21, 25; Tom's mother, 25, 32, 35; Tom's sister, 26; Tom's stepfather, 26, 35

Knowles, John, 159n2

Koertge, Ron, 63, 76–77

Kristeva, Julia, 5–6, 11

Lee, Latoya A., 132

Levithan, David, 16

Literature and Disability (Hall), 3

Little Women (Alcott), 4, 159n2

lobotomies, 8

Mad Pride movement, 8

McCullers, Carson, 158n1

McGee, Chris, 12, 37, 38, 60, 106

McRuer, Robert, 7, 81, 100, 157n1

media: digital, 108–13, 130–44; participatory, 108–9; problem narratives in digital, 140; resistance and hope in traditional, 113–20; singing along in digital, 130–44; social, 109–12; speechless communication in transformed-traditional, 120–30; traditional analog, 108–9, 113–20, 151; transformed-traditional, 108–9, 120–30, 151; twenty-first-century young adult disability narratives in, 109–10

Member of the Wedding, The (McCullers), 158n1

mental illness, 8, 9, 159–60n3; in *The Bell Jar*, 16–17, 32–33, 36, 159n1,

161n7; in *The Catcher in the Rye*, 16, 17, 32–33, 36, 159n1, 160–62n8; definition of, 8; in *Feed*, 37; in *Inside Out*, 87, 89–90, 93–94, 169n4; in *King Dork*, 34; in *Nick and Norah's Infinite Playlist*, 34; in *The Perks of Being a Wallflower*, 36; in *The Sound and the Fury*, 4–5; in *The Virgin Suicides*, 39. *See also* disability, invisible
Mighty, The, 140; "Living in the Grey Area between Disabled and Able-Bodied (Becca R)," 144
Mingus, Mia, 137–38
Miskec, Jennifer, 12, 37–38, 60, 106
Mitchell, David, 117–18
Mollow, Anna, 81
Murdoch, Stuart, 114–15, 134–35, 148–49, 154, 170n1; ME/CFS, 132, 135–36, 141, 170n2; on Twitter, 131–32; vlogs, 140–43
Muscular Dystrophy Association, 170n6
My Left Foot (Brown), 77

National Public Radio, 139
Netflix, 120
New York Post, 21
Nick and Norah's Infinite Playlist (Cohn, Levithan), 16, 159n1; alienation, 20; Caroline, 20; change or "cure" in, 21; Dev, 28; judgmental nature of narrators, 24–25, 34, 159n1; loneliness, 21, 31; mental illness in, 34; music in, 20–21, 31; Nick, 20–21, 24–25, 28, 31, 34–36, 159n1; Norah, 20–21, 24–25, 28, 31, 34–36, 159n1; nostalgia in, 31; quest for truth, 28; self-consciousness in, 25; sense of infinity, 35–36; sexuality in, 28, 31; *tikkun olam*, 34; Tris, 24
Nijkamp, Marieke, 118–19
"Nothing About Us Without Us," 147–48

Outsiders, The (Hinton), 11–12

Palacio, R. J., 63, 73, 120
Perks of Being a Wallflower, The (Chbosky), 16; abuse in, 27, 34, 159n1; alienation, 19; Bill, 19, 20, 24, 116; Bridget, 20; Carl, 20; change or "cure" in, 20; Charlie, 19–20, 29–30, 33–36, 115–16; Charlie's brother, 30–31; Charlie's "friend," 19; Charlie's parents, 30; Charlie's sister, 23–24, 30–31; Craig, 24; Dave, 20; death in, 27, 159n1; drugs, 31; Helen, 27–29, 33–34, 159; judgmental nature of narrator, 23–24, 33; Mary Elizabeth, 24; mental illness in, 36; Michael, 19–20, 28, 33; Patrick, 20, 24, 28; psychiatrist in, 33–34; quest for truth in, 27; Sam, 24, 27; Sean, 23; self-awareness in, 24; sense of infinity, 35; sexuality in, 24, 27–28, 31; shame in, 24; suicide in, 19, 28, 33; Susan, 20
Peters, G., 134
Philbrick, Rodman, 63
Plath, Sylvia, 12, 17, 27
Pollard, Scott, 3, 150
Portman, Frank, 16
postmodernism, 8
"problem novels," 11, 86, 122; literary representations of disability in, 12; restraints of, 93; simple plot of, 97; trappings of, 12, 106
Pulrang, Andrew, 133

Quayson, Ato, 3, 12, 66

Rashid, Robia, 120
Reason I Jump: The Inner Voice of a Thirteen-Year-Old Boy with Autism, The (Higashida), 116–17; autism-based filters in, 117; preface, 117–18

Resistance & Hope: Essays by Disabled People: Crip Wisdom for the People, 119, 120
Romper, 139
Rorby, Ginny, 86, 90, 92, 165nn1–2
Ryan, Pam Muñoz, 63–64

Salinger, J. D., 12, 16–17
Savage, Dan, 47, 48, 51
Scarlet Letter, The (Hawthorne), 4
Schneider Family Book Awards, 3
Secret Fruit of Peter Paddington, The (Francis), 38–61; Andrew Sinclair, 48–49, 53, 55; Arlene Marple, 58; Bedtime Movies, 46–47, 50–51, 55; Billy Archer, 48–51, 53; Brian Cinder, 53, 58; Bubbles, 57; change or "cure," search for, 45, 47, 55–57, 59–60; Christine, 56–57; Daniela, 58–60; disabling effects of adolescence, 38, 46–47, 52–53, 56; gender exploration in, 50–51; Jackie Myner, 58–59; John Geddes, 60; Margaret, 58; metaphors in, 47–49, 55, 57–58, 60; Mr. Bernard, 55; Mr. Hanlan, 49, 53–54; Nancy, 56–57, 59; nonnormative body issues in, 39, 45, 46–47, 51–54, 56–57, 60, 161n2; original title, 162n1; Peter, 38, 45–54, 163n2; Peter's identity, 47, 51, 53; Peter's mother, 52–55; Peter's nipples, 38, 46, 48–53, 55–56, 59–60; queerness, 38, 46–51, 53–56, 59–60; self-acceptance and self-awareness in, 53, 56–57, 59–60; self-mortification in, 51–52; sexuality in, 38–39, 46–54; social hierarchies in, 57–58; Uncle Ed, 50, 54–55
Separate Peace, A (Knowles), 159n2
Seventeenth Summer (Daly), 158n1–59n2
Sickboy Podcast, 140
Silveri, Scott, 121–22, 147
Smiths, The, 28
Sound and the Fury, The (Faulkner), 4–6; abuse in, 81; Benjy Compson, 4, 6–7, 81; disability in, 4; mental illness in, 4–5; Quentin Compson, 4–7
Speechless, 107, 146–47, 149–51; authentic voices in, 121, 126–27; "B-O-N-BONFIRE," 107, 126, 130; "C-H-CHEATER!", 124, 127; cerebral palsy, 107, 121, 128; Claire, 151–52; creative team, 121, 124; "D-A-T-E-DATE?" 151; "D-I-DING," 129; DiMeo family, 107–8, 122–24, 126, 128–29, 137, 146–49, 151; Dylan, 124, 127, 152; "H-A-HALLOWEEN," 126; "H-E-R-HERO," 125; "The H-U-S-HUSTLE," 126; humor in, 124–25, 152; "I-N-S-INSPIRATIONS," 122, 153; issues with identity in, 127–28; J.J. DiMeo, 107, 121, 122, 125–29, 147, 151–52; "J-J's D-R-DREAM," 127; Jimmy, 107–8, 124–25, 127; Kai, 127; Kenneth, 125–26, 128, 151–52; Lee, 128–29; Maya, 124–30, 147; narrative, 122; "O-S-OSCAR P-A-PARTY," 128; "P-R-O-M-P-PROMPOSAL," 147–48; "P-R-PROM," 152; premier of, 107; "R-A-Y-RAY-CATION," 125; "R-O-ROAD T-R-TRIP," 129; "R-U-N-RUNAWAY," 127; Ray, 107–8, 124, 127, 129–30, 152; rejection of "normal" in, 107–8; "S-H-SHIPPING," 152–53; "S-P-SPECIAL B-BOY T-I-TIME," 127; sexuality in, 127–29, 152–53; "T-H-THE C-L-CLUB," 129; Taylor, 127; as transformed-traditional media, 108; "U-N-R-UNREALISTIC," 127; "W-E-WE'RE B-A-BACK!" 129
SpoonieChat, 133
Stigma: Notes on the Management of Spoiled Identity (Goffman), 101

Stoner & Spaz (Koertge), 63; Ben Bancroft, 76–84, 164n4; cerebral palsy, 76, 78–79; Colleen, 77–84, 164n4; depression in, 164n4; drug use in, 82–83; grandmother, 78–80; *High School Confidential*, 81–82; humor in, 77–78; Marcie, 77–80, 82–84; role of freak in, 63, 77, 82–84; self-acceptance in, 77–82; sexuality in, 80–81
Sweet Whispers, Brother Rush (Hamilton), 63–66; abuse in, 65, 81; Brother Rush, 64; Dab, 64, 65, 81, 84, 163n1; death in, 64–65, 84; disability in, 64–65; Miss Pricherd, 65; porphyria in, 64–65, 163n1; repercussion of slavery, 64, 163n1; self-awareness in, 65; sexuality in, 65; Tree, 64–65; Vy, 64–65
Szasz, Thomas, 8

Tender is the Night (Fitzgerald), 4; Nicole Driver, 4
Too Late to Die Young: Nearly True Tales from a Life (Johnson), 170n6
Trites, Roberta Seelinger, 158n1, 159n2
Trueman, Terry, 86, 93
Twain, Alcott, and the Birth of the Adolescent Reform Novel (Kidd), 158n1
Twain, Mark, 159n1
Twitter, 109; Black, 109–10, 132; disability, 110–12, 131–44; hashtags, 110–12, 131, 138; real-time chats and conversations, 131, 137, 139–40; tweets, 110, 131

Unbroken: 13 Stories Starring Disabled Teens (Nijkamp), 118–19, 147; dust jacket, 118–19

Virgin Suicides, The (Eugenides), 38–45, 60; agency of the Lisbon sisters, 44; Bonnie, 40, 42, 45; Cecilia, 39–41, 43–45; depression in, 40; disabling effects of adolescence, 38, 40–41, 43–44; Dr. Hornicker, 40, 45; elm trees, 44; fish flies, 43; homecoming dance, 42; Joe Hill Conley, 44; journalists in, 44–45; Lisbon house, 41, 43; Lisbon sisters, 38–45; Lux, 40–45; Mary, 40, 42, 45; mental illness in, 39; Mr. and Mrs. Lisbon, 41; Mrs. Buell, 41; Mrs. Scheer, 41, 43; narrators, 39, 41–43, 45; Parkie Denton, 44; rejection of societal norms, 45; sexuality in, 38–45, 60; suicide in, 38–45, 60; Therese, 40, 42, 45; Trip Fontaine, 44

We Need Diverse Books, 119
Wheeler, Elizabeth A., 74, 163–64n3
Willy Wonka and the Chocolate Factory, 125
Wong, Alice, 111, 119, 131, 132, 133, 134, 135, 137, 138
Wonder (Palacio), 63, 74, 84, 122; "Auggie" August, 66–72, 75–76, 78, 81, 121, 163n2; Auggie's sister, 73, 123; craniofacial disorder, 67–68, 70, 121; disability in, 75–76; dynamic of separation in, 73; Ellie, 69; humor in, 66, 69–70, 78; Isabel, 70, 75–76, 124; Jack, 69–70, 73, 163n2–64n3; Julian, 69; Justin, 73; martyrdom in, 123; Maya, 69, 124; Miranda, 73; Mr. Tushman, 71, 75–76; role of the freak in, 63, 66–68, 70–72; school assembly and award presentation, 67–68, 71; self-acceptance in, 75; suicide in, 163n2; Summer, 70, 73
Wonder (film), 120; marketing strategies, 121

Yoshida, K. A., 117–18
young adult novels, 4; authentic voice of, 36; change or "cure" of character

in, 18; disability as the young adult voice, 16–36, 153–54; disability-centered readings, 4; disability-themed, 3; dismissal of, 11–12; first publication of, 11, 158n1; kinship model for understanding, 150–51; literary authenticity in, 18; literary "freaks," 62–84; literary possibilities, 4, 13, 37; literary representations of disability, 47; narrative(s), 4, 7, 10, 12, 17, 74; narrative, controlling, 18; narrative agency in, 7; "normalization" in, 17–18; political possibilities, 4, 13; power that disability brings to, 13; as "problem novels," 11–12, 86; rereading for adolescence, 4; role of the freak in, 63, 66; "special child" in, 62, 63; trauma in, 158–59n1; viability of, 37; villainous freaks in, 62

YouTube, 109